EVIL, SUFFERING, AND PESSIMISM

EVIL, SUFFERING, AND PESSIMISM:

Readings from the Darker Side of Modern Philosophy

EDITED BY
Corey W. Dyck,
Fabio Malfara,
and Ignacio L. Moya

broadview press

BROADVIEW PRESS
Peterborough, Ontario, Canada

Founded in 1985, Broadview Press is a fully independent academic publishing house owned by approximately twenty-five shareholders—almost all of whom are either Broadview employees or Broadview authors. Broadview is supported by a collaboration with Trent University, a liberal arts university located in Peterborough, Ontario—the city where Broadview was founded and continues to operate. Broadview is committed to environmentally responsible publishing and fair business practices.

Library and Archives Canada Cataloguing in Publication

Title: Evil, suffering, and pessimism : readings from the darker side of modern philosophy / edited by Corey W. Dyck, Fabio Malfara, and Ignacio L. Moya.
Names: Dyck, Corey, editor | Malfara, Fabio, editor. | Moya, Ignacio L., editor.
Description: Includes bibliographical references.
Identifiers: Canadiana (print) 20260110388 | Canadiana (ebook) 20260110418 | ISBN 9781554816675 (softcover) | ISBN 9781460408698 (EPUB) | ISBN 9781770489455 (PDF)
Subjects: LCSH: Pessimism. | LCSH: Good and evil. | LCSH: Suffering—Philosophy. | LCSH: Philosophy, Modern.
Classification: LCC B829 .E95 2026 | DDC 149/.6—dc23

Broadview Press handles its own distribution in Canada and the United States:
PO Box 1243, Peterborough, Ontario K9J 7H5, Canada
555 Riverwalk Parkway, Tonawanda, NY 14150, USA
Tel: (705) 482-5915
customerservice@broadviewpress.com

Broadview Press books are imported and distributed in the United Kingdom and European Union by:
Gazelle Book Services Ltd.
White Cross Mills, Hightown, Lancaster, Lancashire, LA1 4XS
sales@gazellebookservices.co.uk

European Union – Responsible Person (for official use only):
eucomply OÜ
Pärnu mnt 139b14
11317 Tallinn, Estonia
hello@eucompliancepartner.com
+33757690241

Canada

Broadview Press acknowledges the financial support of the Government of Canada for our publishing activities.

Edited by Robert M. Martin
Book design by Michel Vrana

PRINTED IN CANADA

1 2 3 4 5 6 7 8 9 10 26 27 28 29 30

CONTENTS

UNIT II. EVIL WITHOUT SIN: UNDERSTANDING SUFFERING

UNIT III. THE WORST OF ALL POSSIBLE WORLDS: THE CHALLENGE OF PESSIMISM

PREFACE

This book is a reader featuring texts in modern philosophy, roughly between 1500 and 1900. It differs dramatically, however, from a typical collection of philosophical texts from this period. The focus of this collection is a cluster of philosophical questions that are not much discussed in a standard course on modern philosophy in the Western tradition: *Is it possible to explain the existence of evil under the supposition of a supremely good creator? Are we ourselves the cause of most of the suffering that befalls us? Is life generally more painful than it is pleasant and, if so, is non-existence preferable to existence? Is happiness ever even attainable?*[1]

Despite not being taken up in introductory courses, these questions occupied some of the best-known philosophers of the modern tradition—figures like G.W. Leibniz, David Hume, Jean-Jacques Rousseau, Immanuel Kant, and Friedrich Nietzsche. More importantly, these questions provoked a number of other thinkers besides to take up their pens, including figures who currently find themselves just outside the modern philosophical canon, such as Pierre Bayle, Voltaire, and Arthur Schopenhauer, as well as some who, until very recently, had been excluded from it, such as Ottobah Cugoano, Mary Astell, and Olga Plumacher. We even find a number of writers who are not primarily identified as philosophers, like Alexander Pope, contributing to the ongoing discussion in important and influential ways.

That this very diverse group of prominent thinkers found such topics to be subjects worth engaging should not be surprising. Modern philosophers upheld a view of philosophy centered on matters of concrete and relatable importance, and their investigations into more theoretical issues were often outgrowths of this guiding interest. In the texts collected here, one will find philosophers bending their intellectual efforts to the darker side of life, asking whether this world might not be *bad*, or even *the worst possible*, or questioning whether life itself is *something that ought to be*. Here too lies an important lesson about how

1 The texts included in this volume are drawn from the history of the Western philosophical tradition but, as at least one of the philosophers featured in it (Arthur Schopenhauer) recognized, the themes considered offer numerous points of contact with Eastern philosophical traditions, including Vedanta and Buddhism.

the moderns understood their discipline. Philosophy was not only a fair-weather friend but also, and especially, a companion in storms and in darkness, and not because it offered entertainment or distraction, but as a way of thinking about, thinking through, and contending with the profoundly unsettling.

This collection takes its inspiration from a number of excellent recent historical studies of modern philosophy. First and foremost is Susan Neiman's *Evil in Modern Thought: An Alternative History of Philosophy* (Princeton: Princeton University Press, 2002), which first used the "problem of evil" as a lens for an alternative approach to the history of modern thought. Unit I of this text parallels her exposition, with some supplemental texts drawn from outside of the canonical figures she focuses on. Second, Mara van der Lugt's *Dark Thoughts: Pessimism and the Problem of Suffering* (Princeton: Princeton University Press, 2021) inspires some of the selections in Unit II, and follows her in definitively foregrounding Bayle's role as the initiator of many debates concerning the themes of this collection. The third book is Frederick Beiser's *Weltschmerz: Pessimism in German Philosophy, 1860–1900* (Oxford: Oxford University Press, 2018), which informs the selection of readings in Unit III. Students who are interested in the topics discussed in this anthology are encouraged to seek these resources out first for further reading.

Note on the Texts: The chapters in this collection are not strictly chronologically ordered, but they are nonetheless intended to be read in the order in which they are presented, and all the context needed to understand a given reading will be provided by the preceding chapters (and the brief introductions to each). The versions of the texts here, whether originally in English or in translation, are sourced from the period to ensure a consistent tone throughout (and references to these are supplied in the concluding Sources), though spelling, punctuation, and idiomatic expressions have been silently modernized throughout to improve readability. The content of any footnotes added by the editors to the texts are enclosed in square brackets. The editors would like to express their gratitude to James Mackey for his assistance in transcribing many of the readings in this collection.

Unit I

THE CASE AGAINST GOD: THEODICY AND THE PROBLEM OF EVIL

Chapter 1

BAYLE ON THE INSOLUBLE PROBLEM OF EVIL

Introduction

IN THIS FIRST UNIT, WE WILL CONSIDER PHILOSOPHICAL engagements with the "problem of evil." The problem itself has a long history stretching well before the modern period. Indeed, we owe its first formulation to the early Christian author Lactantius (c. 250–325), who actually attributes it to Epicurus.[1] In essence, the problem concerns reconciling the existence of evil—whether evil deeds committed by human beings, or simply the occurrence of pain and suffering in the world—with God's supreme goodness, power, and wisdom. Assuming that God exists and that he has these attributes, it is hard to explain the existence of evil in a way that does not compromise one or more of the following: God's goodness (since he apparently wills the existence of evil), his power (since he seems unable to prevent it), or his wisdom (since its existence makes the world he created less perfect). Most of the authors we will survey in the next chapters were not willing to (explicitly) abandon the assumption of God's existence and supreme nature; accordingly, the strategies for resolving the problem have tended to deny that evil exists at all or deny that it owes its existence to God: a strategy adopted by the Christian thinkers St. Anselm (1033–1109) and St. Augustine (354–430), respectively.

It is to Pierre Bayle (1647–1706), an enigmatic French philosopher, that we owe the most provocative presentation of the problem of evil in the early modern period. Bayle was a member of a persecuted French protestant minority and was ultimately forced to flee to Rotterdam,

1 See the second reading, "Paulicians," below, remark *E*.

though he would draw on this experience for his impassioned defenses of toleration in a number of his works. His most important text is the monumental *Dictionnaire historique et critique* (*The Historical and Critical Dictionary*), originally published in 1697 with an expanded second edition following in 1702. The *Dictionary* is a singular work of perhaps unequaled erudition. Laid out as a conventional dictionary, with entries mostly devoted to the life and works of ancient and modern authors, the comparatively brief main text of each entry is accompanied by a host of expansive remarks in footnotes in which Bayle himself, prompted by the exposition, engages with key philosophical and theological issues of his time.

In the set of so-called "Manichean articles," Bayle re-poses the challenge of the problem of evil and offers his own novel response. These controversial entries include "Manicheans" and "Paulicians" (excerpts of which constitute the readings for this chapter) as well as "Marcionites" (not included here). What they all have in common is that they focus on the foundation and the legacy of the Manichean sect, which drew eclectically on Judaic and Christian sources but also on Zoroastrian, Buddhist, and gnostic traditions, among others. This now obscure but once enormously influential religion posited two opposed but equally-powerful cosmological principles—of light and goodness on the one hand and dark and evil on the other—to account for natural phenomena but also for the existence of evil in the world. The Manichean resolution of the problem of evil finds a surprising advocate in Bayle who uses these entries to demonstrate the superiority of the Manichean explanation of evil over anything offered by Christian thinkers. Even so, Bayle uses the apparent success of the Manichean hypothesis in accounting for evil to provoke a fundamental reconsideration of the capability of human reason, with all of its limitations, to arrive at a satisfactory solution to the problem of evil.

As indicated, each entry in Bayle's *Dictionary* consists of a comparatively small, primarily informational account of the subject of the entry, with a set of expansive remarks given in footnotes (and denoted by letters) printed below the main text. In the selections here (and in Chapter 5, below), we have opted not to follow the manner of Bayle's presentation strictly but have given the main text of the entry first, and then provided the text of the most relevant remarks. We have included a few of Bayle's own notes to his various remarks as footnotes, along with our own explanatory footnotes (enclosed in square brackets).

Pierre Bayle, *The Historical and Critical Dictionary*, from "Manicheans"

MANICHEANS, heretics, whose infamous sect, founded by one Manes, began in the 3rd century and established itself in several provinces, and subsisted a very long time. They taught such doctrines as ought to inspire us with the greatest horror. Their weakness did not consist, as at first it may seem, in their doctrine of two principles, one good, and the other bad, but in the particular explications they gave of it, and in the practical consequences they drew from it. It must be confessed that this false tenet, which is much more ancient than Manes, and cannot be maintained by any one who admits the Holy Scripture, either in whole or in part, would not easily be refuted if it were maintained by pagan philosophers well-skilled in disputing [*D*]. It was a happy thing, that St. Augustine, who understood so well all the arts of controversy, abandoned the Manichean heresy; for he would have removed its grossest errors, and framed such a system, as, by his management, would have puzzled the orthodox. Pope Leo I, acted very vigorously against the Manicheans; and his zeal being supported by the Imperial laws, this sect received then a very great blow. It became formidable in Armenia in the 9th century, as I say elsewhere,[2] and it appeared in France in the time of the Albigenses. This cannot be denied; but it is not true that the Albigenses were Manicheans. These, among other errors, taught that the souls of plants are rational; and condemned agriculture as a murdering occupation, but they permitted it to their hearers in favour of their elect. [...]

[*D*] (*it would not easily be refuted if it were maintained by pagan philosophers well skilled in disputing*) By reasons *a priori* they would quickly have been routed: but the reasons *a posteriori* were their strongholds; with these they might have fought a long time, and it would have been difficult to force them. You will understand me better by the explication I shall now provide. The most certain and most clear ideas of order we have, teach us that a being, which exists by itself, which is necessary and

2 [Bayle here refers to the entry "Paulicians," which follows this entry below.]

eternal, must be one, infinite, almighty, and endowed with all kind of perfection. If therefore we consult these ideas, we shall find nothing more absurd than the hypothesis of two eternal principles, independent of one another, one of which has no goodness, and can put a stop to the designs of the other. This is what I call reasons *a priori*; and which necessarily lead us to reject this hypothesis, and to admit only one principle of all things. If nothing but this were required to prove the goodness of a system, the cause would be determined to the frustration of Zoroaster and all his followers. But every system requires these two things to make it preferable: one, that the ideas of it be distinct; the other, that it accounts for what experience teaches us. We must see therefore whether the phenomena of nature can be conveniently explained by the hypothesis of one principle alone. When the Manicheans tell us that since we see in the world many things that are contrary to one another, such as heat and cold, white and black, light and darkness, there must necessarily be two first principles, they argue pitifully; for the opposition between those beings, however confirmed by what we call variations, disorders, and irregularities of nature, cannot make one half an objection against the unity, simplicity, and immutability of God. All these things may be accounted for, either by the different powers God has given to bodies, or by the laws of motion which he has established, or from the concurrence of occasional intelligent causes, by which he is pleased to act. [...] They say that God has united himself to ten most pure intelligences called *Sefira*, and that he acts with them in such a manner, that all the variations and imperfections of effects must be attributed to them. [...] Without being at the expense of such an hypothesis, the simplicity and immutability of the ways of God may be saved; the sole establishment of occasional causes is sufficient for that, provided we are only to explain the phenomena relating to bodies and do not consider man. The heavens, and the rest of the universe, declare the glory, power, and the unity of God; man alone, that master-piece of his creation among things visible, man alone, I say, affords the greatest objection against the unity of God. The matter is thus:

Man is wicked and unhappy: everyone knows it by what he feels in himself, and by the concourse he is obliged to have with his neighbours. He, who lives only five or six years,[3] may be perfectly convinced of these two things; and they who live long and are much engaged in worldly affairs know this still more clearly. Travel affords perpetual lessons upon this subject: they show everywhere the monuments of men's misfortunes and wickednesses: this appears everywhere in the many prisons, hospitals, gallows, and beggars. Here you see the ruins of a flourishing city; elsewhere you cannot even find the ruins of it. [...] Studious men, without going out of their closets, make the greatest discoveries on these two articles; because, in reading history, they take a view of all the ages and countries of the world. History, properly speaking, is nothing but a collection of the crimes and misfortunes of mankind; but we must observe that these two evils, the one moral, and the other physical, do not wholly fill up history, nor all the experience of private persons. There are everywhere some things, that are physically good and morally good; some examples of virtue, and some examples of happiness. And this is that which makes the difficulty; for if there were none but evil and unhappy men, there would be no occasion to have recourse to the hypothesis of two principles: it is the mixture of happiness and virtue with misery and vice, which requires this hypothesis; and this is the stronghold of the sect of Zoroaster. [...]

In order to make it appear how difficult it would be to refute this false system, and that we may conclude that it is necessary to have recourse to revelation to overthrow it, let us feign here a dispute between Melissus and Zoroaster, who were both pagans and great philosophers. Melissus, who acknowledged but one principle, would say, at first, that his system agrees admirably well with the ideas of order. The necessary being is not bounded; and therefore is infinite and almighty, and consequently one; and it would be a monstrous thing, and a contradiction, if he had no goodness, but the greatest of all vices, *viz.* an essential malice. I confess to you, would Zoroaster answer, that your ideas are very well connected, and I am willing to grant, that, in this respect, your hypothesis surpasses mine. I will not insist upon an objection, which I might make use of, which is this: that as infinity must include everything that is real, and malice being

3 At that age, he has played and suffered malicious tricks; he has had grief and sorrow, and has pouted many times, etc.

no less a real thing than goodness, the universe requires that there should be both wicked and good beings; and that, since a sovereign goodness, and a sovereign malice, cannot subsist in one and the same subject, there must be in nature one being essentially good, and another essentially evil. I do not insist, I say, upon this objection; I will allow, that your system is more agreeable to the notions of order than mine. But explain to me, I pray, by your hypothesis, how does it comes to pass, that man is wicked, and so subject to pain and grief? I defy you to find in your principles a reason of this phenomenon, as I can in mine; and now I have regained the advantage I gave you; for, as you surpass me in the beauty of ideas, and in reasons *a priori*, so I surpass you in the explication of phenomena, and in reasons *a posteriori*. And since the principal character of a good system is to account for what experience teaches us, and that the bare incapacity of explaining it is a proof that a hypothesis is not good, how beautiful forever it appears, you must grant that I have hit the mark, by admitting two principles, and that you have not hit it by admitting but one.

Here, without doubt, lies the main point of the whole matter: here Melissus is engaged in a hard conflict [...]. Let us hear Zoroaster continuing his discourse: If a man is the creature of one principle perfectly good, most holy and omnipotent, can he be exposed to diseases, to heat and cold, hunger and thirst, pain and grief? Can he have so many bad inclinations? Can he commit so many crimes? Can perfect holiness produce a criminal creature? Would not omnipotence, joined with infinite goodness, furnish his own work plentifully with good things, and secure it from everything that might be offensive or vexatious?

If Melissus consults the notions of order, he will answer that man was not wicked when God made him. He will say that man was created by God in a happy fate; but he, not following the light of his conscience, which was intended by the author of his being to conduct him in the way of virtue, became so wicked and deserved that God, who is perfectly just as well as perfectly good, should make him feel the effects of his wrath. God therefore is not the cause of moral evil, but he is the cause of physical evil, i.e., of the punishment of moral evil; a punishment, which is so far from being inconsistent with a principle perfectly good, that it flows necessarily from one of his attributes, I mean from his justice, which is no less essential to him than his goodness.

This answer, which is the best that Melissus could make, is good and well-founded, but it may be opposed by reasons that have something in them more specious, and dazzling: for Zoroaster would not fail to represent that, if man were the work of a principle infinitely good and holy, he ought to have been created not only without any actual evil, but also without any inclination to evil, since that inclination is such a defect, as could not have such a principle for its cause. It remains, therefore, that we say that man, coming out of the hands of his Creator, had only the power of determining himself to evil, and that having determined himself to it, he was the sole cause of the crime which he committed and of the moral evil which has introduced itself into the world.

But, (I.) we have no distinct idea that can make us understand that a being, which does not exist of its own accord can nevertheless act fully independently. Zoroaster, therefore, will say that the free will, which was given to man is actually not able to determine itself wholly, since it exists continually and totally by the action of God. (II.) He will put this question: did God foresee that man would make an ill use of his free-will? If you answer yes, he will say that it seems not possible that anything can foresee that which depends wholly upon an indeterminate cause. But I will grant you, he will say, that God did foresee the sin of his creature, and from thence I conclude that he would have hindered him from sinning, for the ideas of order will not suffer us to believe that a cause infinitely good and holy, which can hinder the introduction of moral evil, should not hinder it, especially since by permitting it God was obliged severely to punish his own work. If God did not foresee the fall of man, yet at least he must think it possible: since therefore he saw himself obliged, in case it should happen, to depart from his paternal goodness, and to make his children very miserable, by exercising upon them the office of a severe judge, He would have determined man to moral good as he determined him to that which is physical; he would not have left in the soul of man any power which should incline him to sin, any more than he has left any to incline him to misery as such. This is what our clear and distinct ideas of order lead us to when we follow, step by step, what a principle infinitely good ought to do. For if a goodness, so bounded as that of earthly fathers necessarily requires that they should prevent, as much as possible, the bad use their children may make of the good things they give them; much more will an infinite and almighty goodness prevent the ill effects of his gifts. Instead of giving them free will, it will determine its creatures to that which is good; or, if it gives them a free will, it will always effectually watch over them to keep them from sinning. I believe indeed, that Melissus would not remain silent here, but all that he could answer would be presently opposed by reasons as plausible as his, and so there would be no end of the dispute.[4]

If Melissus had recourse to retortion,[5] he would very much perplex Zoroaster; but should he grant him his two principles, he would leave him an open way to come at the explication of the origin of evil. Zoroaster would go back to the time of the chaos, which is a state, as to his two principles, very like that which Hobbes calls the state of nature, and which he supposes to have preceded the first establishment of societies. In this state of nature one man was a wolf to another, and everything belonged to the first possessor: none was master of anything, except he who was the strongest. To get out of this confusion, everyone agreed to quit his right to the whole, that he might have a property in something; they transacted together, and the war ceased. The two principles, weary of the chaos, where each confounded and overthrew what the other would do, came at last to an agreement: each of them yielded something, each had a share in the production of man and in the laws of the union of the soul. The good principle obtained those which procure to man a thousand pleasures and consented to those which expose man to a thousand sorrows; and if it consented that moral good should be infinitely less in mankind than moral evil, he repaired the damage in some other kind of creatures, in which vice should be much less than virtue. If many men in this life have more misery than happiness, this is recompensed in another state: what they have not under a human shape they

4 All this is more largely discussed in the remarks of the article "Paulicians."

5 [A mode of refutation where it is shown that the objections directed against an opponent also apply to the defended position.]

shall recover under another. By means of this agreement, the chaos was disembroiled, the chaos, I say, a passive principle, which was the field of battle between these two active principles. The poets have represented this disembroiling under the image of a quarrel ended. This is what Zoroaster might allege, boasting that he does not attribute to the good principle the production of a creature at his own pleasure, which was to be so wicked and miserable, but only after he had found by experience that he could do no better nor better oppose the horrible designs of the evil principle. To render his hypothesis the less offensive he might have denied that there was a long war between the two principles, and lay aside all those fights, and prisoners, which the Manicheans speak of. The whole might be reduced to certain knowledge of the two principles. That one could never obtain from the other but such and such conditions. And thus an eternal agreement might have been made upon this footing.

A thousand great difficulties might be objected to this philosopher; but as he would find answers, and after all desire to be furnished with a better hypothesis pretending to have solidly refuted that of Melissus, he would never be brought back into the way of truth. Human reason is too weak for this end: it is a principle of destruction, and not of edification; it is only fit to start doubts and to turn itself all manner of ways to perpetuate a dispute. And I think I am not mistaken if I say of natural revelation, that is, of the light of reason, what divines say of the Mosaical economy: it was only fit to discover to man his weakness, and the necessity of a redeemer, and the law of mercy. It was a schoolmaster (these are their own words) for bringing men to Jesus Christ. Let us say the same of reason: it can only discover to man his ignorance and weakness, and the necessity of another revelation, which is that of the Scripture. There we find what is sufficient to refute unanswerably the hypothesis of two principles and all the objections of Zoroaster. We find there the unity of God, and his infinite perfections; the fall of man, and the consequences of it. Let any one tell us with a pompous show of arguments that it was not possible that moral evil should introduce itself into the world by the work of a principle infinitely good and holy; we shall answer, that this was nevertheless done, and consequently that it is very possible. There is nothing more foolish than to reason against matter of fact; this maxim, *ab actu ad potentiam valet consequentia*,[6] is as clear as this proposition, two and two make four. The Manicheans were sensible of what I have just now observed, and therefore they rejected the Old Testament; but what they retained of the Scripture supplied the orthodox with sufficient arms against them. And so it was not very difficult to confound those heretics, who otherwise childishly entangled themselves when they came to particulars. Now since the Scripture affords us the best solutions, I cannot be blamed for saying that it would be difficult to gain the victory over a heathen philosopher in this cause.

6 [It is permitted to infer from what is actually so to its possibility (Latin).]

Pierre Bayle, *The Historical and Critical Dictionary*, from "Paulicians"

PAULICIANS. Thus were the Manicheans in Armenia called, when one Paul became their head in the 7th century. They arrived at so great a power, either by the weakness of the government, or by the protection of the Saracens, or even by the favour of the emperor Nicephorus, who favoured that sect very much, that at last, being persecuted by the empress Theodora, the wife of Basil I, they were in a condition to build towns and to take up arms against their princes. Those wars were long and bloody under the empire of Basil the Macedonian, that is, at the end of the 9th century. And yet there was so great a slaughter of those heretics under the empress Theodora that it seemed they would never be able to rise again. It is thought that the preachers whom they sent into Bulgaria, settled there the Manichean heresy, and that from thence it spread itself soon after into the other parts of Europe. They condemned the worship of saints and the images of the cross, but this was not their principal character. Their fundamental doctrine was that of two co-eternal principles independent of one another. This doctrine at first hearing creates horror, and consequently it is strange that the Manichean sect could seduce so great a part of the world. But on the other side, it is so difficult to answer their objections about the origin of evil [*E*], that we must not wonder that the hypothesis of two principles, the one good and the other bad, should have dazzled the eyes of several ancient philosophers and found so many followers in Christendom, where the doctrine which teaches the enmity of the devils to the true God is always accompanied with the doctrine which teaches rebellion and fall of one part of the good angels. This hypothesis of two principles would probably have made a greater progress, if the particulars of it had been given less crudely explained, and if it had not been attended with several odious practices, or if there had been as many disputes then about predestination as there are at this day [*F*] in which the Christians accuse one another either of making God the author of sin or of depriving him of the government of the world. The pagans could better answer than the Christians to the objections of the Manicheans, but some of their philosophers found it a difficult thing. I shall observe in what sense the orthodox seem to admit two first principles, and in what sense it cannot be said that, according to the Manicheans, God is the author of sin. [...] The ancient Fathers were not ignorant that the question concerning the origin of evil is a most perplexing one. They could not resolve it by the Platonic hypothesis, which was at bottom a type of Manicheism, since it admitted of two principles. Thus, they found themselves obliged to have recourse to the privilege of the free will of men; but the more we reflect on that way of solving the difficulty, the more we find the natural light of philosophy ties and entangles this Gordian knot [*M*]. [...]

> [*E*] (*it is so difficult to answer the objections of the Manicheans about the origin of evil*) I have prepared my readers to see here three observations which I would have placed in the article of the Manicheans but that I had a mind to avoid prolixity in that place. Let us now perform our promise, and not frustrate the expectation of those who have a mind to go after our reference. I shall place below by themselves the second and third observation: but here follows the first.
>
> The Fathers of the church, who have so well refuted the Marcionites, the Manicheans, and in general all those who admitted two principles, have not well answered the objections which relate to the origin of evil. They should have abandoned all the reasons *a priori*, as the outlying parts of a place, which may be troubled and cannot be maintained; they should have contented themselves with reasons *a posteriori*, and placed all their forces behind this entrenchment. The Old and New Testament are two parts of revelation, which mutually confirm one another; since therefore these heretics acknowledged the divine authority of the New, it was no difficult matter to prove to them the divine authority of the Old, after which it was easy to destroy their objections by showing that they are contrary to experience. According to Scripture, there is but one good principle, and yet moral and physical evil have been introduced among mankind; it is not therefore contrary to the nature of a good principle to permit the introduction of moral evil and to punish crimes, for it is not more evident that four and four are eight than it is evident that if a thing come to pass then it is possible. *Ab actu ad potentiam valet consequentia*, is one of the clearest and most uncontestable axioms in metaphysics.[7] This is

7 See the article "Manicheans," remark *D*, above.

an impregnable rampart and this is sufficient to render the cause of the orthodox victorious, although their reasons *a priori* may be refuted. But some will wonder: may they be so refuted? I will answer: yes. The manner of introducing evil under the empire of a sovereign being, infinitely good, infinitely holy, and infinitely powerful, is not only inexplicable but incomprehensible, and all that is objected against the reasons why this being has permitted evil is more agreeable to natural light, and the ideas we have of order, than these reasons are. Let us consider this passage of Lactantius, which contains an answer to an objection of Epicurus.

> "'God,' says Epicurus, 'is either willing to remove evil and is not able, or he is able and not willing, or he is neither willing nor able, or else he is both willing and able. If he is willing and not able, he must then be weak, which cannot be affirmed of God. If he is able and not willing he must be envious, which is likewise contrary to the nature of God. If he is neither willing nor able, he must be both envious and weak, and consequently not God. If he is both willing and able, which only can agree with the notion of God, whence then proceeds evil? Or, why does he not remove it?' I know, that the greatest part of philosophers, who assert a providence, are commonly embarrassed with this argument, and almost forced against their will to acknowledge that God does not concern himself with the administration of the world, which is the very thing that Epicurus drives at. But we easily overthrow this formidable argument by clear reason. For God can do whatever he pleases, and there is not weakness or envy in him; consequently, he is able to remove evil but is not willing, and yet for all that, is not envious. He does not remove evil for this reason, because withal (as I have shown) he bestows wisdom, and there is more good and satisfaction in wisdom, than there is painfulness in evil. By wisdom likewise we come to know God, and by that knowledge attain to immortality, which is the chief good. And therefore unless we first know evil we shall not be able to know good. But neither Epicurus nor any other has observed this: if evil be removed, wisdom must also

> be removed; no trace of virtue will remain; because virtue consists in bearing with and overcoming the sharpness of evil, we should be deprived of the greatest, the most real, and proper good. It is evident, therefore, that all things, evil as well as good, were intended for the benefit of mankind."[8]

The whole strength of the objection could not be more sincerely represented; Epicurus himself could not have proposed it with greater clearness and strength. But the answer of Lactantius is pitiful, and it is not only weak, but full of errors, and perhaps of heresies. It supposes that God must produce evil because otherwise he would not be able to communicate to us either wisdom or virtue, or the knowledge of what is good. Can anything be shown more monstrous than this doctrine? Does it not overthrow all that divines tell us about the happiness of paradise and the state of innocence? They tell us that Adam and Eve in this happy state felt, without any mixture of uneasiness, all the pleasures which that delicious and charming place, the garden of Eden, where God placed them, could afford them. They add that, if they had not sinned, they and all their posterity should have enjoyed this happiness without being subject either to diseases or sorrows, and that neither the elements nor animals had ever done them any harm. It was their sin that exposed them to cold and heat, to hunger and thirst, to pain and sorrow, and to the mischiefs which certain beasts do to us. So far is it from being true, that virtue and wisdom cannot subsist in a man without physical evil, as Lactantius affirms, that, on the contrary, it must be maintained, that man has been subject to this evil only because he renounced virtue and wisdom. If the doctrine of Lactantius were good, we must necessarily suppose that the good angels are subject to a thousand inconveniences, and that the souls of the blessed do alternately pass from joy to sorrow, so that even in the mansions of glory and in the bosom of the beatific vision none are secured

8 [Lactantius (c. 250–325) was an early Christian author and advisor to the Roman emperor Constantine I. This quotation is taken from his *De ira Dei* (*On the Anger of God*).]

from adversity. Nothing is more contrary to the unanimous sentiment of divines, and to right reason, than this doctrine.

It is even true in sound philosophy that it is no way necessary that our soul should feel evil to the end that it may relish what is good, and that it should pass successively from pleasure to pain, and from pain to pleasure, that it may be able to discern that pain is an evil, and that pleasure is a good thing. And thus Lactantius does not less oppose the light of nature than the opinions of divines. We know by experience, that our soul cannot feel at one and the same time both pleasure and pain; it must therefore at first either have felt pain before pleasure, or pleasure before pain. If its first sensation was that of pleasure, then it found that state to be agreeable though it was ignorant of pain; and if its first sensation was that of pain, it found that state to be uneasy although it was ignorant of pleasure. Suppose then that its first sensation lasted several years without interruption, you may conceive that during that time it was in an easy condition or in one that was uneasy. And do not cite experience to me; do not tell me that a pleasure which lasts long becomes insipid and that pain in time becomes supportable, for I will answer you that this proceeds from a change in the organ, which makes that sensation which continues the same, as to kind, to be different as to degree. If you have had at first a sensation of six degrees, it will not continue to be six at the end of two hours or to the end of a year, but only one degree or one quarter of a degree; thus custom blunts the edge of our sensations. Their degrees correspond to the concussions on the parts of the brain, and this concussion is weakened by frequent repetitions, from whence it comes to pass that the degrees of sensation are diminished. But if pain or joy were communicated to us in the same degree successively for a hundred years, we should be as unhappy or as happy the hundredth year as the first day, which plainly proves that a creature may be happy with a continued good or unhappy with a continued evil, and that the alternative which Lactantius speaks of is a bad solution of the difficulty. It is not founded upon the nature of good and evil, nor upon the nature of the subject which receives them, nor upon the nature of the cause which produces them. Pleasure and pain are no less proper to be communicated the second moment than the first, and the third moment than the second, and so all of the rest. Our soul is also as susceptible to them after it has felt them one moment as it was before it felt them, and God who gives them is no less capable of producing them the second time than the first. This is what we learn from the natural ideas we have of these objects. Christian theology confirms this invincibly since it teaches us that the torments of the damned shall be eternal and continued, and as sharp at the end of a hundred thousand years as the first day, and that on the contrary the pleasures of paradise shall last eternally and continually without ever abating. I would gladly know whether supposing a thing which is very easy, as that there were two suns in the world, of which one should rise when the other sets, we must not conclude that darkness would be unknown to mankind. According to this fine philosophy of Lactantius, we must also conclude that a man could not know the light, that he would not know it is day and that he sees the objects before him, etc.

What I have just now said proves invincibly, I think, that there is no advantage to be gained against our Paulicians by representing to them that God has mingled good and evil only as he foresaw that a pure and unmixed good would seem to us insipid in a little time. They will answer that this property is not contained in the idea we have of a good thing, and that it is directly contrary to the common doctrine about the happiness of paradise. And as to the experience which teaches us only too well namely (1), that the joys of this life are not felt but in proportion as they deliver us from a troublesome state, and (2) that they draw after them disgust when they have continued a little while, they will maintain that this phenomenon is inexplicable unless we have recourse to the hypothesis of two principles. For if we depend, they will say, only upon one cause, almighty, infinitely good, and infinitely free, and which disposes universally of all beings, according to the good pleasure of his own will, we ought not to feel any evil, all our good ought to be pure, and we ought never to have the least disgust. The author of our being, if he is infinitely beneficent, ought to take a continual pleasure in making us happy and preventing everything that may disturb or diminish our joy: for it is a character essentially contained in the idea of supreme goodness. The fibers of our brain, cannot be the cause that God weakens our pleasures; for according to you, he is the only author of matter; he is almighty, and nothing can hinder him from acting according to the full extent of his infinite goodness; he needs only to will that our pleasures should not depend upon the fibers of our brain; and if he wills that they should depend upon them, he can preserve these fibers eternally in the same state, he needs only to will either that they should not wear out at all or that the damage they suffer should be quickly repaired. You cannot therefore explain what we experience but by the hypothesis of two principles. If we feel pleasure, it is the good principle that gives it to us; but if we do not feel it perfectly pure, and if we are quickly disgusted with it, it is because there is an ill principle that thwarts the good. The latter, to be even with him, makes our pains less grievous by custom and gives us always some hopes in the greatest evils. This, and the good use that is often made of prosperity, are phenomena which are admirably explained according to the Manichean hypothesis. These are things which lead us to suppose that the two principles made an agreement which reciprocally limits their operations. The good principle cannot do us all the good he desires: it was necessary that in order to do us a great deal of good, he should consent that his adversary should do us as much evil; for without this consent the chaos would have continued a chaos and no creature would have ever have felt that which is good. Thus, supreme goodness finding it a better way for its own satisfaction to see the world sometimes happy and sometimes miserable than never to see it happy, made an agreement which produced the mixture of good and evil we now see in mankind. By ascribing to your principle an almighty power, and the glory of enjoying eternity alone, you have deprived him of an attribute which goes before all the rest; for *optimus*, the best, always precedes *maximus*, the greatest, in the manner of the most learned nations when they speak of God. You suppose, that having nothing to hinder him from loading his creatures with good things, he oppresses them with evils; and if any of them be advanced before others, it is that their fall may be the greater. We clear him from any guilt in all this matter, we explain without impeaching his goodness, all that can be said of the inconstancy of fortune, the jealousy of nemesis, and the continual sport which Aesop makes the employment of God: he exalts things, says Aesop, that are low, and abases things that are high. We say however that the good principle could obtain no more from his adversary: his goodness extended as far as it could; if he does us no more good, it is because he cannot and we have no reason, therefore, to complain.

Who will not wonder at and deplore the fate of our reason? Behold here the Manicheans who, with a hypothesis altogether absurd and contradictory, explain what we experience one hundred times better than the orthodox do with the supposition, so just, so necessary, and so singularly true, of one first principle which is infinitely good and almighty. [...]

Thus you may see it is not without reason that I urge that we must only oppose to these sects, this maxim: *ab actu ad potentiam valet consequentia*, and this short enthymeme: *this has come to pass, therefore it is not repugnant to the holiness and goodness of God*. I observe that we cannot join issue in this dispute upon any other foot without some disadvantage. The reasons for the permission of sin which are not taken from the mysteries revealed in Scripture, have this defect, however good they be, that they may be opposed by other reasons more convincing and more agreeable to the ideas we have of order. For instance, if you say that God permitted sin to manifest his wisdom, which shines the more brightly by the disorders which the wickedness of men produces every day than it would have done in a state of innocence; it may be answered that this is to compare the deity to a father who would suffer his children to break their legs on purpose to show to all the city his great art in setting their broken bones; or to a king who should suffer seditions and factions to increase through all his kingdom that he might purchase the glory of quelling them. The conduct of this father and monarch is so contrary to the clear and distinct ideas according to which we judge goodness and wisdom, and in general of the whole duty of a father and a king, that our reason cannot conceive how God can make use of the same. But you will say, "the ways of God are not our ways."[9] Keep to that then, this is a text of Scripture and do not reason any more. Do not any more tell us that without the fall of the first man the justice and mercy of God would have remained unknown; for you will be answered that there was nothing more easy than to make man know these two attributes. The bare idea of a being infinitely

9 Isaiah 55.8.

perfect clearly informs sinful man that God possesses all the virtues that are worthy of a nature infinite in all respects; how much more would it have informed an innocent man that God is infinitely just? But, you will say, then he would have never punished anybody. But, I say, by this very thing his justice would have been known as this would have been a continued act, a perpetual exercise of that virtue. None would have deserved to be punished, and consequently the forbearing of all punishment would have been an exercise of justice. I desire you to answer me: there are two princes, whereof one suffers his subjects to fall into misery, that he may deliver them when they have sufficiently languished under it; and the other preserves them always in a prosperous state. Is not the latter much better and more merciful than the other? Those who teach the immaculate conception of the Virgin, prove demonstratively that God poured upon her his mercy and the benefits of redemption more than upon other man. One need not be a metaphysician to know this: a plough-man clearly perceives that it is a much greater goodness to hinder a man from falling into a ditch than to let him fall in and then take him out an hour after; and that it is much better to hinder an assassin from killing a man than to break him upon the wheel after he has been permitted to commit the murder. [...] All this serves to admonish us that we must not engage with the Manicheans till we have before all things laid down the doctrine *of the exaltation of faith, and the abasing of reason.*

Those who say that God permitted sin, because he could not hinder it without destroying that free will which he had given to man, and which was the best present he had made him, venture very much. The reason they give is lovely and there is in it a certain *I know not what* which dazzles the eyes, something that appears great: but nevertheless it may be opposed by such reasons as are more suited to the capacity of all men, and more founded upon good sense and the ideas of order. Without having read the fine treatise of Seneca concerning benefits,[10] any one knows by the light of nature that it is essential to a benefactor not to bestow such favours which he knows will be abused in such a manner that they serve only to the ruin of him on whom they

10 [*De beneficiis* (*On Benefits*) by the Stoic philosopher Seneca (c. 4 BCE–65 CE).]

are bestowed. There is no enemy so inveterate who would not upon these terms load his enemy with such specious favours. It is essential to a benefactor to spare nothing to make the person happy with his benefits, whom he honours with them. If he could confer on him the knowledge of making good use of them and yet should refuse it to him, he would very ill sustain the character of a benefactor; neither would he better sustain it if, being able to keep his client from abusing benefits, he should not hinder him by curing his bad inclinations. These are ideas which are known as well to the common people as to the philosophers. I confess that if one could not prevent the ill use of a favour except by breaking the arms and legs of one's clients, or by shackling their feet with irons in a dungeon, one would not be obliged to prevent it but it would be better to refuse them the benefit; but if one can prevent it by changing the heart, and by giving a man a preference for good things, one ought to do it: now this is what God might easily do, if he pleased. [...]

There is no good mother who, having given leave to her daughters to go to a ball, would not revoke that leave if she were sure that they would yield to enticement and leave their maidenhood behind them. And every mother who knowing that this would certainly come to pass but nevertheless suffers them to go to a ball, being contented with exhorting them to virtue and threatening them with disgrace if they should not return maids, would at least justly bring upon herself the blame of neither loving her daughters nor chastity. It would be in vain for her to say, in her own justification, that she had no mind to restrain the liberty of her daughters nor to show any distrust of them: she would be answered that this management was very preposterous and better suits a provoked step-mother than a mother, and that it would have been better to keep her daughters in her sight than to give them the privilege of liberty to such bad purposes and to grant them such marks of her confidence. This reveals the rashness of those who offer by way of explanation the regard which, they say, God showed for the free will of the first man. They had better believe, and be silent, than allege such reasons as may be refuted by the examples I have just now made use of. [...] By these reasons it were easy to show that the free will of the first man, which was preserved to him sound and entire, in the circumstances wherein he was to make use of it to his own loss, to the ruin of mankind, to the eternal damnation of the greatest part of his posterity, and to the introduction of a terrible deluge of evils, of guilt and punishment, was not a good gift. We shall never understand, that this privilege could be preserved to him by an effect of goodness and out of love for holiness. Those who say that it was necessary that there should be free beings to the end that God might be loved with a love of choice, are conscious to themselves that this hypothesis does not satisfy reason; for when it is foreseen, that those free beings will choose not the love of God but sin, one may plainly perceive that the intended end is defeated and that, therefore, it is in no way necessary that free will should be preserved. I shall examine this again in the remark [*M*].

[*F*] (*if there had been as many disputes then about predestination as there are at this day*) If the Manicheans should go no further they would renounce their principal advantages. For their most terrible objections are these following. (1) It cannot be conceived that the first man could receive from a good principle the faculty of doing ill. This faculty is vicious and everything that can produce evil is bad, since evil cannot proceed but from a bad cause; and therefore the free will of Adam proceeded from two contrary principles: inasmuch as he could take the right way, he depended upon a good principle; but inasmuch as he could embrace evil, he depended upon an ill principle. (2) It is impossible to comprehend that God did only permit sin; for a bare permission of sin added nothing to free will and was not a means to foresee whether Adam would persevere in his innocence or fall from it. Besides, according to the idea we have of a created being we cannot comprehend that it can be a principle of action, that it can move itself, and that receiving in every moment of its duration its existence and the existence of its faculties wholly from another cause, it should create in itself any modalities by a power peculiar to itself. These modalities must be either not distinct from the substance of the soul, as the new philosophers will have it, or distinct from the substance of the soul as the Peripatetics affirm. If they be not distinct, they cannot be produced but by the cause, which can produce the very substance of the soul; but it is manifest that man himself is not this cause, neither can he be. If they are distinct, then they are created beings, produced out of nothing, since they are not composed of the soul nor of any other pre-existent nature; they cannot, therefore, be produced but by a cause that can create. Not all the sects of philosophy agree that man is not, nor can be, such a cause. Some think that the motion which excites him proceeds from some other cause, and that nevertheless he can stop it and fix it upon a certain object. This is contradictory, since there is no less power required to stop that which is in motion than to move that which is at rest. Seeing, therefore, a creature cannot be moved by a bare permission of action, and has not in itself a principles of motion, it is absolutely necessary that God should move it; he must therefore do something else than barely permit man to sin. (3) This may be proved by a new reason: *viz.* that it cannot be comprehended, that a bare permission should bring contingent events out of the class of things merely possible, nor that it should put the deity in a capacity of being certainly sure that the creature will sin. A mere permission cannot be the foundation of the divine prescience. This is what obliges the greatest part of the divines to suppose that God made a decree which imports that the creature will sin and which according to them is the foundation of prescience. Others think that the decree imports that the creature shall be placed in such circumstances in which God has foreseen that it will sin. Thus, some think that God foresaw the sin by reason of his decree; others, that he made the decree because he foresaw the sin. Howsoever this be explained, it follows clearly that God was willing that man should sin, and that he preferred this to the perpetual duration of innocence which it was so easy for him to bring about and ordain. Reconcile this, if you can, with the goodness he ought to have for his creatures, and the infinite love he ought to have for holiness. (4) But if you say with those that come nearer to a method that would justify providence by saying that God did not foresee the fall of Adam, you will gain but little by it; for at least he knew very certainly that the first man ran the risk of losing his innocence and of thereby introducing into the world all the evils of punishment and guilt which followed his apostacy. Neither his goodness, nor his holiness, nor his wisdom could permit that he should run the hazard of these events; for our reason convinces us very evidently that a mother who should suffer her daughters to go to a ball, when she knew most certainly that they would run a great hazard with respect to their honour, shows thereby that she neither loved her daughters nor chastity: and if it be supposed, that she has an infallible preservative against all temptations, and that she gives it not to her daughters when she sends them to a ball, it is most evident that she is guilty and that she takes but little care that her daughters should preserve their maidenhood. Let us carry on the comparison a little further: if that mother should go to this ball, and through a window should see and hear that one of her daughters defends herself but weakly in the corner of a closet against the solicitations of a young gallant; if even when she sees that her daughter is but one step from yielding to the desires of the tempter, she should not go then to assist her and deliver her from the snare, would not everyone have reason to say that she acts like a cruel step-mother, and that she would not scruple to sell the honour of her own daughter? This is a representation of the conduct which the Socinians[11] attribute to God. They cannot say that he knew the sin of the first man but as a possible event; he knew all the particulars of the temptation, and he must needs have known a moment before Eve yielded that she was going to ruin herself; he must, I say, have known it with such a certainty as renders one inexcusable if he does not prevent the evil, and allows him not to say, "I had reason to believe that this would not happen, I had still great hopes." There are no people of so little experience but, without seeing what passes in the heart and knowing the matter any otherwise than by signs, may be sure that a woman is ready to yield if they see through a window how she defends herself when really her fall is near. Before the moment of her consent there are certain indications concerning which they are not deceived. How much greater reason have we to think that God who knew all the thoughts of Eve as they came into her mind (this knowledge the Socinians do not deny him) could not doubt but she was just ready to yield. He would therefore let her sin, and this even at the time when he foresaw she would certainly

11 [Socinianism, named after its founders Lelio Sozzini (1525–62) and Fausto Sozzini (1539–1604), was a broadly Christian belief system that rejected, among other things, divine foreknowledge (especially of the freely-willed actions on the part of human beings.)]

sin. The sin of Adam was yet more certainly foreseen; for the example of Eve gave some light the better to foresee the fall of her husband. If God had wanted to preserve man and his innocence, and to prevent all the miseries which were to be the infallible consequence of sin, would he not at least have fortified the husband after the wife had fallen? Would he not have given him another wife, sound and perfect, instead of that which had suffered herself to be seduced? Let us say therefore that the Socinian system, by depriving God of prescience, reduces him to slavery and to a pitiful form of government and does not remove the grand difficulty which it is supposed to remove and which drives these heretics to deny the foreknowledge of contingent events. [...]

Let us come at last to the text of this remark.[12] The disputes which have arisen in the West among Christians since the Reformation have so clearly shown that a man does not know which side to take when he would solve the difficulties about the origin of evil, and that a Manichean at this day would be more terrible than in former times because he would refute us all one by one. [...] [F]or, [the Manichean might say,] if you examine your system carefully, you will acknowledge, that you as well as I admit two principles, the one of good and the other of evil; but instead of placing them as I do, in the two subjects, you join them together in one and the same substance, which is monstrous and impossible. The only principle which you admit determined from all eternity, according to you, that man should sin and that the first sin should be infectious; that it should produce without end and without intermission all imaginable crimes over the face of the whole earth, as a result of which he prepared for mankind in this life all the miseries that can be conceived such as pestilence, war, famine, pain, vexation, and after this life a Hell, where all men almost shall be eternally tormented after such a manner as makes our hair stand on end when we read descriptions of it. If such a principle is besides perfectly good, and loves holiness infinitely, must we not acknowledge, that the same God is at one and the same time, perfectly good and perfectly bad, and that he loves vice no less than he does virtue? Now is it not more reasonable to divide these two opposite qualities, and to give all that is good to

12 [That is, to the text to which this remark is appended.]

the one principle, and all that is bad to another principle? Human history will prove nothing to the disadvantage of the good principle. I do not say, as you do, that of his own will, and only because it was his good pleasure, he subjected mankind to sin and misery, when nothing hindered him from making them holy and happy: I suppose he did not consent to this but to shun a greater evil, and that he did it as it were in his own defense. This clears him of guilt. He saw that the evil principle would destroy all; he opposed him as much as he could, and by agreement he obtained the state to which things are now reduced. He acted like a monarch, who to avoid the ruin of all his dominions, is obliged to sacrifice one part of them to the good of the other. This is a grand inconvenience, which at first frightens human reason, to talk of a first principle, and a necessary being, as of a thing that does not all it has a mind to, and which is forced for want of power to submit to conjunctures; but it is a greater imperfection still to resolve voluntarily to do evil when one can do good. This is what might be said by this heretic. I shall conclude with the good use for which I made these remarks.

It is more useful than one would think to humble the reason of man by showing him with what force the most foolish heresies, such as those of the Manicheans are, may confound it and embroil the most fundamental truths. This should teach the Socinians, who make reason the rule of faith, that they throw themselves into the way of error, which only tends by degrees to make them deny or doubt of all things, and that they lay themselves open to being beaten by the most execrable people. What must be done then? Men must captivate their understandings to the obedience of faith, and never dispute about some things. [...]

[*M*] (*the more we reflect ... the more we find that the natural light ... ties and entangles this Gordian knot*) I found it so by experience, as I was reading this article again to make it ready for a second edition, some new thoughts came into my mind, which convince me anew, and more strongly than ever, that the best answer that can be naturally returned to the question, "Why did God permit that man should sin?" is this: "I do not know, I only believe that he had some reasons for it very worthy of his infinite wisdom, but they are incomprehensible to me." With such an answer you will stop the most obstinate disputers; for if they will go on they must talk alone, and so they will soon hold their tongues. If you should enter the lists with them, and undertake to maintain that the inviolable privileges of free will have been the true reason which moved God to permit men to sin, you would be forced to answer their objections to their satisfaction; and I do not know how you could well do it, for they might object two things which seem most evident to reason:

I. The first is, that God having caused his creatures to exist by an effect of his goodness, he gave them also, under the character of a bountiful cause, all the perfections which are proper for every kind. We must therefore say that he expressed a greater love for those who received very excellent qualities from him than for those who received less excellent qualities. He has, therefore, out of a particular goodness bestowed free will upon men, since that quality raises them above all the beings that are upon the earth. But we cannot conceive, how a gracious and beneficent being can make a considerable present without designing to increase thereby the happiness of those who receive it, and consequently that bountiful being ought to put them in a condition of getting such an advantage by it, and keep them, if it be possible, from being utterly ruined and destroyed by it. But, if there is no other way of preventing that than by revoking the gift, that gift ought to be revoked; whereby the character of patron and benefactor may be much better preserved than by any other means. This is not changing one's mind with respect to the recipient, but retaining without any shadow of variation the good-will with which that present was given. The same goodness which moves one to give a thing which he thinks will make happy those that shall enjoy it, moves him likewise to take it away as soon as he observes that it makes them unhappy; and if he has time enough, and a sufficient power, he will not put off the withdrawing of his gift until it proves the cause of misery, but he will take it away before it has done any harm. What has been said follows from the ideas of order, and the notions whereby we may judge of the essence and characters of goodness in whatever subject it is to be found, whether in the creator or in a creature, a father, master, or king, etc. From thence comes this dilemma: either God has given free will to men as an effect of his goodness, or without any goodness.

You cannot say that he did it without any goodness, so you say that he has done it with great goodness; but it does necessarily result from this that he should have deprived them of it at any rate, rather than wait until it should prove their eternal damnation by the production of sin, which is a monster he does essentially abhor. And if he has been so patient as to leave so dismal a present in their hands until the evil happened, it is a sign either that his goodness was altered, even before they left the right path, which you dare not say; or that free will was not given them out of goodness, which is against the supposition granted in the above-mentioned dilemma.

Regard ought to be had to a strong obligation—it should never be dispensed with but in cases of necessity; but men in such cases ought to have no such regard. If a son should see his father ready to throw himself out the window, either in a fit of frenzy or because he is troubled in his mind, he would do well to chain him if he could not restrain him otherwise. If a queen should fall into the water, any footman that should get her out of it, either by embracing her or taking her by the hair, though he should pluck off above one half of it, would do a very good action; she would certainly not complain of his want of respect to her. If anyone should suffer a lady finely dressed to fall down a precipice, would it not be a very foolish excuse to say that it had not been possible to stop her without spoiling her ribbons and head-dress? Upon such an occasion as that, restraint and violence are an effect of goodness, and if a man were to be snatched, even against his will, out of the jaws of death it would be a piece of charity to do it, even though you should run the hazard of putting one of his limbs out of joint if he could not be saved any other way; that man, when his passion is over, will not fail to thank you for it. [...] What I have said concerning the right which men have, by virtue of the laws of charity, to thwart and use violence towards those whom they preserve from death by that means, is truer still with respect to fathers. They would be altogether wanting to their duty, if they did not take away from a son a knife or a sword wherewith he is ready to wound himself. They ought, notwithstanding his tears, to snatch away those presents from him, and in a certain course of life they are obliged to bring him off by force, and even to implore the assistance of the temporal power. If they neglect the welfare of their sons, alleging for their excuse that they will use no violence, as if their sons were slaves, they show that they have no love or know not how to use it right.

It does clearly appear from all these things that those who would submit to the judgement of reason the conduct of divine providence with respect to the permission of the first sin, would infallibly lose their cause if they had nothing to say but that the privileges of free will ought not to be violated. They would be answered: how can you conceive that God is the father of men, and yet say that he had rather save them the short and inconsiderable trouble of forcing them to renounce an agreeable conversation, in which they were ready to make an ill use of their liberty, than prevent their eternal damnation which they incur by the ill use of their free will? Where do you find such ideas of paternal goodness? To have a regard to the free will of a man, and carefully to abstain from laying any restraint upon his inclination when he is going to lose his innocence forever and to be eternally damned, do you call that a lawful observation of the privileges of liberty? You would be less unreasonable, if you should say to a man who takes a fall near you and breaks his leg, "what hindered us from preventing your fall is that we were afraid to undo some folds of your robe; we had so great a respect for its symmetry, that we would not attempt to discompose it and we thought it was much better to let you run the hazard of breaking your bones."

I will not deny but that the permission of making use of a thing, and of abusing it,[13] has sometimes had the character of a most special favour; but then that permission implies the impunity of the abuse. This then signifies nothing in the present case.

II. But the second thing which I am to propose will give more trouble to the defendants than the other. I have argued hitherto upon this principle: when those whom we love cannot be preserved from death, or infamy, or some other great evil, unless we make them feel a lesser pain, we are obliged to make them feel it. To indulge them in their capricious or bad inclinations would be rather an act of cruelty than of goodness; and as they would infallibly be angry as soon as they come to know the consequences of it, so they would be ready to thank those who did hurt

13 The right way of conferring a benefit is not to permit the abuse of it, but to add to it the art of making good use of it. Otherwise a present is a body without a soul [...].

them so much for their good. The evidence of those propositions is obvious to everybody, and it cannot be doubted that Adam and Eve would have looked upon God's restraint to keep them from falling as a new favour as great as the previous one.

This is what principles my first observation runs upon, but now I take another way: I grant to the adversaries all their demands. Let them say that since man had received the privilege of liberty he was to have the entire possession and use of it, and no manner of restraint was to be put upon him. Let them say it was not a proper time to save a man by pulling him by the arm, or by the hair, by throwing him upon the ground, [etc.]. Let them say that the free will of man was a barrier altogether inviolable, and a privilege which it was not lawful to strike at. I will grant it. But was there no other means of preventing the fall of man? God was not to oppose a corporeal motion, which is a troublesome opposition: a mere act of the will was the thing in question. But all the philosophers say that the will cannot be forced [...]; and it is a contradiction to say that a volition is forced, for every act of the will is essentially voluntary. Now it is infinitely more easy for God to imprint in the souls of men such an act of the will as he thinks fit, than it is for us to fold a napkin, therefore, etc. Here is another observation more forcible still. All divines own that God can infallibly produce a good act of the will in a human soul without depriving it of the use of liberty. A preventing delectation, the suggestion of an idea which weakens the impression of the tempting object, and a thousand other preliminary means of acting upon the mind and the sensitive soul move the rational soul infallibly to make a good use of its liberty, and to follow the right way without being invincibly forced to it. [...] [These divines] must therefore acknowledge that a divine help so reasonably bestowed upon Adam, and so tempered that it had infallibly prevented his fall, would have been very consistent with the use of liberty, and had been no restraint upon him, nor disagreeable to him, and had left sufficient room for merit.

Thus the defendants are driven from all their entrenchments. Perhaps their last answer will be that God owes nothing to his creatures, and that he was not bound to bestow a necessitating or infallible grace upon them. But why then did they say before that he was to have a regard for human liberty? If he was obliged to preserve that prerogative of men, he must needs owe something to his own work. But not to insist upon that argument *ad hominem*, one may answer them, that if he owes nothing to his creatures, he is altogether bound to himself, and can do nothing against his essence. But it is essential to the holiness of God,[14] and to his infinite and almighty goodness, not to suffer the introduction of moral and physical evil.

Well, will they reply at last, "shall the thing formed say to him that formed it, why hast Thou made me thus?" This is well said: we should have stopped there. We are come again to the beginning of the lists; it had been better to stay there for it is needless to engage in a dispute if, after having run for some time, one must at last shut up one's self in one's own thesis. The doctrine which the Manicheans oppose ought to be looked upon by the orthodox as a truth in fact, clearly revealed, and since it must at last be confessed that the causes and reasons of it cannot be apprehended, it is better to own it from the very beginning and stop there, and to look upon the objections of philosophers as vain wrangling, and oppose nothing to them but silence together with the shield of faith.

14 That is, it seems so to the light of our weak reason.

Chapter 2

PHILOSOPHICAL OPTIMISM: LEIBNIZ AND POPE

Introduction

BAYLE'S CLAIM THAT THE PROBLEM OF EVIL WAS INSOLUBLE for human reason proved very controversial. In spite of Bayle's own profession of faith in the Christian God, some took his conclusion that we can only have a *non-rational* basis (i.e., in revelation or Scripture) for our insight into the compatibility of God's existence and the existence of evil as amounting to a defense of the *rationality* of atheism. Foremost among those provoked by Bayle's discussion was Gottfried Wilhelm Leibniz (1649–1716), the German polymath, who in 1710 published his *Essais de Théodicée sur la bonté de Dieu, la liberté de l'homme et l'origine du mal* (*Theodicy: Essays on the Goodness of God, the Freedom of Man, and the Origin of Evil*). This is the only book Leibniz published in his lifetime, and in it he responds directly and at length to Bayle, contending that the compatibility of God's existence with the existence of evil may be *above* the power of human reason to understand in all its details, but is nonetheless not *contrary* to human reason, or a non-rational article of faith as Bayle suggests.

Leibniz argues for this by considering what we can know about the attributes of God but also what was involved in God's choice to "create" the world in the first place. Like Bayle, Leibniz conceives of God as supremely wise, omnipotent, and perfectly good. In bringing the present world into existence, God would have been able to understand all possible worlds—that is, all possible combinations of things that might exist and their states—on account of his wisdom, and because of his omnipotence, he could bring any of these into existence (or make a possible world *actual*). However, God's goodness means that he only would, indeed *could*, have chosen the *best* of these worlds to make actual. Of course, the world God chose to make actual is just our world, and so we can be confident that this world is *the best of all possible worlds*.

Leibniz's position has become known as *philosophical optimism* (from the Latin *optimus*, or "best"), and Leibniz uses it to reply to Bayle's skeptical concerns about the problem of evil. Leibniz does not, like previous Christian thinkers, deny that evil exists in the actual world, but he thinks the foregoing considerations reassure us that the world in which evil occurs is the best of all possible; indeed, Leibniz goes as far as to claim that removing some evil from this world could only make the world *worse*, all things considered. This suffices to justify the existence of moral evil, or sin, in the world; the existence of physical evil, or human suffering, is justified inasmuch as it is God's punishment for moral evil, which Leibniz contends is the product of our own freedom (properly understood). This optimistic perspective would later find an influential proponent in the English poet Alexander Pope (1688–1744), particularly in the first Epistle of his didactic poem "An Essay on Man" (published in 1733–34). Pope's conclusion that "Whatever is, is right" echoes that of Leibniz, even if Pope does not rely on specifically Leibnizian grounds in making the case for it. (In this chapter we have opted to present the selection from Pope's "Essay" before that from Leibniz's *Theodicy*, as the former offers a more literary introduction to philosophical optimism.)

Alexander Pope, from "An Essay on Man"

Epistle I

Awake, my St. John! leave all meaner things
To low ambition, and the pride of kings.
Let us (since life can little more supply
Than just to look about us and to die)
Expatiate free o'er all this scene of man;
A mighty maze! but not without a plan;
A wild, where weeds and flowers promiscuous shoot;
Or garden tempting with forbidden fruit.
Together let us beat this ample field,
Try what the open, what the covert yield;
The latent tracts, the giddy heights, explore
Of all who blindly creep, or sightless soar;
Eye Nature's walks, shoot Folly as it flies,
And catch the manners living as they rise;
Laugh where we must, be candid where we can;
But vindicate the ways of God to man.

I. Say first, of God above, or man below
What can we reason, but from what we know?
Of man, what see we but his station here,
From which to reason, or to which refer?
Through worlds unnumbered though the God be known,
'Tis ours to trace Him only in our own.
He, who through vast immensity can pierce,
See worlds on worlds compose one universe,
Observe how system into system runs,
What other planets circle other suns,
What varied being peoples every star,
May tell why Heaven has made us as we are.
But of this frame, the bearings, and the ties,
The strong connections, nice dependencies,
Gradations just, has thy pervading soul
Looked through? or can a part contain the whole?

Is the great chain, that draws all to agree,
And drawn supports, upheld by God, or thee?

II. Presumptuous man! the reason wouldst thou find,
Why formed so weak, so little, and so blind?
First, if thou canst, the harder reason guess,
Why formed no weaker, blinder, and no less;
Ask of thy mother earth, why oaks are made
Taller or stronger than the weeds they shade?
Or ask of yonder argent fields above,
Why Jove's satellites are less than Jove?
Of systems possible, if 'tis confest
That wisdom infinite must form the best,
Where all must full or not coherent be,
And all that rises, rise in due degree;
Then in the scale of reasoning life, 'tis plain,
There must be, somewhere, such a rank as man:
And all the question (wrangle e'er so long)
Is only this, if God has placed him wrong?
Respecting man, whatever wrong we call,
May, must be right, as relative to all.
In human works, though laboured on with pain,
A thousand movements scarce one purpose gain;
In God's one single can its end produce;
Yet serves to second too some other use.
So man, who here seems principal alone,
Perhaps acts second to some sphere unknown,
Touches some wheel, or verges to some goal;
'Tis but a part we see, and not a whole.
When the proud steed shall know why man restrains
His fiery course, or drives him o'er the plains:
When the dull ox, why now he breaks the clod,
Is now a victim, and now Egypt's god:
Then shall man's pride and dullness comprehend
His actions', passions', being's, use and end;
Why doing, suffering, checked, impelled; and why
This hour a slave, the next a deity.
Then say not man's imperfect, Heaven in fault;
Say rather man's as perfect as he ought:

His knowledge measured to his state and place;
His time a moment, and a point his space.
If to be perfect in a certain sphere,
What matter, soon or late, or here or there?
The blest today is as completely so,
As who began a thousand years ago.

III. Heaven from all creatures hides the book of Fate,
All but the page prescribed, their present state:
From brutes what men, from men what spirits know:
Or who could suffer being here below?
The lamb thy riot dooms to bleed today,
Had he thy reason, would he skip and play?
Pleased to the last, he crops the flowery food,
And licks the hand just raised to shed his blood.
Oh, blindness to the future! kindly given,
That each may fill the circle, marked by Heaven:
Who sees with equal eye, as God of all,
A hero perish, or a sparrow fall,
Atoms or systems into ruin hurled,
And now a bubble burst, and now a world.
    Hope humbly, then; with trembling pinions soar;
Wait the great teacher Death; and God adore.
What future bliss, He gives not thee to know,
But gives that hope to be thy blessing now.
Hope springs eternal in the human breast:
Man never is, but always to be blest:
The soul, uneasy and confined from home,
Rests and expatiates in a life to come.
    Lo, the poor Indian! whose untutored mind
Sees God in clouds, or hears Him in the wind;
His soul, proud science never taught to stray
Far as the solar walk, or milky way;
Yet simple Nature to his hope has given,
Behind the cloud-topped hill, an humbler heaven;
Some safer world in depth of woods embraced,
Some happier island in the watery waste,
Where slaves once more their native land behold,
No fiends torment, no Christians thirst for gold.

To be, contents his natural desire,
He asks no angel's wing, no seraph's fire;
But thinks, admitted to that equal sky,
His faithful dog shall bear him company.

IV. Go, wiser thou! and, in thy scale of sense,
Weigh thy opinion against providence;
Call imperfection what thou fanciest such,
Say, here He gives too little, there too much;
Destroy all creatures for thy sport or gust,
Yet cry, if man's unhappy, God's unjust;
If man alone engross not Heaven's high care,
Alone made perfect here, immortal there:
Snatch from His hand the balance and the rod,
Re-judge His justice, be the God of God.
In pride, in reasoning pride, our error lies;
All quit their sphere, and rush into the skies.
Pride still is aiming at the blest abodes,
Men would be angels, angels would be gods.
Aspiring to be gods, if angels fell,
Aspiring to be angels, men rebel:
And who but wishes to invert the laws
Of order, sins against the Eternal Cause.

V. Ask for what end the heavenly bodies shine,
Earth for whose use? Pride answers, "'Tis for mine:
For me kind Nature wakes her genial power,
Suckles each herb, and spreads out every flower;
Annual for me, the grape, the rose renew
The juice nectareous, and the balmy dew;
For me, the mine a thousand treasures brings;
For me, health gushes from a thousand springs;
Seas roll to waft me, suns to light me rise;
My footstool earth, my canopy the skies."
    But errs not Nature from this gracious end,
From burning suns when livid deaths descend,
When earthquakes swallow, or when tempests sweep
Towns to one grave, whole nations to the deep?
"No, ('tis replied) the first Almighty Cause

Acts not by partial, but by general laws;
The exceptions few; some change since all began;
And what created perfect?"—Why then man?
If the great end be human happiness,
Then Nature deviates; and can man do less?
As much that end a constant course requires
Of showers and sunshine, as of man's desires;
As much eternal springs and cloudless skies,
As men for ever temperate, calm, and wise.
If plagues or earthquakes break not Heaven's design,
Why then a Borgia, or a Catiline?
Who knows but He, whose hand the lightning forms,
Who heaves old ocean, and who wings the storms;
Pours fierce ambition in a Cæsar's mind,
Or turns young Ammon loose to scourge mankind?
From pride, from pride, our very reasoning springs;
Account for moral, as for natural things:
Why charge we heaven in those, in these acquit?
In both, to reason right is to submit.
    Better for us, perhaps, it might appear,
Were there all harmony, all virtue here;
That never air or ocean felt the wind;
That never passion discomposed the mind.
But all subsists by elemental strife;
And passions are the elements of life.
The general order, since the whole began,
Is kept in nature, and is kept in man.

VI. What would this man? Now upward will he soar,
And little less than angel, would be more;
Now looking downwards, just as grieved appears
To want the strength of bulls, the fur of bears
Made for his use all creatures if he call,
Say what their use, had he the powers of all?
Nature to these, without profusion, kind,
The proper organs, proper powers assigned;
Each seeming want compensated of course,
Here with degrees of swiftness, there of force;
All in exact proportion to the state;

Nothing to add, and nothing to abate.
Each beast, each insect, happy in its own:
Is Heaven unkind to man, and man alone?
Shall he alone, whom rational we call,
Be pleased with nothing, if not blessed with all?
    The bliss of man (could pride that blessing find)
Is not to act or think beyond mankind;
No powers of body or of soul to share,
But what his nature and his state can bear.
Why has not man a microscopic eye?
For this plain reason, man is not a fly.
Say what the use, were finer optics given,
To inspect a mite, not comprehend the heaven?
Or touch, if tremblingly alive all o'er,
To smart and agonize at every pore?
Or quick effluvia darting through the brain,
Die of a rose in aromatic pain?
If Nature thundered in his opening ears,
And stunned him with the music of the spheres,
How would he wish that Heaven had left him still
The whispering zephyr, and the purling rill?
Who finds not Providence all good and wise,
Alike in what it gives, and what denies?

VII. Far as Creation's ample range extends,
The scale of sensual, mental powers ascends:
Mark how it mounts, to man's imperial race,
From the green myriads in the peopled grass:
What modes of sight betwixt each wide extreme,
The mole's dim curtain, and the lynx's beam:
Of smell, the headlong lioness between,
And hound sagacious on the tainted green:
Of hearing, from the life that fills the flood,
To that which warbles through the vernal wood:
The spider's touch, how exquisitely fine!
Feels at each thread, and lives along the line:
In the nice bee, what sense so subtly true
From poisonous herbs extracts the healing dew?
How instinct varies in the grovelling swine,

Compared, half-reasoning elephant, with thine!
'Twixt that, and reason, what a nice barrier,
For ever separate, yet for ever near!
Remembrance and reflection how allayed;
What thin partitions sense from thought divide:
And middle natures, how they long to join,
Yet never passed the insuperable line!
Without this just gradation, could they be
Subjected, these to those, or all to thee?
The powers of all subdued by thee alone,
Is not thy reason all these powers in one?

VIII. See, through this air, this ocean, and this earth,
All matter quick, and bursting into birth.
Above, how high, progressive life may go!
Around, how wide! how deep extend below?
Vast chain of being! which from God began,
Natures ethereal, human, angel, man,
Beast, bird, fish, insect, what no eye can see,
No glass can reach; from Infinite to thee,
From thee to nothing. On superior powers
Were we to press, inferior might on ours:
Or in the full creation leave a void,
Where, one step broken, the great scale's destroyed:
From Nature's chain whatever link you strike,
Tenth or ten thousandth, breaks the chain alike.
    And, if each system in gradation roll
Alike essential to the amazing whole,
The least confusion but in one, not all
That system only, but the whole must fall.
Let earth unbalanced from her orbit fly,
Planets and suns run lawless through the sky;
Let ruling angels from their spheres be hurled,
Being on being wrecked, and world on world;
Heaven's whole foundations to their center nod,
And nature tremble to the throne of God.
All this dread order break—for whom? for thee?
Vile worm!—Oh, madness! pride! impiety!

IX. What if the foot, ordained the dust to tread,
Or hand, to toil, aspired to be the head?
What if the head, the eye, or ear repined
To serve mere engines to the ruling mind?
Just as absurd for any part to claim
To be another, in this general frame:
Just as absurd, to mourn the tasks or pains,
The great directing Mind of All ordains.
    All are but parts of one stupendous whole,
Whose body Nature is, and God the soul;
That, changed through all, and yet in all the same;
Great in the earth, as in the ethereal frame;
Warms in the sun, refreshes in the breeze,
Glows in the stars, and blossoms in the trees,
Lives through all life, extends through all extent,
Spreads undivided, operates unspent;
Breathes in our soul, informs our mortal part,
As full, as perfect, in a hair as heart:
As full, as perfect, in vile man that mourns,
As the rapt seraph that adores and burns:
To him no high, no low, no great, no small;
He fills, he bounds, connects, and equals all.

X. Cease, then, nor order imperfection name:
Our proper bliss depends on what we blame.
Know thy own point: this kind, this due degree
Of blindness, weakness, Heaven bestows on thee.
Submit. In this, or any other sphere,
Secure to be as blest as thou canst bear:
Safe in the hand of one disposing Power,
Or in the natal, or the mortal hour.
All nature is but art, unknown to thee;
All chance, direction, which thou canst not see;
All discord, harmony not understood;
All partial evil, universal good:
And, spite of pride, in erring reason's spite,
One truth is clear, whatever is, is right.

Gottfried Wilhelm Leibniz, from *Theodicy: Essays on the Goodness of God, the Freedom of Man, and the Origin of Evil*

Preface

There are two famous labyrinths where our reason very often goes astray: one concerns the great question of the Free and the Necessary, above all in the production and the origin of Evil; the other consists in the discussion of continuity and of the indivisibles which appear to be the elements thereof, and where the consideration of the infinite must enter in. The first perplexes almost all the human race, the other exercises philosophers only. I shall have perchance at another time an opportunity to declare myself on the second, and to point out that, for lack of a true conception of the nature of substance and matter, people have taken up false positions leading to insurmountable difficulties, difficulties which should properly be applied to the overthrow of these very positions. But if the knowledge of continuity is important for speculative enquiry, that of necessity is nonetheless so for practical application; and it, together with the questions therewith connected, to wit, the freedom of man and the justice of God, forms the object of this treatise. [...]

I hope to remove all [of the difficulties that beset the origin of evil]. I will point out that absolute necessity, which is called also logical and metaphysical and sometimes geometrical, and which would alone be formidable in this connection, does not exist in free actions, and that thus freedom is exempt not only from constraint but also from real necessity. I will show that God himself, although he always chooses the best, does not act by an absolute necessity, and that the laws of nature laid down by God, founded upon the fitness of things, keep the mean between geometrical truths, absolutely necessary, and arbitrary decrees; which Bayle and other modern philosophers have not sufficiently understood. Further I will show that there is an indifference in freedom, because there is no absolute necessity for one course or the other; but yet that there is never an indifference of perfect equipoise. And I will demonstrate that there is in free actions a perfect spontaneity beyond all that has been conceived hitherto. Finally I will make it plain that the hypothetical and the moral necessity which subsist in free actions are open to no objection [...].

Likewise concerning the origin of evil in its relation to God, I offer a vindication of his perfections that shall extol not less his holiness, his justice and his goodness than his greatness, his power and his independence. I show how it is possible for everything to depend upon God, for him to co-operate in all the actions of creatures, even, if you will, to create these creatures continually, and nevertheless not to be the author of sin. Here also it is demonstrated how the privative nature of evil should be understood. Much more than that, I explain how evil has a source other than the will of God, and that one is right therefore to say of moral evil that God wills it not, but simply permits it. Most important of all, however, I show that it has been possible for God to permit sin and misery, and even to co-operate therein and promote it, without detriment to his holiness and his supreme goodness: although, generally speaking, he could have avoided all these evils. [...]

Part One

1. [...] The *difficulties* [relating to evil] are distinguishable into two classes. The one kind springs from man's freedom, which appears incompatible with the divine nature; and nevertheless freedom is deemed necessary, in order that man may be deemed guilty and open to punishment. The other kind concerns the conduct of God, and seems to make him participate too much in the existence of evil, even though man be free and participate also therein. And this conduct appears contrary to the goodness, the holiness and the justice of God, since God co-operates in evil, as well physical as moral, and co-operates in each of them both morally and physically; and since it seems that these evils are manifested in the order of nature as well as in that of grace, and in the future and eternal life as well as, indeed, more than, in this transitory life.

2. To present these difficulties in brief, it must be observed that freedom is opposed, to all appearance, by determination or certainty of any kind whatever; and nevertheless the common dogma of our philosophers states that the truth of contingent futurities[1] is determined. The

1 [That is, propositions that make claims about contingent states of affairs in the future. The question is whether God's foreknowledge of the truth of all such propositions in advance of their occurrence renders the future determined.]

foreknowledge of God renders all the future certain and determined, but his providence and his foreordinance, whereon foreknowledge itself appears founded, do much more: for God is not as a man, able to look upon events with unconcern and to suspend his judgement, since nothing exists save as a result of the decrees of his will and through the action of his power. And even though one leaves out of account the co-operation of God, all is perfectly connected in the order of things, since nothing can come to pass unless there be a cause so disposed as to produce the effect, this taking place no less in voluntary than in all other actions. According to which it appears that man is compelled to do the good and evil that he does, and in consequence that he deserves therefore neither recompense nor chastisement: thus is the morality of actions destroyed and all justice, divine and human, shaken.

3. But even though one should grant to man this freedom wherewith he arrays himself to his own hurt, the conduct of God could not but provide matter for a criticism supported by the presumptuous ignorance of men, who would wish to exculpate themselves wholly or in part at the expense of God. It is objected that all the reality and what is termed the substance of the act in sin itself is a production of God, since all creatures and all their actions derive from him that reality they have. Whence one could infer not only that he is the physical cause of sin, but also that he is its moral cause, since he acts with perfect freedom and does nothing without a complete knowledge of the thing and the consequences that it may have. Nor is it enough to say that God has made for himself a law to co-operate with the wills or resolutions of man, whether we express ourselves in terms of the common opinion or in terms of the system of occasional causes. Not only will it be found strange that he should have made such a law for himself, of whose results he was not ignorant, but the principal difficulty is that it seems the evil will itself cannot exist without co-operation, and even without some predetermination, on his part, which contributes towards begetting this will in man or in some other rational creature. For an action is not, for being evil, the less dependent on God. Whence one will come at last to the conclusion that God does all, the good and the evil, indifferently; unless one pretend with the Manicheans that there are two principles, the one good and the other evil. Moreover, according to the general opinion of theologians and philosophers, conservation being a perpetual creation, it will be said that man is perpetually created corrupt and erring. There are, furthermore, modern Cartesians who claim that God is the sole agent, of whom

created beings are only the purely passive organs; and Bayle builds not a little upon that idea.

4. But even granting that God should co-operate in actions only with a general co-operation, or even not at all, at least in those that are bad, it suffices, so it is said, to inculpate him and to render him the moral cause that nothing comes to pass without his permission. To say nothing of the fall of the angels, he knows all that which will come to pass, if, having created man, he places him in such and such circumstances; and he places him there notwithstanding. Man is exposed to a temptation to which it is known that he will succumb, thereby causing an infinitude of frightful evils, by which the whole human race will be infected and brought as it were into a necessity of sinning, a state which is named 'original sin.' Thus the world will be brought into a strange confusion, by this means death and diseases being introduced, with a thousand other misfortunes and miseries that in general afflict the good and the bad; wickedness will even hold sway and virtue will be oppressed on earth, so that it will scarce appear that a providence governs affairs. But it is much worse when one considers the life to come, since but a small number of men will be saved and since all the rest will perish eternally. Furthermore these men destined for salvation will have been withdrawn from the corrupt mass through an unreasoning election, whether it be said that God in choosing them has had regard to their future actions, to their faith or to their works, or one claim that he has been pleased to give them these good qualities and these actions because he has predestined them to salvation. For though it be said in the most lenient system that God wished to save all men, and though in the other systems commonly accepted it be granted, that he has made his Son take human nature upon him to expiate their sins, so that all they who shall believe in him with a lively and final faith shall be saved, it still remains true that this lively faith is a gift of God; that we are dead to all good works; that even our will itself must be aroused by a prevenient grace, and that God gives us the power to will and to do. And whether that be done through a grace efficacious of itself, that is to say, through a divine inward motion which wholly determines our will to the good that it does; or whether there be only a sufficient grace, but such as does not fail to attain its end, and to become efficacious in the inward and outward circumstances wherein the man is and has been placed by God: one must return to the same conclusion that God is the final reason of salvation, of grace, of faith and of election in Jesus Christ. And be the election the cause or the result of God's design to

give faith, it still remains true that he gives faith or salvation to whom he pleases, without any discernible reason for his choice, which falls upon but few men.

5. So it is a terrible judgement that God, giving his only Son for the whole human race and being the sole author and master of the salvation of men, yet saves so few of them and abandons all others to the devil his enemy, who torments them eternally and makes them curse their Creator, though they have all been created to diffuse and show forth his goodness, his justice and his other perfections. And this outcome inspires all the more horror, as the sole cause why all these men are wretched to all eternity is God's having exposed their parents to a temptation that he knew they would not resist; as this sin is inherent and imputed to men before their will has participated in it; as this hereditary vice impels their will to commit actual sins; and as countless men, in childhood or maturity, that have never heard or have not heard enough of Jesus Christ, saviour of the human race, die before receiving the necessary succor for their withdrawal from this abyss of sin. These men too are condemned to be for ever rebellious against God and plunged in the most horrible miseries, with the wickedest of all creatures, though in essence they have not been more wicked than others, and several among them have perchance been less guilty than some of that little number of elect, who were saved by a grace without reason, and who thereby enjoy an eternal felicity which they had not deserved. Such in brief are the difficulties touched upon by sundry persons; but Bayle was the one who insisted on them the most, as will appear subsequently when we examine his passages. I think that now I have recorded the main essence of these difficulties: but I have deemed it fitting to refrain from some expressions and exaggerations which might have caused offence, while not rendering the objections any stronger.

6. Let us now turn the medal and let us also point out what can be said in answer to those objections; and here a course of explanation through fuller dissertation will be necessary: for many difficulties can be opened up in few words, but for their discussion one must dilate upon them. Our end is to banish from men the false ideas that represent God to them as an absolute prince employing a despotic power, unfitted to be loved and unworthy of being loved. These notions are the more evil in relation to God inasmuch as the essence of piety is not only to fear him but also to love him above all things: and that cannot come about unless there be knowledge of his perfections capable of arousing the love which

he deserves, and which makes the felicity of those that love him. Feeling ourselves animated by a zeal such as cannot fail to please him, we have cause to hope that he will enlighten us, and that he will himself aid us in the execution of a project undertaken for his glory and for the good of men. [...]

7. *God is the first reason of things*: for such things as are bounded, as all that which we see and experience, are contingent and have nothing in them to render their existence necessary, it being plain that time, space and matter, united and uniform in themselves and indifferent to everything, might have received entirely other motions and shapes, and in another order. Therefore one must seek the reason for the existence of the world, which is the whole assemblage of *contingent* things, and seek it in the substance which carries with it the reason for its existence, and which in consequence is *necessary* and eternal. Moreover, this cause must be intelligent: for this existing world being contingent and an infinity of other worlds being equally possible, and holding, so to say, equal claim to existence with it, the cause of the world must needs have had regard or reference to all these possible worlds in order to fix upon one of them. This regard or relation of an existent substance to simple possibilities can be nothing other than the *understanding* which has the ideas of them, while to fix upon one of them can be nothing other than the act of the *will* which chooses. It is the *power* of this substance that renders its will efficacious. Power relates to *being*, wisdom or understanding to *truth*, and will to *good*. And this intelligent cause ought to be infinite in all ways, and absolutely perfect in *power*, in *wisdom* and in *goodness*, since it relates to all that which is possible. Furthermore, since all is connected together, there is no ground for admitting more than *one*. Its understanding is the source of *essences*, and its will is the origin of *existences*. There in few words is the proof of one only God with his perfections, and through him of the origin of things.

8. Now this supreme wisdom, united to a goodness that is no less infinite, cannot but have chosen the best. For as a lesser evil is a kind of good, even so a lesser good is a kind of evil if it stands in the way of a greater good; and there would be something to correct in the actions of God if it were possible to do better. As in mathematics, when there is no maximum nor minimum, in short nothing distinguished, everything is done equally, or when that is not possible nothing at all is done: so it may be said likewise in respect of perfect wisdom, which is no less orderly than mathematics, that if there were not the best (*optimum*) among all

possible worlds, God would not have produced any. I call 'World' the whole succession and the whole agglomeration of all existent things, lest it be said that several worlds could have existed in different times and different places. For they must needs be reckoned all together as one world or, if you will, as one Universe. And even though one should fill all times and all places, it still remains true that one might have filled them in innumerable ways, and that there is an infinitude of possible worlds among which God must needs have chosen the best, since he does nothing without acting in accordance with supreme reason.

9. Some adversary not being able to answer this argument will perchance answer the conclusion by a counter-argument, saying that the world could have been without sin and without sufferings; but I deny that then it would have been *better*. For it must be known that all things are *connected* in each one of the possible worlds: the universe, whatever it may be, is all of one piece, like an ocean: the least movement extends its effect there to any distance whatsoever, even though this effect become less perceptible in proportion to the distance. Therein God has ordered all things beforehand once for all, having foreseen prayers, good and bad actions, and all the rest; and each thing *as an idea* has contributed, before its existence, to the resolution that has been made upon the existence of all things; so that nothing can be changed in the universe (any more than in a number) save its essence or, if you will, save its *numerical individuality*. Thus, if the smallest evil that comes to pass in the world were missing in it, it would no longer be this world; which, with nothing omitted and all allowance made, was found the best by the Creator who chose it.

10. It is true that one may imagine possible worlds without sin and without unhappiness, and one could make some like Utopian or Sevarambian romances: but these same worlds again would be very inferior to ours in goodness. I cannot show you this in detail. For can I know and can I present infinities to you and compare them together? But you must judge with me *ab effectu*,[2] since God has chosen this world as it is. [...]

12. Use has ever been made of comparisons taken from the pleasures of the senses when these are mingled with that which borders on pain, to prove that there is something of like nature in intellectual pleasures. A little acid, sharpness or bitterness is often more pleasing than sugar;

2 [That is, reasoning *from the effect*, or in this case from the fact that God has chosen this world to make actual.]

shadows enhance colours; and even a dissonance in the right place gives relief to harmony. We wish to be terrified by rope-dancers on the point of falling and we wish that tragedies shall well-nigh cause us to weep. Do men relish health enough, or thank God enough for it, without having ever been sick? And is it not most often necessary that a little evil render the good more discernible, that is to say, greater?

13. But it will be said that evils are great and many in number in comparison with the good: that is erroneous. It is only want of attention that diminishes our good, and this attention must be given to us through some admixture of evils. If we were usually sick and seldom in good health, we should be wonderfully sensible of that great good and we should be less sensible of our evils. But is it not better, notwithstanding, that health should be usual and sickness the exception? Let us then by our reflection supply what is lacking in our perception, in order to make the good of health more discernible. Had we not the knowledge of the life to come, I believe there would be few persons who, being at the point of death, were not content to take up life again, on condition of passing through the same amount of good and evil, provided always that it were not the same kind: one would be content with variety, without requiring a better condition than that wherein one had been.

14. When one considers also the fragility of the human body, one looks in wonder at the wisdom and the goodness of the Author of Nature, who has made the body so enduring and its condition so tolerable. That has often made me say that I am not astonished men are sometimes sick, but that I am astonished they are sick so little and not always. This also ought to make us the more esteem the divine contrivance of the mechanism of animals, whose Author has made machines so fragile and so subject to corruption and yet so capable of maintaining themselves: for it is Nature which cures us rather than medicine. Now this very fragility is a consequence of the nature of things, unless we are to will that this kind of creature, reasoning and clothed in flesh and bones, be not in the world. But that, to all appearance, would be a defect which some philosophers of old would have called *vacuum formarum*, a gap in the order of species. [...]

20. But it is necessary also to meet the more speculative and metaphysical difficulties which have been mentioned, and which concern the cause of evil. The question is asked first of all, whence does evil come? [...] The ancients attributed the cause of evil to *matter*, which they believed uncreated and independent of God: but we, who derive all

being from God, where shall we find the source of evil? The answer is, that it must be sought in the ideal nature of the creature, insofar as this nature is contained in the eternal verities which are in the understanding of God, independently of his will. For we must consider that there is an *original imperfection in the creature* before sin, because the creature is limited in its essence; whence ensues that it cannot know all, and that it can deceive itself and commit other errors. Plato said in *Timaeus* that the world originated in Understanding united to Necessity. Others have united God and Nature. This can be given a reasonable meaning. God will be the Understanding; and the Necessity, that is, the essential nature of things, will be the object of the understanding, insofar as this object consists in the eternal verities. But this object is inward and abides in the divine understanding. And therein is found not only the primitive form of good, but also the origin of evil: the Region of the Eternal Verities must be substituted for matter when we are concerned with seeking out the source of things.

This region is the ideal cause of evil (as it were) as well as of good: but, properly speaking, the formal character of evil has no *efficient* cause, for it consists in privation, as we shall see, namely, in that which the efficient cause does not bring about. [...]

21. Evil may be taken metaphysically, physically and morally. *Metaphysical evil* consists in mere imperfection, *physical evil* in suffering, and *moral evil* in sin. Now although physical evil and moral evil be not necessary, it is enough that by virtue of the eternal verities they be possible. And as this vast Region of Verities contains all possibilities it is necessary that there be an infinitude of possible worlds, that evil enter into diverse of them, and that even the best of all contain a measure thereof. Thus has God been induced to permit evil.

22. But someone will say to me: why speak you to us of 'permitting'? Is it not God that doeth the evil and that willeth it? Here it will be necessary to explain what 'permission' is, so that it may be seen how this term is not employed without reason. But before that one must explain the nature of will, which has its own degrees. Taking it in the general sense, one may say that *will* consists in the inclination to do something in proportion to the good it contains. This will is called *antecedent* when it is detached, and considers each good separately in the capacity of a good. In this sense it may be said that God tends to all good, as good [...], and that by an antecedent will. He is earnestly disposed to sanctify and to save all men, to exclude sin, and to prevent damnation. It may even be

said that this will is efficacious *of itself (per se)*, that is, in such sort that the effect would ensue if there were not some stronger reason to prevent it: for this will does not pass into final exercise (*ad summum conatum*), else it would never fail to produce its full effect, God being the master of all things. Success entire and infallible belongs only to the *consequent will*, as it is called. This it is which is complete; and in regard to it this rule obtains, that one never fails to do what one wills, when one has the power. Now this consequent will, final and decisive, results from the conflict of all the antecedent wills, of those which tend towards good, even as of those which repel evil; and from the concurrence of all these particular wills comes the total will. So in mechanics compound movement results from all the tendencies that concur in one and the same moving body, and satisfies each one equally, insofar as it is possible to do all at one time. [...] In this sense also it may be said that the antecedent will is efficacious in a sense and even effective with success.

23. Thence it follows that God wills *antecedently* the good and *consequently* the best. And as for evil, God wills moral evil not at all, and physical evil or suffering he does not will absolutely. Thus it is that there is no absolute predestination to damnation; and one may say of physical evil, that God wills it often as a penalty owing to guilt, and often also as a means to an end, that is, to prevent greater evils or to obtain greater good. The penalty serves also for amendment and example. Evil often serves to make us savour good the more; sometimes too it contributes to a greater perfection in him who suffers it, as the seed that one sows is subject to a kind of corruption before it can germinate: this is a beautiful similitude, which Jesus Christ himself used.

24. Concerning sin or moral evil, although it happens very often that it may serve as a means of obtaining good or of preventing another evil, it is not this that renders it a sufficient object of the divine will or a legitimate object of a created will. It must only be admitted or *permitted* insofar as it is considered to be a certain consequence of an indispensable duty: as for instance if a man who was determined not to permit another's sin were to fail of his own duty, or as if an officer on guard at an important post were to leave it, especially in time of danger, in order to prevent a quarrel in the town between two soldiers of the garrison who wanted to kill each other.

25. The rule which states, *non esse facienda mala, ut eveniant bona*,[3] and which even forbids the permission of a moral evil with the end of obtaining a physical good, far from being violated, is here proved, and its source and its reason are demonstrated. One will not approve the action of a queen who, under the pretext of saving the State, commits or even permits a crime. The crime is certain and the evil for the State is open to question. Moreover, this manner of giving sanction to crimes, if it were accepted, would be worse than a disruption of some one country, which is liable enough to happen in any case, and would perchance happen all the more by reason of such means chosen to prevent it. But in relation to God nothing is open to question, nothing can be opposed to *the rule of the best*, which suffers neither exception nor dispensation. It is in this sense that God permits sin: for he would fail in what he owes to himself, in what he owes to his wisdom, his goodness, his perfection, if he followed not the grand result of all his tendencies to good, and if he chose not that which is absolutely the best, notwithstanding the evil of guilt, which is involved therein by the supreme necessity of the eternal verities. Hence the conclusion that God wills all good *in himself antecedently*, that he wills the best *consequently* as an *end*, that he wills what is indifferent, and physical evil, sometimes as a *means*, but that he will only permit moral evil as the *sine quo non* or as a hypothetical necessity which connects it with the best. Therefore the *consequent will* of God, which has sin for its object, is only *permissive*. [...]

34. The physical co-operation of God and of creatures with the will contributes also to the difficulties existing in regard to freedom. I am of the opinion that our will is exempt not only from constraint but also from necessity. Aristotle has already observed that there are two things in freedom, to wit, spontaneity and choice, and therein lies our mastery over our actions. When we act freely we are not being forced, as would happen if we were pushed on to a precipice and thrown from top to bottom; and we are not prevented from having the mind free when we deliberate, as would happen if we were given a draught to deprive us of discernment. There is *contingency* in a thousand actions of Nature; but when there is no judgement in him who acts there is no *freedom*. And if we had judgement not accompanied by any inclination to act, our soul would be an understanding without will.

3 [Evil should not be done so that good things can come to pass (Latin).]

35. It is not to be imagined, however, that our freedom consists in an indetermination or an indifference of equipoise, as if one must needs be inclined equally to the side of yes and of no and in the direction of different courses, when there are several of them to take. This equipoise in all directions is impossible: for if we were equally inclined towards the courses A, B and C, we could not be equally inclined towards A and towards not A. This equipoise is also absolutely contrary to experience, and in scrutinizing oneself one will find that there has always been some cause or reason inclining us towards the course taken, although very often we be not aware of that which prompts us: just in the same way one is hardly aware why, on issuing from a door, one has placed the right foot before the left or the left before the right.

36. But let us pass to the difficulties. Philosophers agree today that the truth of contingent futurities is determinate, that is to say that contingent futurities are future, or that they will be, that they will happen: for it is as sure that the future will be, as it is sure that the past has been. It was true already a hundred years ago that I should write today, as it will be true after a hundred years that I have written. Thus the contingent is not, because it is future, any the less contingent; and *determination*, which would be called certainty if it were known, is not incompatible with contingency. Often the certain and the determinate are taken as one thing, because a determinate truth is capable of being known: thus it may be said that determination is an objective certainty.

37. This determination comes from the very nature of truth, and cannot injure freedom: but there are other determinations taken from elsewhere, and in the first place from the foreknowledge of God, which many have held to be contrary to freedom. They say that what is foreseen cannot fail to exist, and they say so truly; but it follows not that what is foreseen is necessary, for *necessary truth* is that whereof the contrary is impossible or implies contradiction. Now this truth which states that I shall write tomorrow is not of that nature, it is not necessary. Yet supposing that God foresees it, it is necessary that it come to pass; that is, the consequence is necessary, namely, that it exist, since it has been foreseen; for God is infallible. This is what is termed a *hypothetical necessity*. But our concern is not this necessity: it is an *absolute necessity* that is required, to be able to say that an action is necessary, that it is not contingent, that it is not the effect of a free choice. Besides it is very easily seen that foreknowledge in itself adds nothing to the determination of the truth of contingent futurities, save that this determination is known:

and this does not augment the determination or the 'futurition' (as it is termed) of these events, that whereon we agreed at the outset. [...]

43. But if the foreknowledge of God has nothing to do with the dependence or independence of our free actions, it is not so with the foreordinance of God, his decrees, and the sequence of causes which, as I believe, always contribute to the determination of the will. And if I am for the Molinists[4] in the first point, I am for the predeterminators in the second, provided always that predetermination be taken as not necessitating. In a word, I am of opinion that the will is always more inclined towards the course it adopts, but that it is never bound by the necessity to adopt it. That it will adopt this course is certain, but it is not necessary. The case corresponds to that of the famous saying, *Astra inclinant, non necessitant*,[5] although here the similarity is not complete. For the event towards which the stars tend (to speak with the common herd, as if there were some foundation for astrology) does not always come to pass, whereas the course towards which the will is more inclined never fails to be adopted. Moreover the stars would form only a part of the inclinations that co-operate in the event, but when one speaks of the greater inclination of the will, one speaks of the result of all the inclinations. It is almost as we have spoken above of the consequent will in God, which results from all the antecedent wills.

44. Nevertheless, objective certainty or determination does not bring about the necessity of the determinate truth. All philosophers acknowledge this, asserting that the truth of contingent futurities is determinate, and that nevertheless they remain contingent. The thing indeed would imply no contradiction in itself if the effect did not follow; and therein lies contingency. The better to understand this point, we must take into account that there are two great principles of our arguments. The one is the principle of *contradiction*, stating that of two contradictory propositions the one is true, the other false; the other principle is that of the *determinant reason*: it states that nothing ever comes to pass without there being a cause or at least a reason determining it, that is, something to give an *a priori* reason why it is existent rather than non-existent,

---

4 [Followers of Luis de Molina (1532–1600), who took God's knowledge of contingent possibilities to be a "middle knowledge," distinct from the knowledge of necessary truths and so consistent with the freedom of the human will.]

5 [The stars incline without necessitating (Latin), an astrologer's excuse frequently quoted by Leibniz.]

and in this wise rather than in any other. This great principle holds for all events, and a contrary instance will never be supplied: and although more often than not we are insufficiently acquainted with these determinant reasons, we perceive nevertheless that there are such. Were it not for this great principle we could never prove the existence of God, and we should lose an infinitude of very just and very profitable arguments whereof it is the foundation; moreover, it suffers no exception, for otherwise its force would be weakened. Besides, nothing is so weak as those systems where all is unsteady and full of exceptions. That fault cannot be laid to the charge of the system I approve, where everything happens in accordance with general rules that at most are mutually restrictive.

45. We must therefore not imagine with some Schoolmen, whose ideas tend towards the chimerical, that free contingent futurities have the privilege of exemption from this general rule of the nature of things. There is always a prevailing reason which prompts the will to its choice, and for the maintenance of freedom for the will it suffices that this reason should incline without necessitating. That is also the opinion of all the ancients, of Plato, of Aristotle, of St. Augustine. The will is never prompted to action save by the representation of the good, which prevails over the opposite representations. This is admitted even in relation to God, the good angels and the souls in bliss: and it is acknowledged that they are nonetheless free in consequence of that. God fails not to choose the best, but he is not constrained so to do: nay, more, there is no necessity in the object of God's choice, for another sequence of things is equally possible. For that very reason the choice is free and independent of necessity, because it is made between several possibles, and the will is determined only by the preponderating goodness of the object. This is therefore not a defect where God and the saints are concerned: on the contrary, it would be a great defect, or rather a manifest absurdity, were it otherwise, even in men here on earth, and if they were capable of acting without any inclining reason. Of such absurdity no example will ever be found; and even supposing one takes a certain course out of caprice, to demonstrate one's freedom, the pleasure or advantage one thinks to find in this conceit is one of the reasons tending towards it.

46. There is therefore a freedom of contingency or, in a way, of indifference, provided that by 'indifference' is understood that nothing necessitates us to one course or the other; but there is never any *indifference of equipoise*, that is, where all is completely even on both sides, without any inclination towards either. Innumerable great and small movements,

internal and external, co-operate with us, for the most part unperceived by us. And I have already said that when one leaves a room there are such and such reasons determining us to put the one foot first, without pausing to reflect. [...]

52. All is therefore certain and determined beforehand in man, as everywhere else, and the human soul is a kind of *spiritual automaton*, although contingent actions in general and free action in particular are not on that account necessary with an absolute necessity, which would be truly incompatible with contingency. Thus neither futurition in itself, certain as it is, nor the infallible prevision of God, nor the predetermination either of causes or of God's decrees destroys this contingency and this freedom. That is acknowledged in respect of futurition and prevision, as has already been set forth. Since, moreover, God's decree consists solely in the resolution he forms, after having compared all possible worlds, to choose that one which is the best, and bring it into existence together with all that this world contains, by means of the all-powerful word *Fiat*,[6] it is plain to see that this decree changes nothing in the constitution of things: God leaves them just as they were in the state of mere possibility, that is, changing nothing either in their essence or nature, or even in their accidents, which are represented perfectly already in the idea of this possible world. Thus that which is contingent and free remains no less so under the decrees of God than under his prevision.

53. But could God himself (it will be said) then change nothing in the world? Assuredly he could not now change it, without derogation to his wisdom, since he has foreseen the existence of this world and of what it contains, and since, likewise, he has formed this resolution to bring it into existence: for he cannot be mistaken nor repent, and it did not behoove him to form an imperfect resolution applying to one part and not the whole. Thus, all being ordered from the beginning, it is only because of this hypothetical necessity, recognized by everyone, that after God's prevision or after his resolution nothing can be changed: and yet the events in themselves remain contingent. For (setting aside this supposition of the futurition of the thing and of the prevision or of the resolution of God, a supposition which already lays it down as a fact that the thing will happen [...]), the event has nothing in it to render it necessary and to suggest that no other thing might have happened in its stead. And as for the connection between causes and effects, it only inclined, without

6 [Let it be (Latin), as in God's act of creation.]

necessitating, the free agency, as I have just explained; thus it does not produce even a hypothetical necessity, save in conjunction with something from outside, to wit, this very maxim, that the prevailing inclination always triumphs. [...]

Part Three

241. Now at last I have disposed of the cause of moral evil; *physical evil*, that is, sorrows, sufferings, miseries, will be less troublesome to explain, since these are results of moral evil. [...] It is true that one often suffers through the evil actions of others; but when one has no part in the offence one must look upon it as a certainty that these sufferings prepare for us a greater happiness. The question of *physical evil*, that is, of the origin of sufferings, has difficulties in common with that of the origin of *metaphysical evil*, examples whereof are furnished by the monstrosities and other apparent irregularities of the universe. But one must believe that even sufferings and monstrosities are part of order; and it is well to bear in mind not only that it was better to admit these defects and these monstrosities than to violate general laws [...], but also that these very monstrosities are in the rules, and are in conformity with general acts of will, though we be not capable of discerning this conformity. It is just as sometimes there are appearances of irregularity in mathematics which issue finally in a great order when one has finally got to the bottom of them: that is why I have already in this work observed that according to my principles all individual events, without exception, are consequences of general acts of will. [...]

288. I have proved that free will is the proximate cause of the evil of guilt, and consequently of the evil of punishment; although it is true that the original imperfection of creatures, which is already presented in the eternal ideas, is the first and most remote cause. Bayle nevertheless always disputes this use of the notion of free will; he will not have the cause of evil ascribed to it. One must listen to his objections, but first it will be well to throw further light on the nature of freedom. I have shown that freedom, according to the definition required in the schools of theology, consists in intelligence, which involves a clear knowledge of the object of deliberation; in spontaneity, whereby we determine; and in contingency, that is, in the exclusion of logical or metaphysical necessity. Intelligence is, as it were, the soul of freedom, and the rest is as its body and foundation. The free substance is self-determining and that

according to the motive of good perceived by the understanding, which inclines it without compelling it: and all the conditions of freedom are comprised in these few words. It is nevertheless well to point out that the imperfection present in our knowledge and our spontaneity, and the infallible determination that is involved in our contingency, destroy neither freedom nor contingency.

289. Our knowledge is of two kinds, distinct or confused. Distinct knowledge, or *intelligence*, occurs in the actual use of reason; but the senses supply us with confused thoughts. And we may say that we are immune from bondage insofar as we act with a distinct knowledge, but that we are the slaves of passion insofar as our perceptions are confused. In this sense we have not all the freedom of spirit that were to be desired, and we may say with St. Augustine that being subject to sin we have the freedom of a slave. Yet a slave, slave as he is, nevertheless has freedom to choose according to the state wherein he is, although more often than not he is under the stern necessity of choosing between two evils, because a superior force prevents him from attaining the goods whereto he aspires. That which in a slave is effected by bonds and constraint in us is effected by passions, whose violence is sweet but nonetheless pernicious. In truth we will only that which pleases us: but unhappily what pleases us now is often a real evil, which would displease us if we had the eyes of the understanding open. Nevertheless that evil state of the slave, which is also our own, does not prevent us, any more than him, from making a free choice of that which pleases us most, in the state to which we are reduced, in proportion to our present strength and knowledge.

290. As for spontaneity, it belongs to us insofar as we have within us the source of our actions, as Aristotle rightly conceived. The impressions of external things often, indeed, divert us from our path, and it was commonly believed that, at least in this respect, some of the sources of our actions were outside ourselves. I admit that one is bound to speak thus, adapting oneself to the popular mode of expression, as one may, in a certain sense, without doing violence to truth. But when it is a question of expressing oneself accurately I maintain that our spontaneity suffers no exception and that external things have no physical influence upon us, I mean in the strictly philosophical sense. [...]

301. The spontaneity of our actions can therefore no longer be questioned; and Aristotle has defined it well, saying that an action is *spontaneous* when its source is in him who acts. '*Spontaneum est, cujus*

principium est in agente.'[7] Thus it is that our actions and our wills depend entirely upon us. It is true that we are not directly the masters of our will, although we be its cause; for we do not choose volitions, as we choose our actions by our volitions. Yet we have a certain power also over our will, because we can contribute indirectly towards willing another time that which we would fain will now, as I have here already shown: that, however, is no *velleity*,[8] properly speaking. There also we have a mastery, individual and even perceptible, over our actions and our wills, resulting from a combination of spontaneity with intelligence.

302. Up to this point I have expounded the two conditions of freedom mentioned by Aristotle, that is, *spontaneity* and *intelligence*,[9] which are found united in us in deliberation, whereas beasts lack the second condition. But the Schoolmen demand yet a third, which they call *indifference*. And indeed one must admit it, if indifference signifies as much as 'contingency'; for I have already said here that freedom must exclude an absolute and metaphysical or logical necessity. But, as I have declared more than once, this indifference, this contingency, this non-necessity, if I may venture so to speak, which is a characteristic attribute of freedom, does not prevent one from having stronger inclinations towards the course one chooses; nor does it by any means require that one be absolutely and equally indifferent towards the two opposing courses.

303. I therefore admit indifference only in the one sense, implying the same as contingency, or non-necessity. But, as I have declared more than once, I do not admit an indifference of equipoise, and I do not think that one ever chooses when one is absolutely indifferent. Such a choice would be, as it were, mere chance, without determining reason, whether apparent or hidden. But such a chance, such an absolute and actual fortuity, is a chimera which never occurs in nature. All wise men are agreed that chance is only an apparent thing, like fortune: only ignorance of causes gives rise to it. But if there were such a vague indifference, or rather if we were to choose without having anything to prompt us to the choice, chance would then be something actual, resembling what, according to Epicurus, took place in that little deviation of the atoms, occurring without cause or reason. [...]

---

7 ["That action is spontaneous whose principle is in the agent" (Latin)]

8 [That is, an instance of willing that does not issue in an action.]

9 [This account can be found in Aristotle's *Nicomachean Ethics*, especially at the outset of Book III.]

320. This false idea of freedom, conceived by those who, not content with exempting it, I do not say from constraint, but from necessity itself, would also exempt it from certainty and determination, that is, from reason and perfection, nevertheless pleased some Schoolmen, people who often become entangled in their own subtleties, and take the straw of terms for the grain of things. They assume some chimerical notion, whence they think to derive some use, and which they endeavour to maintain by quibblings. Complete indifference is of this nature: to concede it to the will is to grant it a privilege of the kind that some Cartesians and some mystics find in the divine nature, of being able to do the impossible, to produce absurdities, to cause two contradictory propositions to be true simultaneously. To claim that a determination comes from a complete indifference absolutely indeterminate is to claim that it comes naturally from nothing. Let it be assumed that God does not give this determination: it has accordingly no fountainhead in the soul, nor in the body, nor in circumstances, since all is assumed to be indeterminate; and yet there it is, appearing and existing without preparation, nothing making ready for it, no angel, not even God himself, being able to see or to show how it exists. That would be not only the emergence of something from nothing, but its emergence thence *of itself*. [...]

365. The whole difficulty here has therefore only come from a wrong idea of contingency and of freedom, which was thought to have need of a complete indifference or equipoise, an imaginary thing, of which neither a notion nor an example exists, nor ever can exist. Apparently Descartes had been imbued with the idea in his youth, at the College of la Flèche. That caused him to say (part I of his *Principles*, art. 41): 'Our thought is finite, and the knowledge and omnipotence of God, whereby he has not only known from all eternity everything that is, or that can be, but also has willed it, is infinite. Thus we have enough intelligence to recognize clearly and distinctly that this power and this knowledge are in God; but we have not enough so to comprehend their extent that we can know how they leave the actions of men entirely free and indeterminate.' The continuation has already been quoted above. 'Entirely free', that is right; but one spoils everything by adding 'entirely indeterminate'. One has no need of infinite knowledge in order to see that the foreknowledge and the providence of God allow freedom to our actions, since God has foreseen those actions in his ideas, just as they are, that is, free. [...] But there is no knowledge, however infinite it be, which can reconcile the knowledge and providence of God with actions of an indeterminate cause, that is to

say, with a chimerical and impossible being. The actions of the will are determined in two ways, by the foreknowledge or providence of God, and also by the dispositions of the particular immediate cause, which lie in the inclinations of the soul. [...]

367. Indeed, confusion springs, more often than not, from ambiguity in terms, and from one's failure to take trouble over gaining clear ideas about them. That gives rise to these eternal, and usually mistaken, contentions on necessity and contingency, on the possible and the impossible. But provided that it is understood that necessity and possibility, taken metaphysically and strictly, depend solely upon this question, whether the object in itself or that which is opposed to it implies contradiction or not; and that one takes into account that contingency is consistent with the inclinations, or reasons which contribute towards causing determination by the will; provided also that one knows how to distinguish clearly between necessity and determination or certainty, between metaphysical necessity, which admits of no choice, presenting only one single object as possible, and moral necessity, which constrains the wisest to choose the best; finally, provided that one is rid of the chimera of complete indifference, which can only be found in the books of philosophers, and on paper (for they cannot even conceive the notion in their heads, or prove its reality by an example in things) one will easily escape from a labyrinth whose unhappy Daedalus was the human mind. That labyrinth has caused infinite confusion, as much with the ancients as with those of later times[.] [...]

Chapter 3

ATROCIOUS EVIL: VOLTAIRE, ROUSSEAU, AND CUGOANO

Introduction

PHILOSOPHICAL OPTIMISM MIGHT OFFER A CONVINCING, AND comforting, explanation of the occurrence of everyday sorts of evil. An appeal to a larger order of things can help to contextualize our own sufferings and reassure us of their lesser importance within the bigger picture. Moreover, there is certainly a grain of truth to the optimistic claim that the human susceptibility to morally evil intentions and actions should not be greeted with surprise or strike us as an argument against a larger order in the world but is rather wholly to be expected given the imperfection that is constitutive of human nature. Where philosophical optimism is arguably much less successful, and sympathetic, is when it comes to large-scale cases of evil and suffering. Indeed, concerning what has been called *atrocious* evil, whether the result of human action or of natural causes, philosophical optimism can seem to be trivializing and highly insensitive. These failings of philosophical optimism were made all too evident for some by a natural disaster that struck Europe in the middle of the eighteenth century.

On the morning of 1 November 1755, a Saturday, an earthquake occurred that impacted Spain, Morocco, and Portugal, with the city of Lisbon being particularly affected. The magnitude of the earthquake has been estimated as at least 7.7 on the Richter scale. Notably, the earthquake occurred on All Saints Day, a Christian religious holiday, for which many households and churches had set out candles which were upset in the earthquake, starting fires throughout the city. Additionally, as the epicenter of the earthquake was in the Atlantic Ocean, the earthquake triggered a tsunami that destroyed the harbor, engulfed the city center, and sent a wave up the Tagus river that caused extensive destruction. It is estimated that between 10,000 and 40,000 of Lisbon's residents died, in addition to other losses throughout Portugal (not to mention in Spain and Northern Africa).

The occurrence of such a destructive natural event, on the European continent, provoked a number of Enlightenment philosophers to wonder how such a disaster could be explained in terms of a larger, purposive order of the world. One of these, François-Marie Arouet (1694–1778), better known by his pen-name Voltaire, was moved to write a poem on the occasion entitled "Poème sur le désastre de Lisbonne" ("Poem on the Lisbon Disaster"), in which he condemned the attempts of some philosophers, in the spirit of Pope and Leibniz, to justify the earthquake. Voltaire would subsequently write his famous *Candide, ou l'Optimisme* (*Candide, or: On Optimism*, published in 1759) in which he satirized optimistic thinkers like Leibniz. However, Voltaire did not speak for all of his enlightened colleagues on this, as Jean-Jacques Rousseau (1712–78) defended a version of the optimistic position in a letter to Voltaire in response to his poem. As Rousseau emphasizes (quite consistently with his own negative appraisal of the nature of modern humanity), natural disasters might be much less harmful were it not for human action (in densely populating certain areas)—accordingly, destructive natural disasters are less of an indictment of the order of nature than they are of the wisdom of the human being and the process of civilization.

Significantly, the adequacy of optimism for justifying the occurrence of atrocious *moral* evil was also considered, in the form of the profound moral evils that made up the transatlantic slave trade. It was not the *philosophes* of the French Enlightenment who recognized how the atrocious evil of the slave trade eluded any optimistic justification, but instead a former slave, Ottobah Cugoano (c. 1757–c. 1791) who exposed the bankruptcy of any justification of the institution of slavery and the trade in human beings. This is accomplished in Cugoano's treatise, *Thoughts and Sentiments on the Evil and Wicked Traffic of the Slavery and Commerce of the Human Species* (1787), which begins with his own harrowing account of his kidnapping and enslavement. Having subsequently escaped slavery, Cugoano exposes the evils involved in the slave trade, from the African kidnappers through to the European merchants and planters, all the way to the magistrates and princes under whose auspices the whole business takes place; yet, it is a purported optimistic justification of slavery that provides the occasion for the work altogether. James Tobin (1736/37–1817), who owned a plantation and slaves in Nevis, had written a defense of slavery, entitled *Cursory Remarks upon the Reverend Mr. Ramsay's Essay on the Treatment and Conversion of African Slaves in the Sugar Colonies* (1785), to which Cugoano directly responds. Among Tobin's shocking arguments in defense of the practice is the optimistic argument that slavery is perhaps only an evil considered from our limited perspective: were we to see things from God's perspective it might be revealed to be something "originally interwoven into the constitution of the *present* world, for purposes wholly unknown to its short-sighted inhabitants" (*Cursory Remarks*, p. 7). Cugoano's exposure of the undeniable evils of slavery, designed to puncture the "insensibility" of his European readers, is thus an indictment of philosophical optimism and its ability to justify atrocious moral evil.

Voltaire, "On the Lisbon Disaster"

Unhappy mortals! Dark and mourning earth!
Affrighted gathering of human kind!
Eternal lingering of useless pain!
Come, ye philosophers, who cry, "All's well,"
And contemplate this ruin of a world.
Behold these shreds and cinders of your race,
This child and mother heaped in common wreck,
These scattered limbs beneath the marble shafts—
A hundred thousand whom the earth devours,
Who, torn and bloody, palpitating yet,
Entombed beneath their hospitable roofs,
In racking torment end their stricken lives.
To those expiring murmurs of distress,
To that appalling spectacle of woe,
Will ye reply: "You do but illustrate
The iron laws that chain the will of God"?
Say ye, o'er that yet quivering mass of flesh:
"God is avenged: the wage of sin is death"?
What crime, what sin, had those young hearts conceived
That lie, bleeding and torn on mother's breast?
Did fallen Lisbon deeper drink of vice
Than London, Paris, or sunlit Madrid?
In these men dance; at Lisbon yawns the abyss.
Tranquil spectators of your brothers' wreck,
Unmoved by this repellent dance of death,
Who calmly seek the reason of such storms,
Let them but lash your own security;
Your tears will mingle freely with the flood.
When earth its horrid jaws half open shows,
My plaint is innocent, my cries are just.
Surrounded by such cruelties of fate,
By rage of evil and by snares of death,
Fronting the fierceness of the elements,
Sharing our ills, indulge me my lament.
"'Tis pride," ye say—"the pride of rebel heart,

To think we might fare better than we do."
Go, tell it to the Tagus' stricken banks;
Search in the ruins of that bloody shock;
Ask of the dying in that house of grief,
Whether 'tis pride that calls on heaven for help
And pity for the sufferings of men.
"All's well," ye say, "and all is necessary."
Think ye this universe had been the worse
Without this hellish gulf in Portugal?
Are ye so sure the great eternal cause,
That knows all things, and for itself creates,
Could not have placed us in this dreary clime
Without volcanoes seething' neath our feet?
Would you forbid it use its clemency?
Are not the means of the great artisan
Unlimited for shaping his designs?
The master I would not offend, yet wish
This gulf of fire and sulphur had outpoured
Its baleful flood amid the desert wastes.
God I respect, yet love the universe.
Not pride, alas, it is, but love of man,
To mourn so terrible a stroke as this.

Would it console the sad inhabitants
Of these aflame and desolated shores
To say to them: "Lay down your lives in peace;
For the world's good your homes are sacrificed;
Your ruined palaces shall others build,
For other peoples shall your walls arise;
The North grows rich on your unhappy loss;
Your ills are but a link in general law;
To God you are as those low creeping worms
That wait for you in your predestined tombs"?
What speech to hold to victims of such ruth!
Add not such cruel outrage to their pain.

Nay, press not on my agitated heart
These iron and irrevocable laws,
This rigid chain of bodies, minds, and worlds.

Dreams of the bloodless thinker are such thoughts.
God holds the chain: is not himself enchained;
By his indulgent choice is all arranged;
Implacable he's not, but free and just.
Why suffer we, then, under one so just?
There is the knot your thinkers should undo.
Think ye to cure our ills denying them?
All peoples, trembling at the hand of God,
Have sought the source of evil in the world.
When the eternal law that all things moves
Doth hurl the rock by impact of the winds,
With lightning rends and fires the sturdy oak,
They have no feeling of the crashing blows;
But I, I live and feel, my wounded heart
Appeals for aid to him who fashioned it.

Children of that Almighty Power, we stretch
Our hands in grief towards our common sire.
The vessel, truly, is not heard to say:
"Why should I be so vile, so coarse, so frail?"
Nor speech nor thought is given unto it.
The urn that, from the potter's forming hand,
Slips and is shattered has no living heart
That yearns for bliss and shrinks from misery.
"This misery," ye say, "is others' good."
Yes; from my mouldering body shall be born
A thousand worms, when death has closed my pain.
Fine consolation this in my distress!
Grim speculators on the woes of men,
Ye double, not assuage, my misery.
In you I mark the nerveless boast of pride
That hides its ill with pretext of content.

I am a puny part of the great whole.
Yes; but all animals condemned to live,
All sentient things, born by the same stern law,
Suffer like me, and like me also die.

The vulture fastens on his timid prey,
And stabs with bloody beak the quivering limbs:
All's well, it seems, for it. But in a while
An eagle tears the vulture into shreds;
The eagle is transfixed by shaft of man;
The man, prone in the dust of battlefield,
Mingling his blood with dying fellow-men,
Becomes in turn the food of ravenous birds.
Thus the whole world in every member groans:
All born for torment and for mutual death.
And o'er this ghastly chaos you would say
The ills of each make up the good of all!
What blessedness! And as, with quaking voice,
Mortal and pitiful, yet cry, "All's well,"
The universe belies you, and your heart
Refutes a hundred times your mind's conceit.

All dead and living things are locked in strife.
Confess it freely—evil stalks the land,
Its secret principle unknown to us.
Can it be from the author of all good?
Are we condemned to weep by tyrant law
Of black Typhon or barbarous Ahriman?
These odious monsters, whom a trembling world
Made gods, my spirit utterly rejects.

But how conceive a God supremely good,
Who heaps his favours on the sons he loves,
Yet scatters evil with as large a hand?
What eye can pierce the depth of his designs?
From that all-perfect Being came not ill:
And came it from no other, for he's lord:
Yet it exists. O stern and numbing truth!
O wondrous mingling of diversities!
A God came down to lift our stricken race:
He visited the earth and changed it not!
One sophist says he had not power to change;
"He had," another cries, "but willed it not:
In time he will no doubt." And, while they prate,

The hidden thunders, belched from underground,
Fling wide the ruins of a hundred towns
Across the smiling face of Portugal.
God either smites the inborn guilt of man,
Or, arbitrary lord of space and time,
Devoid alike of pity and of wrath,
Pursues the cold designs he has conceived.
Or else this formless stuff, recalcitrant,
Rears in itself inalienable faults;
Or else God tries us, and this mortal life
Is but the passage to eternal spheres.
'Tis transitory pain we suffer here,
And death its merciful deliverance.
Yet, when this dreadful passage has been made,
Who will contend he has deserved the crown?
Whatever side we take we needs must groan;
We nothing know, and everything must fear.
Nature is dumb, in vain appeal to it;
The human race demands a word of God.
'Tis his alone to illustrate his work,
Console the weary, and illume the wise.
Without him man, to doubt and error doomed,
Finds not a reed that he may lean upon.
From Leibniz learn we not by what unseen
Bonds, in this best of all imagined worlds,
Endless disorder, chaos of distress,
Must mix our little pleasures thus with pain;
Nor why the guiltless suffer all this woe
In common with the most abhorrent guilt.
'Tis mockery to tell me all is well.
Like learned doctors, nothing do I know.
Plato has said that men did once have wings
And bodies proof against all mortal ill;
That pain and death were strangers to their world.
How have we fallen from that high estate!
Man crawls and dies: all is but born to die:
The world's the empire of destructiveness.
This frail construction of quick nerves and bones
Cannot sustain the shock of elements;

This temporary blend of blood and dust
Was put together only to dissolve;
This prompt and vivid sentiment of nerve
Was made for pain, the minister of death:
Thus in my ear does nature's message run.
Plato and Epicurus I reject,
And turn more hopefully to learned Bayle.
With even poised scale Bayle bids me doubt.
He, wise and great enough to need no creed,
Has slain all systems—combats even himself:
Like that blind conqueror of Philistines,
He sinks beneath the ruin he has wrought.
What is the verdict of the vastest mind?
Silence: the book of fate is closed to us.

Man is a stranger to his own research;
He knows not whence he comes, nor wither goes.
Tormented atoms in a bed of mud,
Devoured by death, a mockery of fate.
But thinking atoms, whose far-seeing eyes,
Guided by thought, have measured the faint stars,
Our being mingles with the infinite;
Ourselves we never see, or come to know.
This world, this theatre of pride and wrong,
Swarms with sick fools who talk of happiness.
With plaints and groans they follow up the quest,
To die reluctant, or be born again.
At fitful moments in our pain-racked life
The hand of pleasure wipes away our tears;
But pleasure passes like a fleeting shade,
And leaves a legacy of pain and loss.
The past for us is but a fond regret,
The present grim, unless the future's clear.
If thought must end in darkness of the tomb,
All will be well one day—so runs our hope.
All *now* is well, is but an idle dream.
The wise deceive me: God alone is right.
With lowly sighing, subject in my pain,
I do not fling myself 'gainst Providence.

Once did I sing, in less lugubrious tone,
The sunny ways of pleasure's genial rule;
The times have changed, and, taught by growing age,
And shoring of the frailty of mankind,
Seeking a light amid the deepening gloom,
I can but suffer, and will not repine.

A caliph once, when his last hour had come,
This prayer addressed to him he reverenced:
"To thee, sole and all-powerful king, I bear
What thou dost lack in thy immensity—
Evil and ignorance, distress and sin."
He might have added one thing further—hope.

Jean-Jacques Rousseau, from "A Letter from M. Rousseau to M. de Voltaire"

18 August 1756.
Your two last poems, Sir, reached me in this solitude; but, though all my friends are acquainted with the passion I have for your writings, I know not from whom these pieces could come, unless from yourself. I have found in them both pleasure and instruction, and discovered the hand of a master; thinking myself indebted to you, at once, for the copy and the work. I cannot say that every part appears to me equally good; but the things which displease me, serve only to make me place greater confidence in those which give me delight. It is not without pain that I sometimes arm my reason against the charms of your poetry, but it is with a view to render my admiration more worthy of your works, that I thus endeavour not to admire them indiscriminately.

I will do more, Sir. I will tell you ingenuously, not the beauties which I think I perceive in your two poems—the task is too great for my indolence—nor even the faults—which it is possible persons of greater judgment than I may find in them—but the displeasure which at present affects the taste I have for your lessons. And I will tell it to you, while I am still moved by a first perusal in which my heart listened attentively to yours; loving you as a brother, honouring you as my master, flattering myself, in short, that you will discover in my intentions the frankness of an ingenuous mind, and in my discourse, the voice of a friend to truth who is speaking to a philosopher. Besides, the more your second poem enchants me, the more freely can I take part against the first. For if you have not been afraid to oppose yourself, why should I be afraid of being of your opinion? I ought not to think you can make any great dependence on sentiments you have so well refuted.

The whole cause of my complaint is in your poem on the fatal disaster which has befallen Lisbon because I expected from it results more worthy of the humanity with which you seem to have been inspired. You reproach Pope and Leibniz with insulting mankind under their misfortunes by maintaining that everything is good, and expatiate so amply on the picture of our miseries that you aggravate the sense of them. Instead of the consolation I hoped for, you have only given me affliction.

One would think you were afraid I should not sufficiently feel my own unhappiness, and seem to think that you give me much tranquility in proving that every thing is evil.

Be not mistaken, Sir, the very contrary happened to what you seem to have proposed. That optimism, which appears to you so cruel, consoles me, under the very miseries which you describe as insupportable.

Mr. Pope's poem alleviates my evils, and induces me to patience. Yours embitters my sorrows, excites my complaints, and, depriving me of everything but a doubtful hope, reduces me to despair.

Amidst this strange opposition which subsists between what you lay down and what I experience, calm the perplexity with which I am agitated, and tell me who is misled either by sentiment or reason. "Man, have patience," say Pope and Leibniz, "The evils you experience are the necessary effect of your nature, and the constitution of the universe. That benevolent and eternal being which governs, will protect you. Of all possible systems, he has chosen that which contains the least evil with the greatest good. Or (to say the same thing more crudely, if it be necessary) if he has not done better, it is because it was out of his power."

Now what says your poem? "Continue, unhappy wretch, to suffer. If there be a God, who has created you, he is, without doubt, omnipotent. He could have prevented all the evils you suffer. You must not hope, therefore, they will ever have an end, for we cannot see why you exist except to suffer and to die." I do not know what such a doctrine can contain that is more consolatory than optimism, or even fatalism. For my own part, I confess it appears still more cruel than Manicheanism. If the difficulty attending the origin of evil obliges you to alter any of the perfections of the Deity, why would you justify his power at the expense of his goodness? Were I to choose between the two errors, I should certainly prefer the former.

You would not have your work looked upon as a poem against providence, and I shall beware of calling it such. However, you have called a performance, in which I pleaded the cause of mankind against themselves, a book written against mankind.[1] I am not to learn that a distinction is necessary to be made between the intentions of an author, and the consequences which may be deduced from his doctrines. The just defense of myself obliges me only to observe to you that my end, in describing the

1 [This was Voltaire's description of Rousseau's *Discourse on the Origin and the Foundation of Inequality of Mankind*; see Chapter 6, below.]

miseries of mankind, was, in my opinion, excusable and even commendable, for I showed in what manner men brought their own misfortunes on themselves, and consequently how they might avoid them.

I see not where we must look for the source of moral evil except in man, a free, improved and yet corrupted being. And, as to physical evils, if matter cannot be at once susceptible and impenetrable, as it appears to me it cannot, they must be unavoidable in every system of which man constitutes a part, and then the question is not, why is man not perfectly happy, but why does he exist? Again, I think I have shown that, with the exception of death, which can be called an evil only because of the preparations that are made preceding it, most of our physical evils are our own work. Without leaving the subject of Lisbon, you must agree, for example, that nature never assembled there twenty thousand houses of six or seven stories high; and that, if the inhabitants of that great city had been more equally dispersed, and more lightly lodged, the damage would have been much less, and perhaps none at all. Everybody would have fled at the first shock, and would have been seen the next day twenty leagues away, as gay as if nothing had happened. But as it was, everyone was obliged to stay, obstinately determined to remain near the ruins, exposed to new shocks, because what they would have had to leave was worth more than what they could take away. How many unhappy persons must have perished in that disaster, merely from persisting, some to take their clothes, some their papers, and others their money! Is it not well known that the person of a man has become the least part of him, and that there is hardly any trouble in saving it when he has lost everything else?

You could have wished (and who would not have wished the same) that the earthquake had happened in the middle of a desert rather than in Lisbon. Can it be doubted that earthquakes happen also in deserts? But no notice is taken of them, because they do no harm to the gentry of the cities, the only persons of whom any account is made. Not that they do much even to the animals and savages dispersed throughout those solitary wilds, who are neither afraid of the falling of tiles, nor the tottering of houses. But what signifies such a privilege? Will it therefore be said that the order of things ought to be changed to accord with our caprices, that nature ought to be submitted to our laws, and that we have nothing more to do than to build a city in a certain spot to secure it forever from earthquakes?

There are many events which strike us more or less according to the way in which they are considered, and which become much less horrible than they first appeared when they are examined more closely. I have learned from *Zadig*,[2] and nature daily confirms the truth of it, that an untimely death is not always a real evil, and that it may sometimes pass for a relative good. Among the number of those who perished under the ruins of Lisbon, many of them, undoubtedly, avoided greater misfortunes; and, notwithstanding the occasion which such a subject affords for emotive and poetic description, it is not certain that any one individual of those unfortunate persons actually suffered more than he might have done, if, according to the ordinary course of things, he had received the stroke of death through the lingering anguish of disease. In a word, could their end be more lamentable than that of a dying man tormented by fruitless solicitudes, whose heirs and lawyers hardly permit to breathe, whom the physicians murder in his bed at their ease, and to whom the barbarous priests administer the bitterest potion of death and artfully make the patient taste it drop by drop even to the very dregs? For my part, look which way I will, I see that the evils, to which we are exposed by nature, are much less cruel than those which we unnecessarily add to them.

But however ingenious we may be in fomenting our miseries by dint of curious institutions, we have not yet been able to improve ourselves to such a degree as to make life a burden, and to cause us generally to prefer annihilation to existence. For with such a preference, discouragement and despair would soon have taken hold of the greater part of mankind, and the human race could not have long subsisted. Now, if it be better for us to be than not to be, this would be sufficient to justify our existence, even if we can expect no indemnification for the evils we are to endure, and if those evils were as great as you describe them. But, on this subject, it is difficult to find sincerity among men or good calculators among philosophers. This is because the latter, in making an estimate of the good and bad of human life, always forget the delightful sentiment of existence, which is independent of every other sensation, and because the vanity of despising death, leads the others to undervalue life, just as those women who, having dirty gowns and a pair of scissors at hand, claim to prefer holes to stains. [...]

To return, Sir, to the system you have attacked, I believe that it cannot be suitably examined without carefully distinguishing the particular evil, the existence of which no philosopher ever denied, from the general

2 [A philosophical play by Voltaire.]

evil, which is denied by the optimist. The question is not whether individuals suffer, but whether the existence of the universe is, on the whole, good or not, and whether our particular sufferings are not unavoidable in the constitution of that universe. Thus, it appears to me that the addition of a single article will render the proposition exact, that is, instead of saying *Tout est bien* ('all is good'), we should say *Le tout est bien* ('the whole is good'), or *Tout est bien pour le tout* ('all is good for the whole'). It is thus very evident that nobody can bring a direct proof either for or against it. For these proofs depend on a perfect knowledge of the constitution of the world and of the design of its Author, and such knowledge is incontestably above the reach of the human understanding.

The true principles of optimism cannot be deduced either from the properties of matter, or the mechanism of the universe, but only by induction from the perfections of God who presides over the whole, so that we cannot prove the existence of God from the system of Pope, but the system of Pope from the existence of God. And, without contradiction, the question about the origin of evil is derived from that of providence. If one of these questions has been treated no better than the other, it is because we have always reasoned so badly about providence that the absurdities of the argument have confused all the corollaries that might be deduced from this important and consolatory tenet [...].

Ottobah Cugoano, from *Thoughts and Sentiments on the Evil and Wicked Traffic of the Slavery and Commerce of the Human Species*

As several learned gentlemen of distinguished abilities, as well as eminent for their great humanity, liberality and candour, have written various essays against that infamous traffic of the African Slave Trade, carried on with the West India planters and merchants, to the great shame and disgrace of all Christian nations wherever it is admitted in any of their territories, or in any place or situation amongst them; it cannot be amiss that I should thankfully acknowledge these truly, worthy and humane gentlemen with the warmest sense of gratitude, for their beneficent and laudable endeavours towards a total suppression of that infamous and iniquitous traffic of stealing, kidnapping, buying, selling, and cruelly enslaving men!

Those who have endeavoured to restore to their fellow-creatures the common rights of nature, of which especially the poor unfortunate Black People have been so unjustly deprived, cannot fail in meeting with the applause of all good men, and the approbation of that which will forever redound to their honour; they have the warrant of that which is divine: *Open thy mouth, judge righteously, plead the cause of the poor and needy; for the liberal deviseth liberal things, and by liberal things shall stand.*[3] And they can say with the pious Job, *Did not I weep for him that was in trouble; was not my soul grieved for the poor?*[4]

The kind exertions of many benevolent and Humane gentlemen, against the iniquitous traffic of slavery and oppression, has been attended with much good to many, and must redound with great honour to themselves, to humanity and their country; their laudable endeavours have been productive of the most beneficent effects in preventing that savage barbarity from taking place in free countries at home. In this, as well as in many other respects, there is one class of people (whose virtues of probity and humanity are well known) who are worthy of universal

3 [Proverbs 31.8–9.]

4 [Job 30.25.]

approbation and imitation, because, like men of honour, and Humanity, they have jointly agreed to carry on no slavery and savage barbarity among them; and, since the last war, some mitigation of slavery has been obtained in some respective districts of America, though not in proportion to their own vaunted claims of freedom; but it is to be hoped, that they will yet go on to make a further and greater reformation. However, notwithstanding all that has been done and written against it, that brutish barbarity and unparalleled injustice, is still carried on to a very great extent in the colonies, and with an avidity as insidious, cruel and oppressive as ever. The longer that men continue in the practice of evil and wickedness, they grow the more abandoned; for nothing in history can equal the barbarity and cruelty of the tortures and murders committed under various pretenses in modern slavery, except the annals of the Inquisition and the bloody edicts of Popish massacres.

It is therefore manifest, that something else ought yet to be done; and what is required, is evidently the incumbent duty of all men of enlightened understanding, and of every man that has any claim or affinity to the name of Christian, that the base treatment which the African Slaves undergo, ought to be abolished; and it is moreover evident, that the whole, or any part of that iniquitous traffic of slavery, can nowhere, or in any degree, be admitted, but among those who must eventually resign their own claim to any degree of sensibility and humanity, for that of barbarians and ruffians.

But it would be needless to arrange an history of all the base treatment which the African Slaves are subjected to, in order to show the exceeding wickedness and evil of that insidious traffic, as the whole may easily appear in every part, and at every view, to be wholly and totally inimical to every idea of justice, equity, reason and humanity. What I intend to advance against that evil, criminal and wicked traffic of enslaving men, are only some Thoughts and Sentiments which occur to me, as being obvious from the scriptures of Divine Truth, or such arguments as are chiefly deduced from thence, with other such observations as I have been able to collect. Some of these observations may lead into a larger field of consideration, than that of the African Slave Trade alone; but those causes from wherever they originate, and become the production of slavery, the evil effects produced by it, must show that its origin and source is of a wicked and criminal nature.

No necessity, or any situation of men, however poor, pitiful and wretched they may be, can warrant them to rob others, or oblige them to become thieves, because they are poor, miserable and wretched. But the robbers of men, the kidnappers, ensnarers and slave-holders, who take away the common rights and privileges of others to support and enrich themselves, are universally those pitiful and detestable wretches; for the ensnaring of others, and taking away their liberty by slavery and oppression, is the worst kind of robbery, as most opposite to every precept and injunction of the Divine Law, and contrary to that command which enjoins that *all men should love their neighbours as themselves, and that they should do unto others, as they would that men should do to them.* As to any other laws that slave-holders may make among themselves, as respecting slaves, they can be of no better kind, nor give them any better character, than what is implied in the common report—that there may be some honesty among thieves. This may seem a harsh comparison, but the parallel is so coincident that, I must say, I can find no other way of expressing my Thoughts and Sentiments, without making use of some harsh words and comparisons against the carriers on of such abandoned wickedness. But, in this little undertaking, I must humbly hope the impartial reader will excuse such defects as may arise from want of better education; and as to the resentment of those who can lay their cruel lash upon the backs of thousands, for a thousand times less crimes than writing against their enormous wickedness and brutal avarice, is what I may be sure to meet with.

However, it cannot but be very discouraging to a man of my complexion in such an attempt as this, to meet with the evil aspersions of some men, who say, "That an African is not entitled to any competent degree of knowledge, or capable of imbibing any sentiments of probity; and that nature designed him for some inferior link in the chain, fitted only to be a slave." But when I meet with those who make no scruple to deal with the human species, as with the beasts of the earth, I must think them not only brutish, but wicked and base; and that their aspersions are insidious and false: And if such men can boast of greater degrees of knowledge, than any African is entitled to, I shall let them enjoy all the advantages of it unenvied, as I fear it consists only in a greater share of infidelity, and that of a blacker kind than only skin deep. And if their complexion be not what I may suppose, it is at least the nearest in resemblance to an infernal hue. A good man will neither speak nor do as a bad man will; but if a man is bad, it makes no difference whether he be a black or a white devil.

By some of such complexion, as whether black or white it matters not, I was early snatched away from my native country, with about eighteen or twenty more boys and girls, as we were playing in a field. We lived but a few days journey from the coast where we were kidnapped, and as we were decoyed and drove along, we were soon conducted to a factory, and from thence, in the fashionable way of traffic, consigned to Grenada. Perhaps it may not be amiss to give a few remarks, as some account of myself, in this transposition of captivity.

I was born in the city of Agimaque, on the coast of Fantyn; my father was a companion to the chief in that part of the country of Fantee, and when the old king died I was left in his house with his family; soon after I was sent for by his nephew, Ambro Accasa, who succeeded the old king in the chiefdom of that part of Fantee known by the name of Agimaque and Assinee. I lived with his children, enjoying peace and tranquillity, about twenty moons, which, according to their way of reckoning time, is two years. I was sent for to visit an uncle, who lived at a considerable distance from Agimaque. The first day after we set out we arrived at Assinee, and the third day at my uncle's habitation, where I lived about three months, and was then thinking of returning to my father and young companion at Agimaque; but by this time I had got well acquainted with some of the children of my uncle's hundreds of relations, and we were some days too venturesome in going into the woods to gather fruit and catch birds, and such amusements as pleased us. One day I refused to go with the rest, being rather apprehensive that something might happen to us; till one of my play-fellows said to me, because you belong to the great men, you are afraid to venture your carcass, or else of the *bounsam*, which is the devil. This enraged me so much, that I set a resolution to join the rest, and we went into the woods as usual; but we had not been above two hours before our troubles began, when several great ruffians came upon us suddenly, and said we had committed a fault against their lord, and we must go and answer for it ourselves before him.

Some of us attempted in vain to run away, but pistols and cutlasses were soon introduced, threatening, that if we offered to stir we should all lie dead on the spot. One of them pretended to be more friendly than the rest, and said, that he would speak to their lord to get us clear, and desired that we should follow him; we were then immediately divided into different parties and drove after him. We were soon led out of the way which we knew, and towards the evening, as we came in light of a town, they told us that this great man of theirs lived there, but pretended it was too late to go and see him that night. Next morning there came three other men, whose language differed from ours and spoke to some of those who watched us all the night, but he that pretended to be our friend with the great man, and some others, were gone away. We asked our keepers what these men had been saying to them, and they answered, that they had been asking them, and us together, to go and feast with them that day, and that we must put off seeing the great man till after; little thinking that our doom was so nigh, or that these villains meant to feast on us as their prey. We went with them again about half a day's journey, and came to a great multitude of people, having different music playing; and all the day after we got there, we were very merry with the music, dancing and singing. Towards the evening, we were again persuaded that we could not get back to where the great man lived till next day; and when bedtime came, we were separated into different houses with different people. When the next morning came, I asked for the men that brought me there, and for the rest of my companions; and I was told that they were gone to the seaside to bring home some rum, guns and powder, and that some of my companions were gone with them, and that some were gone to the fields to do something or other. This gave me strong suspicion that there was some treachery in the case, and I began to think that my hopes of returning home again were all over. I soon became very uneasy, not knowing what to do, and refused to eat or drink for whole days together, till the man of the house told me that he would do all in his power to get me back to my uncle; then I ate a little fruit with him, and had some thoughts that I should be sought after, as I would be then missing at home about five or six days. I enquired every day if the men had come back, and for the rest of my companions, but could get no answer of any satisfaction. I was kept about six days at this man's house, and in the evening there was another man who came and talked with him a good while, and I heard the one say to the other he must go, and the other said the sooner the better; that man came out and told me that he knew my relations at Agimaque, and that we must set out tomorrow morning, and he would convey me there. Accordingly, we set out next day, and travelled till dark, when we came to a place where we had some supper and slept. He carried a large bag with some gold dust, which he said he had to buy some goods at the seaside to take with him to Agimaque. Next day we travelled on, and in the evening came to a town, where I saw several white people, which made me afraid that they would eat me, according to our notion as children in the inland parts of the country. This made me rest very uneasy all the night, and next morning I had some victuals brought, desiring me to eat and make haste, as my guide and kidnapper told me that he had to go to the castle with some company that were going there, as he had told me before, to get some goods. After I was ordered out, the horrors I soon saw and felt, cannot be well described; I saw many of my miserable countrymen chained two and two, some hand-cuffed, and some with their hands tied behind. We were conducted along by a guard, and when we arrived at the castle, I asked my guide what I was brought there for, he told me to learn the ways of the *browfow*, that is the white-faced people. I saw him take a gun, a piece of cloth, and some lead for me, and then he told me that he must now leave me there and went off. This made me cry bitterly, but I was soon conducted to a prison, for three days, where I heard the groans and cries of many, and saw some of my fellow-captives. But when a vessel arrived to conduct us away to the ship, it was a most horrible scene; there was nothing to be heard but rattling of chains, smacking of whips, and the groans and cries of our fellow men. Some would not stir from the ground, when they were lashed and beat in the most horrible manner. I have forgot the name of this infernal fort; but we were taken in the ship that came for us, to another that was ready to sail from Cape Coast. When we were put into the ship, we saw several black merchants coming on board, but we were all driven into our holes and not suffered to speak to any of them. In this situation we continued several days in sight of our native land; but I could find no good person to give any information of my situation to Accasa at Agimaque. And when we found ourselves at last taken away, death was more preferable than life, and a plan was concerted amongst us, that we might burn and blow up the ship, and to perish all together in the flames; but we were betrayed by one of our own countrywomen, who slept with some of the head men of the ship, for it was common for the dirty filthy sailors to take the African women and lie upon their bodies; but the men were chained and pent up in holes. It was the women and boys which were to burn the ship, with the approbation and groans of the rest; though that was prevented, the discovery was likewise a cruel bloody scene.

But it would be needless to give a description of all the horrible scenes which we saw, and the base treatment which we met with in this dreadful captive situation, as the similar cases of thousands, which suffer by this infernal traffic, are well known. Let it suffice to say, that I was thus lost to my dear indulgent parents and relations, and they to me. All my help was cries and tears, and these could not avail; nor suffered long, till one succeeding woe, and dread, swelled up another. Brought from a state of innocence and freedom and, in a barbarous and cruel manner, conveyed to a state of horror and slavery: this abandoned situation may be easier conceived than described. From the time that I was kidnapped and conducted to a factory, and from thence in the brutish, base, but fashionable way of traffic, consigned to Grenada, the grievous thoughts which I then felt, still pant in my heart; though my fears and tears have long since subsided. And yet it is still grievous to think that thousands more have suffered in similar and greater distress, under the hands of barbarous robbers, and merciless taskmasters; and that many even now are suffering in all the extreme bitterness of grief and woe, that no language can describe. The cries of some, and the sight of their misery, may be seen and heard afar; but the deep sounding groans of thousands, and the great sadness of their misery and woe, under the heavy load of oppressions and calamities inflicted upon them, are such as can only be distinctly known to the ears of Jehovah Sabaoth.

This Lord of Hosts, in his great providence, and in great mercy to me, made a way for my deliverance from Grenada.—Being in this dreadful captivity and horrible slavery, without any hope of deliverance, for about eight or nine months, beholding the most dreadful scenes of misery and cruelty, and seeing my miserable companions often cruelly lashed, and as it were cut to pieces, for the most trifling faults; this made me often tremble and weep, but I escaped better than many of them. For eating a piece of sugar cane, some were cruelly lashed, or struck over the face to knock their teeth out. Some of the stouter ones, I suppose often reproved, and grown hardened and stupid with many cruel beatings and lashings, or perhaps faint and pressed with hunger and hard labour, were often committing trespasses of this kind, and when detected, they met with exemplary punishment. Some told me they had their teeth pulled out to deter others, and to prevent them from eating any cane in future. Thus seeing my miserable companions and countrymen in this pitiful, distressed and horrible situation, with all the brutish baseness and barbarity attending it, could not but fill my little mind with horror and indignation. But I must own, to the shame of my own countrymen, that I was first kidnapped and betrayed by some of my own complexion, who were the first cause of my exile and slavery; but if there were no buyers there would be no sellers. So far as I can remember, some of the Africans in my country keep slaves, which they take in war, or for debt; but those which they keep are well fed, and good care taken of them, and treated well; and, as to their clothing, they differ according to the custom of the country. But I may safely say, that all the poverty and misery that any of the inhabitants of Africa meet with among themselves, is far inferior to those inhospitable regions of misery which they meet with in the West Indies, where their hardhearted overseers have neither regard to the laws of God, nor the life of their fellow-men.

Thanks, be to God, I was delivered from Grenada, and that horrid brutal slavery.—A gentleman coming to England, took me for his servant, and brought me away, where I soon found my situation become more agreeable. After coming to England, and seeing others write and read, I had a strong desire to learn, and getting what assistance I could, I applied myself to learn reading and writing, which soon became my recreation, pleasure, and delight; and when my master perceived that I could write some, he sent me to a proper school for that purpose to learn. Since, I have endeavoured to improve my mind in reading and have sought to get all the intelligence I could, in my situation of life, towards the state of my brethren and countrymen in complexion, and of the miserable situation of those who are barbarously sold into captivity and unlawfully held in slavery.

But, among other observations, one great duty I owe to Almighty God, (the thankful acknowledgement I would not omit for any consideration) that, although I have been brought away from my native country, in that torrent of robbery and wickedness, thanks be to God for his good providence towards me; I have both obtained liberty, and acquired the great advantages of some little learning, in being able to read and write; and, what is still infinitely of greater advantage, I trust, to know something of *Him who is that God whose providence rules over all, and who is the only Potent One that rules in the nations over the children of men. It is unto Him who is the Prince of the Kings of the earth, that I would give all thanks*. And, in some manner, I may say with Joseph, as he did with respect to the evil intention of his brethren, when they sold him into Egypt, that whatever evil intentions and bad motives those insidious robbers had in carrying me away from my native country and friends, I trust, was what the Lord intended for my good. In this respect, I am highly indebted to many of the good people of England for learning and principles unknown to the people of my native country. But, above all, what have I obtained from the Lord God of Hosts, the God of the Christians! in that divine revelation of the only true God, and the Saviour of men, what a treasure of wisdom and blessings are involved? How wonderful is the divine goodness displayed in those invaluable books the Old and

New Testaments, that inestimable compilation of books, the Bible? And O what a treasure to have, and one of the greatest advantages to be able to read therein, and a divine blessing to understand![5]

But, to return to my subject, I begin with the Cursory Remarker.[6] This man stiles himself a friend to the West India colonies and their inhabitants, like Demetrius, the silversmith, a man of some considerable abilities, seeing their craft in danger, a craft, however, not so innocent and justifiable as the making of shrines for Diana, though that was base and wicked enough to enslave the minds of men with superstition and idolatry; but his craft, and the gain of those craftsmen, consists in the enslaving both soul and body to the cruel idolatry, and most abominable service and slavery, to the idol of cursed avarice: and as he finds some discoveries of their wicked traffic held up in a light where truth and facts are so clearly seen, as none but the most desperate villain would dare to obstruct or oppose, he therefore sallies forth with all the desperation of an Utopian assailant, to tell lies by a virulent contradiction of facts, and with false aspersions endeavour to calumniate the worthy and judicious essayist of that discovery, a man, whose character is irreproachable.[7] By thus artfully supposing, if he could bring the reputation of the author, who has discovered so much of their iniquitous traffic, into dispute, his work would fall and be less regarded. However, this virulent craftsman has done no great merit to his cause and the credit of that infamous craft; at the appearance of truth, his understanding has got the better of his avarice and infidelity, so far as to draw the following concession: "I shall not be so far misunderstood, by the candid and judicious part of mankind, as to be ranked among the advocates of slavery, as I most sincerely join Mr. Ramsay and every other man of sensibility, in hoping the blessings of freedom will, in due time, be equally diffused over the whole globe."

By this, it would seem that he was a little ashamed of his craftsmen and would not like to be ranked or appear amongst them. But as long

5 [Note removed.]

6 [This refers to James Tobin (1736/37–1817), the author of an anonymous defense of the practice of slavery on the part of West Indian plantation owners, entitled *Cursory Remarks upon the Reverend Mr. Ramsay's Essay on the Treatment and Conversion of African Slaves in the Sugar Colonies* (1785). Cugoano's quotations from Tobin are taken from this text.]

7 [The reference here is to James Ramsey (1733–89), an abolitionist writer whose *An Essay on the Treatment and Conversion of African Slaves in the British Sugar Colonies* (1784) was the target of Tobin's tract.]

as there are any hopes of gain to be made by that insidious craft, he can join with them well enough, and endeavour to justify them in that most abandoned traffic of buying, selling, and enslaving men. He finds fault with a plan for punishing robbers, thieves and vagabonds, who distress their neighbours by their thrift, robbery and plunder, without regarding any laws human or divine, except the rules of their own fraternity, and in that case, according to the proverb, there may be some honour among thieves; but these are the only people in the world that ought to suffer some punishment, imprisonment or slavery; their external complexion, whether black or white, should be no excuse for them to do evil. Being aware of this, perhaps he was afraid that some of his friends, the great and opulent *banditti* of slave-holders in the western part of the world, might be found guilty of more atrocious and complicated crimes, than even those of the highwaymen, the robberies and the petty larcenies committed in England. Therefore, to make the best of this sad dilemma, he brings in a ludicrous invective comparison that it would be "an event which would undoubtedly furnish a new and pleasant compartment to that well known and most delectable print, called, *The world, turn'd up side down*, in which the cook is roasted by the pig, the man saddled by the horse," &c.[8] If he means that the complicated *banditti* of pirates, thieves, robbers, oppressors and enslavers of men, are those cooks and men that would be roasted and saddled, it certainly would be no unpleasant sight to see them well roasted, saddled and bridled too, and no matter by whom, whether he terms them pigs, horses or asses. But there is not much likelihood of this silly, monkeyish comparison as yet being verified, in bringing the opulent pirates and thieves to condign punishment, so that he could very well bring it in to turn it off with a grin. However, to make use of his words, it would be a most delectable sight, when thieves and robbers get the upper side of the world, to see them turned down; and I should not interrupt his mirth, to see him laugh at his own invective monkeyish comparison as long as he pleases.

But again, when he draws a comparison of the many hardships that the poor in Great Britain and Ireland labour under, as well as many of those in other countries; that their various distresses are worse than the West India slaves—it may be true, in part, that some of them suffer greater hardships than many of the slaves; but, bad as it is, the poorest

8 [The title of an English ballad which was also issued in a printed edition in 1646 with illustrations.]

in England would not change their situation for that of slaves. And there may be some masters, under various circumstances, worse off than their servants; but they would not change their own situation for theirs: nor as little would a rich man wish to change his situation of affluence, for that of a beggar: and so, likewise, no freeman, however poor and distressing his situation may be, would resign his liberty for that of a slave, in the situation of a horse or a dog. The case of the poor, whatever their hardships may be, in free countries, is widely different from that of the West India slaves. For the slaves, like animals, are bought and sold, and dealt with as their capricious owners may think fit, even in torturing and tearing them to pieces, and wearing them out with hard labour, hunger and oppression; and should the death of a slave ensue by some other more violent way than that which is commonly the death of thousands, and tens of thousands in the end, the haughty tyrant, in that case, has only to pay a small fine for the murder and death of his slave. The brute creation in general may fare better than man, and some dogs may refuse the crumbs that the distressed poor would be glad of; but the nature and situation of man is far superior to that of beasts; and, in like manner, whatever circumstances poor freemen may be in, their situation is much superior, beyond any proportion, to that of the hardships and cruelty of modern slavery. But where can the situation of any freeman be so bad as that of a slave; or could such be found, or even worse, as he would have it, what would the comparison amount to? Would it plead for his craft of slavery and oppression? Or, rather, would it not cry aloud for some redress, and what every well-regulated society of men ought to hear and consider, that none should suffer want or be oppressed among them? And this seems to be pointed out by the circumstances which he describes; that it is the great duty, and ought to be the highest ambition of all governors, to order and establish such policy, and in such a wise manner that everything should be so managed as to be conducive to the moral, temporal and eternal welfare of every individual from the lowest degree to the highest; and the consequence of this would be, the harmony, happiness and good prosperity of the whole community.

But this crafty author has also, in defense of his own or his employer's craft in the British West India slavery, given sundry comparisons and descriptions of the treatment of slaves in the French islands and settlements in the West Indies and America. And, contrary to what is the true case, he would have it supposed that the treatment of the slaves in the former, is milder than the latter; but even in this, unwarily for his own craft of slavery, all that he has advanced can only add matter for its confutation, and serve to heighten the ardour and wish of every generous mind, that the whole should be abolished. An equal degree of enormity found in one place, cannot justify crimes of as great or greater enormity committed in another. The various depredations committed by robbers and plunderers, on different parts of the globe, may not be all equally alike bad, but their evil and malignancy, in every appearance and shape, can only hold up to view the just observation, that,

Virtue herself hath such peculiar mien,
Vice, to be hated, needs but to be seen.[9]

The farther and wider that the discovery and knowledge of such an enormous evil, as the base and villainous treatment and slavery which the poor unfortunate Black People meet with, is spread and made known, the cry for justice, even virtue lifting up her voice, must rise the louder and higher, for the scale of equity and justice to be lifted up in their defense. *And doth not wisdom cry, and understanding put forth her voice?*[10] But who will regard the voice and hearken to the cry? Not the sneaking advocates for slavery, though a little ashamed of their craft; like the monstrous crocodile weeping over their prey with fine concessions (while gorging their own rapacious appetite) to hope for universal freedom taking place over the globe. Not those inebriated with avarice and infidelity, who hold in defiance every regard due to the divine law, and who endeavour all they can to destroy and take away the natural and common rights and privileges of men. Not the insolent and crafty author for slavery and oppression, who would have us to believe, that the benign command of God in appointing the seventh day for a sabbath of rest for the good purposes of our present and eternal welfare, is not to be regarded. He will exclaim against the teachers of obedience to it; and tells us, that the poor, and the oppressed, and the heavy burdened slave, should not lay down his load that day, but appropriate these hours of sacred rest to labour in some bit of useful ground. His own words are, "to dedicate the unappropriated hours of Sunday to the cultivation of this

9 [This is Cuguono's rendering of a couplet in Epistle II of Alexander Pope's "An Essay on Man" ("Vice is a monster of so frightful mien, / As, to be hated, needs but to be seen").]

10 [Proverbs 8.1.]

useful spot, he is brought up to believe would be the worst of sins, and that the sabbath is a day of absolute and universal rest is a truth he hears frequently inculcated by the curate of the parish," &c. But after bringing it about in this round-about way and manner, whatever the curate has to say of it as a truth, he would have us by no means to regard. This may serve as a specimen of his crafty and detestable production, where infidelity, false aspersions, virulent calumnies, and lying contradictions abound throughout. I shall only refer him to that description which he meant for another, as most applicable and best suited for himself; and so long as he does not renounce his craft, as well as to be somewhat ashamed of his craftsmen and their insensibility, he may thus stand as described by himself: "A man of warm imagination (but strange infatuated unfeeling sensibility) to paint things not as they really are, but as his rooted prejudices represent them, and even to shut his eyes against the convictions afforded him by his own senses."

But such is the insensibility of men, when their own craft of gain is advanced by the slavery and oppression of others, that after all the laudable exertions of the truly virtuous and humane, towards extending the beneficence of liberty and freedom to the much degraded and unfortunate Africans, which is the common right and privilege of all men, in everything that is just, lawful and consistent, we find the principles of justice and equity, not only opposed, and every duty in religion and humanity left unregarded; but that unlawful traffic of dealing with our fellow-creatures as with the beasts of the earth, still carried on with as great assiduity as ever; and that the insidious piracy of procuring and holding slaves is countenanced and supported by the government of sundry Christian nations. This seems to be the fashionable way of getting riches, but very dishonourable; in doing this, the slave-holders are meaner and baser than the African slaves, for while they subject and reduce them to a degree with brutes, they seduce themselves to a degree with devils.

"Some pretend that, the Africans, in general, are a set of poor, ignorant, dispersed, unsociable people; and that they think it no crime to sell one another, and even their own wives and children; therefore they bring them away to a situation where many of them may arrive to a better state than ever they could obtain in their own native country." This specious pretense is without any shadow of justice and truth, and, if the argument was even true, it could afford no just and warrantable matter for any society of men to hold slaves. But the argument is false; there can be no ignorance, dispersion, or unsociableness so found among them, which can be made better by bringing them away to a state of a degree equal to that of a cow or a horse.

But let their ignorance in some things (in which the Europeans have greatly the advantage of them) be what it will, it is not the intention of those who bring them away to make them better by it; nor is the design of slave-holders of any other intention, but that they may serve them as a kind of engines and beasts of burden, that their own ease and profit may be advanced by a set of poor helpless men and women whom they despise and rank with brutes and keep them in perpetual slavery, both themselves and children, and merciful death is the only release from their toil. By the benevolence of some, a few may get their liberty, and by their own industry and ingenuity, may acquire some learning, mechanical trades, or useful business; and some may be brought away by different gentlemen to free countries, where they get their liberty; but no thanks to slave-holders for it. But amongst those who get their liberty, like all other ignorant men, are generally more corrupt in their morals, than they possibly could have been amongst their own people in Africa; for, being mostly among the wicked and apostate Christians, they sooner learn their oaths and blasphemies, and their evil ways, than anything else. Some few, indeed, may eventually arrive at some knowledge of the Christian religion, and the great advantages of it. Such was the case of Ukawsaw Groniosaw, an African prince, who lived in England.[11] He was a long time in a state of great poverty and distress, and must have died at one time for want, if a good and charitable attorney had not supported him. He was long after in a very poor state, but he would not have given his faith in the Christian religion in exchange for all the kingdoms of Africa, if they could have been given to him, in place of his poverty, for it. And such was A. Morrant in America.[12] When a boy, he could stroll away into a desert and prefer the society of wild beasts to the absurd Christianity of his mother's house. He was conducted to the king of the Cherokees, who, in a miraculous manner, was induced by him to embrace the Christian faith. This Morrant was in the British service last

11 [Ukawsaw Gronniosaw (c. 1705–75), also known as James Albert, was a former slave who wrote *A Narrative of the Most Remarkable Particulars in the Life of James Albert Ukawsaw Gronniosaw, an African Prince, as Related by Himself* (1772).]

12 [John Marrant (1755–91), a former slave who became one of the first Black preachers in North America. His story is told in *A Narrative of the Lord's Wonderful Dealings with John Marrant, a Black* (1785, as told to William Aldridge).]

war, and his royal convert, the king of the Cherokee Indians, accompanied General Clinton at the siege of Charles-Town.

These, and all such, I hope thousands, as meet with the knowledge and grace of the Divine clemency, are brought forth quite contrary to the end and intention of all slavery, and, in general, of all slave-holders too. And should it please the Divine goodness to visit some of the poor dark Africans, even in the brutal stall of slavery, and from thence to install them among the princes of his grace, and to invest them with a robe of honour that will hang about their necks for ever; but who can then suppose, that it will be well-pleasing unto him to find them subjected there in that dejected state? Or can the slave-holders think that the Universal Father and Sovereign of Mankind will be well-pleased with them, for the brutal transgression of his law, in bowing down the necks of those to the yoke of their cruel bondage? Sovereign goodness may eventually visit some men even in a state of slavery, but their slavery is not the cause of that event and benignity; and therefore, should some event of good ever happen to some men subjected to slavery, that can plead nothing for men to do evil, that good may come; and should it apparently happen from thence, it is neither sought for nor designed by the enslavers of men. But the whole, business of slavery is an evil of the first magnitude, and a most horrible iniquity to traffic with slaves and souls of men, and an evil, sorry I am, that it still subsists, and more astonishing to think, that it is an iniquity committed amongst Christians, and contrary to all the genuine principles of Christianity, and yet carried on by men denominated thereby.

In a Christian era, in a land where Christianity is planted, where everyone might expect to behold the flourishing growth of every virtue, extending their harmonious branches with universal philanthropy wherever they came; but, on the contrary, almost nothing else is to be seen abroad but the bramble of ruffians, barbarians and slave-holders, grown up to a powerful luxuriance in wickedness. I cannot but wish, for the honour of Christianity, that the bramble grown up among them was known to the heathen nations by a different name, for sure the depredators, robbers and ensnarers of men can never be Christians, but ought to be held as the abhorrence of all men, and the abomination of all mankind, whether Christians or heathens. Every man of any sensibility, whether he be a Christian or an heathen, if he has any discernment at all, must think that for any man, or any class of men, to deal with their fellow-creatures as with the beasts of the field, or to account them as such, however ignorant they may be, and in whatever situation, or wherever they may find them, and whatever country or complexion they may be of, that those men, who are the procurers and holders of slaves, are the greatest villains in the world. And surely those men must be lost to all sensibility themselves, who can think that the stealing, robbing, enslaving, and murdering of men can be no crimes; but the holders of men in slavery are at the head of all these oppressions and crimes. And, therefore, however insensible they may be of it now, and however long they may laugh at the calamity of others, if they do not repent of their evil way and the wickedness of their doings by keeping and holding their fellow-creatures in slavery and trafficking with them as with the brute creation, and to give up and surrender that evil traffic with an awful abhorrence of it, that this may be averred, if they do not, and if they can think, they must and cannot otherwise but expect in one day at last to meet with the full stroke of the long suspended vengeance of heaven, when death will cut them down to a state as mean as that of the most abjected slave, and to a very eminent danger of a far more dreadful fate hereafter, when they have the just reward of their iniquities to meet with.

And now, as to the Africans being dispersed and unsociable, if it was so, that could be no warrant for the Europeans to enslave them; and even though they may have many different feuds and bad practices among them, the continent of Africa is of vast extent, and the numerous inhabitants are divided into several kingdoms and principalities, which are governed by their respective kings and princes, and those are absolutely maintained by their free subjects. Very few nations make slaves of any of those under their government; but such as are taken prisoners of war from their neighbours, are generally kept in that state until they can exchange and dispose of them otherwise; and towards the west coast they are generally procured for the European market and sold. They have a great aversion to murder, or even in taking away the lives of those which they judge guilty of crimes; and, therefore, they prefer disposing of them otherwise better than killing them.[13] This gives their merchants and procurers of slaves a power to travel a great way into the interior parts of the country to buy such as are wanted to be disposed of. These slave-procurers are a set of as great villains as any in the world. They often steal and kidnap

13 It may be true that some of the slaves transported from Africa may have committed crimes in their own country, that require some slavery as a punishment; but, according to the laws of equity and justice, they ought to become free as soon as their labour has paid for their purchase in the West Indies or elsewhere.

many more than they buy at first if they can meet with them by the way; and they have only their certain boundaries to go to, and sell them from one to another; so that if they are sought after and detected, the thieves are seldom found, and the others only plead that they bought them so and so. These kidnappers and slave-procurers, called merchants, are a species of African villains which are greatly corrupted and even vitiated by their intercourse with the Europeans; but, wicked and barbarous as they certainly are, I can hardly think, if they knew what horrible barbarity they were sending their fellow-creatures to, that they would do it. But the artful Europeans have so deceived them, that they are bought by their inventions of merchandise and beguiled into it by their artifice; for the Europeans, at their factories, in some various manner, have always kept some as servants to them, and with gaudy clothes, in a gay manner, as decoy ducks to deceive others, and to tell them that they want many more to go over the sea, and be as they are. So in that respect, wherein it may be said that they will sell one another, they are only ensnared and enlisted to be servants, kept like some of those which they see at the factories, which, for some gewgaws, as presents given to themselves and friends, they are thereby enticed to go; and something after the same manner that East India soldiers are procured in Britain; and the inhabitants here, just as much sell themselves, and one another, as they; and the kidnappers here, and the slave-procurers in Africa, are much alike. But many other barbarous methods are made use of by the vile instigators, procurers and ensnarers of men; and some of the wicked and profligate princes and chiefs of Africa accept of presents, from the Europeans, to procure a certain number of slaves; and thereby they are wickedly instigated to go to war with one another on purpose to get them, which produces many terrible depredations; and sometimes when those engagements are entered into, and they find themselves defeated of their purpose, it has happened that some of their own people have fallen a sacrifice to their avarice and cruelty. And it may be said of the Europeans, that they have made use of every insidious method to procure slaves whenever they can, and in whatever manner they can lay hold of them, and that their forts and factories are the avowed dens of thieves for robbers, plunderers and depredators.

But again, as to the Africans selling their own wives and children, nothing can be more opposite to everything they hold dear and valuable, and nothing can distress them more, than to part with any of their relations and friends. Such are the tender feelings of parents for their children, that, for the loss of a child, they seldom can be rendered happy, even with the intercourse and enjoyment of their friends, for years. For any man to think that it should be otherwise when he may see a thousand instances of a natural instinct, even in the brute creation, where they have a sympathetic feeling for their offspring; it must be great want of consideration not to think that much more than merely what is natural to animals should in a higher degree be implanted in the breast of every part of the rational creation of man. And what man of feeling can help lamenting the loss of parents, friends, liberty, and perhaps property and other valuable and dear connections. Those people annually brought away from Guinea, are born as free, and are brought up with as great a predilection for their own country, freedom and liberty, as the sons and daughters of fair Britain. Their free subjects are trained up to a kind of military service, not so much by the desire of the chief, as by their own voluntary inclination. It is looked upon as the greatest respect they can show to their king, to stand up for his and their own defense in time of need. Their different chieftains, which bear a reliance on the great chief, or king, exercise a kind of government something like that feudal institution which prevailed some time in Scotland. In this respect, though the common people are free, they often suffer by the villainy of their different chieftains, and by the wars and feuds which happen among them. Nevertheless, their freedom and rights are as dear to them, as those privileges are to other people. And it may be said that freedom, and the liberty of enjoying their own privileges, burns with as much zeal and fervour in the breast of an Ethiopian, as in the breast of any inhabitant on the globe.

But the supporters and favourers of slavery make other things a pretense and an excuse in their own defense; such as, that they find that it was admitted under the Divine institution by Moses, as well as the long continued practice of different nations for ages; and that the Africans are peculiarly marked out by some signal prediction in nature and complexion for that purpose.

This seems to be the greatest bulwark of defense which the advocates and favourers of slavery can advance, and what is generally talked of in their favour by those who do not understand it. I shall consider it in that view, whereby it will appear that they deceive themselves and mislead others. Men are never more liable to be drawn into error, than when truth is made use of in a guileful manner to seduce them. Those who do not believe the scriptures to be a Divine revelation, cannot, consistently with themselves, make the law of Moses, or any mark or prediction they can find respecting any particular set of men, as found in the sacred writings, any reason that one class of men should enslave another. In that respect, all that they have to enquire into should be whether it be right or wrong that any part of the human species should enslave another; and when that is the case, the Africans, though not so learned, are just as wise as the Europeans; and when the matter is left to human wisdom, they are both liable to err. But what the light of nature and the dictates of reason, when rightly considered, teach, is that no man ought to enslave another; and some who have been rightly guided thereby have made noble defenses for the universal natural rights and privileges of all men. But in this case, when the learned take neither revelation nor reason for their guide, they fall into as great and worse errors than the unlearned; for they only make use of that system of Divine wisdom, which should guide them into truth, when they can find or pick out anything that will suit their purpose, or that they can pervert to such—the very means of leading themselves and others into error. And, in consequence thereof, the pretenses that some men make use of for holding of slaves must be evidently the grossest perversion of reason, as well as an inconsistent and diabolical use of the sacred writings. For it must be a strange perversion of reason, and a wrong use or disbelief of the sacred writings, when anything found there is so perverted by them, and set up as a precedent and rule for men to commit wickedness. They had better have no reason, and no belief in the scriptures, and make no use of them at all, than only to believe, and make use of that which leads them into the most abominable evil and wickedness of dealing unjustly with their fellow men.

But this will appear evident to all men that believe the scriptures, that every reason necessary is given that they should be believed; and, in this case, that they afford us this information:

"That all mankind did spring from one original, and that there are no different species among men. For God who made the world, hath made one blood all the nations of men that dwell on all the face of the earth."[14]

Wherefore we may justly infer, as there are no inferior species, but all of one blood and of one nature, that there does not an inferiority subsist, or depend, on their colour, features or form, whereby some men make a pretense to enslave others; and consequently, as they have all one creator, one original, made of one blood, and all brethren descended from one father, it never could be lawful and just for any nation, or people, to oppress and enslave another. [...]

14 [Compare Acts 17.26.]

Chapter 4

HUME AND KANT ON THE IMPOSSIBILITY OF THEODICY

Introduction

THERE IS NO QUESTION THAT THE TASK OF VINDICATING "the conduct of God," to use Leibniz's phrase, became more difficult in the wake of the Lisbon disaster. Only the most devoted disciples were willing to go out on a limb to defend Leibniz's optimism in the face of such a challenge. Interestingly, this resulted in the pendulum swinging back in the direction of Bayle's position. Bayle, it will be recalled, had contended that we can know both that God exists and that evil exists, and that since it is *actually* the case that both exist together, it must also be *possible* for them to do so; yet understanding *how* the two are possible together is a mystery that only serves to humble the pretensions of our reason. Bayle's position, or something close to it, would find two influential defenders in the second half of the eighteenth century, namely, David Hume (1711–77) and Immanuel Kant (1724–1804). Both Hume and Kant would agree with Bayle that an understanding of how the existence of evil is reconcilable with divine goodness is beyond our capacities, though both depart from Bayle in important respects as well.

Hume's discussion occurs in a posthumously published text, the *Dialogues concerning Natural Religion*. This was a text Hume had written but suppressed during his lifetime, due to the fact that it contains an extended critique of traditional arguments for God's existence, such as the design argument (Hume had already been widely suspected of being an atheist). As the title indicates, the text is written as a dialogue among three characters: Cleanthes, a "natural theologian" or someone who thinks that key religious convictions can be adequately known through the application of reason; Demea, a theist who, unlike Cleanthes, thinks that some religious truths remain mysterious to human reason (and so require recourse to Scripture); and Philo, an empiricist or a thinker who assigns a priority to experience as a source of knowledge (and who is often taken to be Hume's own mouthpiece in the text). This empiricistic commitment is clear in Philo's approach to the question of how we come to know the divine attributes (particularly the goodness of God). As Philo claims, before we are in a position to investigate the matter through reason, our experience already reveals to us a world that appears poorly designed to suit human ends, a world, that is, from which it would not be rational to infer the existence of an architect who is supreme in goodness, power, and wisdom. This skeptical conclusion is further supported by what Philo dubs the four "circumstances," or states of affairs in the world that constitute the source of considerable evils for the human being but which, on rational inspection, do not seem to be necessary constituents of the world. This is to say that a world in which these circumstances are present will always strike human reason as incompatible with the claim that it was created by a supremely good, powerful, and wise being.

Kant defends a similarly skeptical position in his 1791 essay "*Über das Mißlingen aller philosophischen Versuche in der Theodicee*" ("On the Failure of All Philosophical Attempts at Theodicy"). Interestingly, in an essay from 1756, Kant had defended Leibniz in the immediate aftermath of Lisbon; however, by the time of his essay on theodicy he had become less optimistic. Kant's aim in the later essay is to offer a systematic argument for why every attempted philosophical explanation of evil, or "counter-purposiveness," must fail. The bulk of the essay is devoted to providing an exhaustive classification of the types of counter-purposiveness and the possible explanatory strategies, and then showing why each is unsuccessful. However, Kant also suggests, in the second part of the essay, that human reason's inability to explain such counter-purposiveness is nothing less than what God intended, and we can understand this divine decree as being issued in the biblical Book of Job itself, which Kant proceeds to interpret. The devout and once-prosperous Job had seen his life turned upside down by God in response to Satan's challenge that Job only worshipped God because of his prosperity. Throughout his trials, Job never abandons the conviction of his conscience that he was blameless for his suffering. For

Kant, Job's case offers both a negative and positive lesson: negatively, it shows Job's presumptuousness in complaining of unjust treatment since we cannot pretend to understand God's reasons for bringing about a world in which evil exists. Positively, however, Kant highlights Job's unwavering conviction in his own blamelessness—despite his friends' efforts to convince him that he must have committed some sin to account for his suffering. Kant praises Job's refusal to accommodate his moral principles to his religious beliefs, even as Job's conviction points to and reinforces a universal moral order which God sustains but is also subject to.

David Hume, *Dialogues concerning Natural Religion*, Part XI

I scruple not to allow, said Cleanthes, that I have been apt to suspect the frequent repetition of the word, *infinite*, which we meet with in all theological writers, to savour more of panegyric than of philosophy, and that any purposes of reasoning, and even of religion, would be better served, were we to rest contented with more accurate and more moderate expressions. The terms, *admirable*, *excellent*, *superlatively great*, *wise*, and *holy*; these sufficiently fill the imaginations of men; and anything beyond, besides that it leads into absurdities, has no influence on the affections or sentiments. Thus, in the present subject, if we abandon all human analogy, as seems your intention, Demea, I am afraid we abandon all religion, and retain no conception of the great object of our adoration. If we preserve human analogy, we must forever find it impossible to reconcile any mixture of evil in the universe with infinite attributes; much less, can we ever prove the latter from the former. But supposing the author of nature to be finitely perfect, though far exceeding mankind; a satisfactory account may then be given of natural and moral evil, and every untoward phenomenon be explained and adjusted. A less evil may then be chosen, in order to avoid a greater; inconveniencies be submitted to, in order to reach a desirable end; and in a word, benevolence, regulated by wisdom, and limited by necessity, may produce just such a world as the present. You, Philo, who are so prompt at starting views, and reflections, and analogies; I would gladly hear, at length, without interruption, your opinion of this new theory; and if it deserve our attention, we may afterwards, at more leisure, reduce it into form.

My sentiments, replied Philo, are not worth being made a mystery of; and therefore, without any ceremony, I shall deliver what occurs to me, with regard to the present subject. It must, I think, be allowed, that, if a very limited intelligence, whom we shall suppose utterly unacquainted with the universe, were assured, that it were the production of a very good, wise, and powerful being, however finite, he would, from his conjectures, form *beforehand* a different notion of it from what we find it to be by experience; nor would he ever imagine, merely from these attributes of the cause, of which he is informed, that the effect could be so full of vice and misery and disorder, as it appears in this life. Supposing now, that this person were brought into the world, still assured, that it was the workmanship of such a sublime and benevolent being; he might, perhaps, be surprised at the disappointment; but would never retract his former belief, if founded on any very solid argument; since such a limited intelligence must be sensible of his own blindness and ignorance, and must allow, that there may be many solutions of those phenomena, which will forever escape his comprehension. But supposing, which is the real case with regard to man, that this creature is not antecedently convinced of a supreme intelligence, benevolent, and powerful, but is left to gather such a belief from the appearances of things; this entirely alters the case, nor will he ever find any reason for such a conclusion. He may be fully convinced of the narrow limits of his understanding; but this will not help him in forming an inference concerning the goodness of superior powers, since he must form that inference from what he knows, not from what he is ignorant of. The more you exaggerate his weakness and ignorance, the more diffident you render him, and give him the greater suspicion, that such subjects are beyond the reach of his faculties. You are obliged, therefore, to reason with him merely from the known phenomena, and to drop every arbitrary supposition or conjecture.

Did I show you a house or palace, where there was not one apartment convenient or agreeable; where the windows, doors, fires, passages, stairs, and the whole economy of the building were the source of noise, confusion, fatigue, darkness, and the extremes of heat and cold; you would certainly blame the contrivance, without any farther examination. The architect would in vain display his subtilty, and prove to you, that if this door or that window were altered, greater ills would ensue. What he says, may be strictly true: The alteration of one particular, while the other parts of the building remain, may only augment the inconveniencies. But still you would assert in general, that, if the architect had had skill and good intentions, he might have formed such a plan of the whole, and might have adjusted the parts in such a manner, as would have remedied all or most of these inconveniencies. His ignorance, or even your own ignorance of such a plan, will never convince you of the impossibility of it. If you find many inconveniencies and deformities in the building, you will always, without entering into any detail, condemn the architect.

In short, I repeat the question: Is the world, considered in general, and as it appears to us in this life, different from what a man or such a limited being would, *beforehand*, expect from a very powerful, wise, and benevolent Deity? It must be strange prejudice to assert the contrary. And from thence I conclude, that, however consistent the world may be, allowing certain suppositions and conjectures, with the idea of such a Deity, it can never afford us an inference concerning his existence. The consistency is not absolutely denied, only the inference. Conjectures, especially where infinity is excluded from the divine attributes, may, perhaps, be sufficient to prove a consistency; but can never be foundations for any inference.

There seem to be *four* circumstances, on which depend all, or the greatest part of the ills, that molest sensible creatures; and it is not impossible but all these circumstances may be necessary and unavoidable. We know so little beyond common life, or even of common life, that, with regard to the economy of a universe, there is no conjecture, however wild, which may not be just; nor any one, however plausible, which may not be erroneous. All that belongs to human understanding, in this deep ignorance and obscurity, is to be sceptical, or at least cautious; and not to admit of any hypothesis, whatever; much less, of any which is supported by no appearance of probability. Now this I assert to be the case with regard to all the causes of evil, and the circumstances, on which it depends. None of them appear to human reason, in the least degree, necessary or unavoidable; nor can we suppose them such, without the utmost license of imagination.

The *first* circumstance which introduces evil, is that contrivance or economy of the animal creation, by which pains, as well as pleasures, are employed to excite all creatures to action, and make them vigilant in the great work of self-preservation. Now pleasure alone, in its various degrees, seems to human understanding sufficient for this purpose. All animals might be constantly in a state of enjoyment; but when urged by any of the necessities of nature, such as thirst, hunger, weariness; instead of pain, they might feel a diminution of pleasure, by which they might be prompted to seek that object, which is necessary to their subsistence. Men pursue pleasure as eagerly as they avoid pain; at least, might have been so constituted. It seems, therefore, plainly possible to carry on the business of life without any pain. Why then is any animal ever rendered susceptible of such a sensation? If animals can be free from it an hour, they might enjoy a perpetual exemption from it; and it required as particular a contrivance of their organs to produce that feeling, as to endow them with sight, hearing, or any of the senses. Shall we conjecture, that such a contrivance was necessary, without any appearance of reason? And shall we build on that conjecture as on the most certain truth?

But a capacity of pain would not alone produce pain, were it not for the *second* circumstance, *viz.* the conducting of the world by general laws; and this seems no wise necessary to a very perfect being. It is true; if everything were conducted by particular volitions, the course of nature would be perpetually broken, and no man could employ his reason in the conduct of life. But might not other particular volitions remedy this inconvenience? In short, might not the Deity exterminate all ill, wherever it were to be found; and produce all good, without any preparation or long progress of causes and effects?

Besides, we must consider, that, according to the present economy of the world, the course of nature, though supposed exactly regular, yet to us appears not so, and many events are uncertain, and many disappoint our expectations. Health and sickness, calm and tempest, with an infinite number of other accidents, whose causes are unknown and variable, have a great influence both on the fortunes of particular persons and on the prosperity of public societies: and indeed all human life, in a manner, depends on such accidents. A being, therefore, who knows the secret springs of the universe, might easily, by particular volitions, turn all these accidents to the good of mankind, and render the whole world happy, without discovering himself in any operation. A fleet, whose purposes were salutary to society, might always meet with a fair wind: good princes enjoy sound health and long life: persons, born to power and authority, be framed with good tempers and virtuous dispositions. A few such events as these, regularly and wisely conducted, would change the face of the world; and yet would no more seem to disturb the course of nature or confound human conduct, than the present economy of things, where the causes are secret, and variable, and compounded. Some small touches, given to Caligula's brain in his infancy, might have converted him into a Trajan: one wave, a little higher than the rest, by burying Caesar and his fortune in the bottom of the ocean, might have restored liberty to a considerable part of mankind. There may, for aught we know, be good reasons, why providence interposes not in this manner; but they are unknown to us: and though the mere supposition, that such reasons exist, may be sufficient to *save* the conclusion concerning the divine attributes, yet surely it can never be sufficient to *establish* that conclusion.

If everything in the universe be conducted by general laws, and if animals be rendered susceptible of pain, it scarcely seems possible but some ill must arise in the various shocks of matter, and the various concurrence and opposition of general laws: But this ill would be very rare, were it not for the *third* circumstance, which I proposed to mention, *viz.* the great frugality with which all powers and faculties are distributed to every particular being. So well adjusted are the organs and capacities of all animals, and so well fitted to their preservation, that, as far as history or tradition reaches, there appears not to be any single species, which has yet been extinguished in the universe. Every animal has the requisite endowments; but these endowments are bestowed with so scrupulous an economy, that any considerable diminution must entirely destroy the creature. Wherever one power is increased, there is a proportional abatement in the others. Animals, which excel in swiftness, are commonly defective in force. Those which possess both are either imperfect in some of their senses, or are oppressed with the most craving wants. The human species, whose chief excellency is reason and sagacity, is of all others the most necessitous and the most deficient in bodily advantages; without clothes, without arms, without food, without lodging, without any convenience of life, except what they owe to their own skill and industry. In short, nature seems to have formed an exact calculation of the necessities of her creatures, and like a *rigid master*, has afforded them little more powers or endowments, than what are strictly sufficient to supply those necessities. An *indulgent parent* would have bestowed a large stock, in order to guard against accidents, and secure the happiness and welfare of the creature, in the most unfortunate concurrence of circumstances. Every course of life would not have been so surrounded with precipices, that the least departure from the true path, by mistake or necessity, must involve us in misery and ruin. Some reserve, some fund would have been provided to ensure happiness; nor would the powers and the necessities have been adjusted with so rigid an economy. The author of nature is inconceivably powerful: his force is supposed great, if not altogether inexhaustible: nor is there any reason, as far as we can judge, to make him observe this strict frugality in his dealings with his creatures. It would have been better, were his power extremely limited, to have created fewer animals, and to have endowed these with more faculties for their happiness and preservation. A builder is never esteemed prudent, who undertakes a plan, beyond what his stock will enable him to finish.

In order to cure most of the ills of human life, I require not that man should have the wings of the eagle, the swiftness of the stag, the force of the ox, the arms of the lion, the scales of the crocodile or rhinoceros; much less do I demand the sagacity of an angel or cherubim. I am contented to take an increase in one single power or faculty of his soul. Let him be endowed with a greater propensity to industry and labour; a more vigorous spring and activity of mind; a more constant bent to business and application. Let the whole species possess naturally an equal diligence with that which many individuals are able to attain by habit and reflection; and the most beneficial consequences, without any allay of ill, is the immediate and necessary result of this endowment. Almost all the moral, as well as natural evils of human life arise from idleness; and were our species, by the original constitution of their frame, exempt from this vice or infirmity, the perfect cultivation of land, the improvement of arts and manufactures, the exact execution of every office and duty, immediately follow; and men at once may fully reach that state of society, which is so imperfectly attained by the best-regulated government. But as industry is a power, and the most valuable of any, nature seems determined, suitably to her usual maxims, to bestow it on men with a very sparing hand; and rather to punish him severely for his deficiency in it than to reward him for his attainments. She has so contrived his frame that nothing but the most violent necessity can oblige him to labour; and she employs all his other wants to overcome, at least in part, the want of diligence, and to endow him with some share of a faculty, of which she has thought fit naturally to bereave him. Here our demands may be allowed very humble, and therefore the more reasonable. If we required the endowments of superior penetration and judgement, of a more delicate taste of beauty, of a nicer sensibility to benevolence and friendship; we might be told, that we impiously pretend to break the order of nature, that we want to exalt ourselves into a higher rank of being, that the presents which we require, not being suitable to our state and condition, would only be pernicious to us. But it is hard; I dare to repeat it, it is hard, that being placed in a world so full of wants and necessities; where almost every being and element is either our foe or refuses its assistance—we should also have our own temper to struggle with, and should be deprived of that faculty, which can alone fence against these multiplied evils.

The *fourth* circumstance, whence arises the misery and ill of the universe, is the inaccurate workmanship of all the springs and principles of the great machine of nature. It must be acknowledged, that there are few parts of the universe, which seem not to serve some purpose, and whose removal would not produce a visible defect and disorder in the whole.

The parts hang all together; nor can one be touched without affecting the rest, in a greater or less degree. But at the same time, it must be observed, that none of these parts or principles, however useful, are so accurately adjusted, as to keep precisely within those bounds in which their utility consists; but they are, all of them, apt, on every occasion, to run into the one extreme or the other. One would imagine, that this grand production had not received the last hand of the maker; so little finished is every part and so coarse are the strokes with which it is executed. Thus, the winds are requisite to convey the vapours along the surface of the globe, and to assist men in navigation: but how oft, rising up to tempests and hurricanes, do they become pernicious? Rains are necessary to nourish all the plants and animals of the earth: but how often are they defective? How often excessive? Heat is requisite to all life and vegetation; but is not always found in the due proportion. On the mixture and secretion of the humours and juices of the body depend the health and prosperity of the animal: but the parts perform not regularly their proper function. What more useful than all the passions of the mind, ambition, vanity, love, anger? But how oft do they break their bounds, and cause the greatest convulsions in society? There is nothing so advantageous in the universe, but what frequently becomes pernicious, by its excess or defect; nor has nature guarded, with the requisite accuracy, against all disorder or confusion. The irregularity is never, perhaps, so great as to destroy any species; but is often sufficient to involve the individuals in ruin and misery.

On the concurrence, then, of these *four* circumstances does all, or the greatest part of natural evil depend. Were all living creatures incapable of pain, or were the world administered by particular volitions, evil never could have found access into the universe: and were animals endowed with a large stock of powers and faculties, beyond what strict necessity requires; or were the several springs and principles of the universe so accurately framed as to preserve always the just temperament and medium; there must have been very little ill in comparison to what we feel at present. What then shall we pronounce on this occasion? Shall we say, that these circumstances are not necessary, and that they might easily have been altered in the contrivance of the universe? This decision seems too presumptuous for creatures, so blind and ignorant. Let us be more modest in our conclusions. Let us allow, that, if the goodness of the Deity (I mean a goodness like the human) could be established on any tolerable reasons *a priori*, these phenomena, however untoward, would not be sufficient to subvert that principle; but might easily, in some unknown manner, be reconcilable to it. But let us still assert, that as this goodness is not antecedently established, but must be inferred from the phenomena, there can be no grounds for such an inference, while there are so many ills in the universe, and while these ills might so easily have been remedied, as far as human understanding can be allowed to judge on such a subject. I am sceptic enough to allow that the bad appearances, notwithstanding all my reasonings, may be compatible with such attributes as you suppose: but surely they can never prove these attributes. Such a conclusion cannot result from scepticism; but must arise from the phenomena, and from our confidence in the reasonings, which we deduce from these phenomena.

Look round this universe. What an immense profusion of beings, animated and organized, sensible and active! You admire this prodigious variety and fecundity. But inspect a little more narrowly these living existences, the only beings worth regarding. How hostile and destructive to each other! How insufficient all of them for their own happiness! How contemptible or odious to the spectator! The whole presents nothing but the idea of a blind nature, impregnated by a great vivifying principle, and pouring forth from her lap, without discernment or parental care, her maimed and abortive children.

Here the Manichaean system occurs as a proper hypothesis to solve the difficulty: and no doubt, in some respects, it is very specious, and has more probability than the common hypothesis, by giving a plausible account of the strange mixture of good and ill, which appears in life. But if we consider, on the other hand, the perfect uniformity and agreement of the parts of the universe, we shall not discover in it any marks of the combat of a malevolent with a benevolent being. There is indeed an opposition of pains and pleasures in the feelings of sensible creatures: but are not all the operations of nature carried on by an opposition of principles, of hot and cold, moist and dry, light and heavy? The true conclusion is, that the original source of all things is entirely indifferent to all these principles, and has no more regard to good above ill than to heat above cold, or to drought above moisture, or to light above heavy.

There may *four* hypotheses be framed concerning the first causes of the universe; *that* they are endowed with perfect goodness, *that* they have perfect malice, *that* they are opposite and have both goodness and malice, *that* they have neither goodness nor malice. Mixed phenomena can never prove the two former unmixed principles. And the uniformity and steadiness of general laws seem to oppose the third. The fourth, therefore, seems by far the most probable.

What I have said concerning natural evil will apply to moral with little or no variation; and we have no more reason to infer that the rectitude of the supreme being resembles human rectitude than that his benevolence resembles the human. Nay, it will be thought, that we have still greater cause to exclude from him moral sentiments, such as we feel them; since moral evil, in the opinion of many, is much more predominant above moral good than natural evil above natural good.

But even though this should not be allowed, and though the virtue, which is in mankind, should be acknowledged much superior to the vice; yet so long as there is any vice at all in the universe, it will very much puzzle you anthropomorphites how to account for it. You must assign a cause for it, without having recourse to the first cause. But as every effect must have a cause, and that cause another; you must either carry on the progression *in infinitum*, or rest on that original principle, who is the ultimate cause of all things—

Hold! Hold! cried Demea: Whither does your imagination hurry you? I joined in alliance with you, in order to prove the incomprehensible nature of the divine being, and refute the principles of Cleanthes, who would measure every thing by a human rule and standard. But I now find you running into all the topics of the greatest libertines and infidels; and betraying that holy cause, which you seemingly espoused. Are you secretly, then, a more dangerous enemy than Cleanthes himself?

And are you so late in perceiving it? replied Cleanthes. Believe me, Demea; your friend Philo, from the beginning, has been amusing himself at both our expense; and it must be confessed, that the injudicious reasoning of our vulgar theology has given him but too just a handle of ridicule. The total infirmity of human reason, the absolute incomprehensibility of the divine nature, the great and universal misery and still greater wickedness of men; these are strange topics surely to be so fondly cherished by orthodox divines and doctors. In ages of stupidity and ignorance, indeed, these principles may safely be espoused; and perhaps, no views of things are more proper to promote superstition, than such as encourage the blind amazement, the diffidence, and melancholy of mankind. But at present—

Blame not so much, interposed Philo, the ignorance of these reverend gentlemen. They know how to change their style with the times. Formerly it was a most popular theological topic to maintain, that human life was vanity and misery, and to exaggerate all the ills and pains, which are incident to men. But of late years, divines, we find, begin to retract this position, and maintain, though still with some hesitation, that there are more goods than evils, more pleasures than pains, even in this life. When religion stood entirely upon temper and education, it was thought proper to encourage melancholy; as indeed, mankind never have recourse to superior powers so readily as in that disposition. But as men have now learned to form principles, and to draw consequences, it is necessary to change the batteries, and to make use of such arguments as will endure, at least some scrutiny and examination. This variation is the same (and from the same causes) with that which I formerly remarked with regard to scepticism.

Thus Philo continued to the last his spirit of opposition, and his censure of established opinions. But I could observe, that Demea did not at all relish the latter part of the discourse; and he took occasion soon after, on some pretense or other, to leave the company.

Immanuel Kant, from "On the Failure of All Philosophical Attempts at Theodicy"

By a *theodicy* is understood the defense of the supreme wisdom of the author of the world against the accusation of that wisdom by reason, from what is counter-purposive in the world. This is called *defending the cause of God* though, at bottom, it may be nothing more than the cause of our presumptuous reason mistaking its limits, which cause is indeed not the very best one, but must be so far approved since the human being (setting aside that self-conceit), as a rational being, has a right to prove all assertions, all the doctrines which reverence imposes on him, before he submits himself to them, in order that this reverence may be sincere and not hypocritical.

To this justification, now, is required that the would-be advocate of God should prove: either that that which we judge in the world as counter-purposive, is not so; or that, were it so, it must by no means be judged as a fact, but as an inevitable consequence of the nature of things; or lastly, that it must at least be considered not as the deed of the supreme author of all things, but merely of those mundane beings, to whom something can be imputed, that is, human beings (and perhaps of higher, good or evil, spiritual beings as well).

The author of a theodicy agrees, then, that this action shall be brought before the court of reason; he engages himself as counsel for the defendant, by formally refuting all the charges preferred by the plaintiff; and he must not, during the legal proceeding, put him off through a decree of the incompetency of the tribunal of reason (*exceptionem fori*[1]); that is, he must not dispatch the charges by imposing on the plaintiff a concession of the supreme wisdom of the author of the world, which would immediately dismiss as groundless, even without inquiry, all doubts that may be raised against it. Rather, he must attend to the objections and, as they by no means derogate from the conception of the supreme wisdom, [...] render everything comprehensible by clearing them up and removing them. There is one thing, however, that he has no occasion to enter into, namely, proving the supreme wisdom of God from what experience teaches of

1 [Exception to the court (Latin), a challenge to a court's jurisdiction over an individual.]

this world. For in this he would absolutely not succeed, as omniscience is requisite in order to cognize that perfection in a given world (as it gives to cognize itself in experience) such that it may be said with certainty that there is nowhere any greater possible in the creation and its government.

But that which is counter-purposive in the world, which may be opposed to the wisdom of its author, is of a threefold nature:

I. The absolutely counter-purposive, which cannot be approved and desired by wisdom as an end, nor as a means.
II. The conditionally counter-purposive, which is consistent with the wisdom of a will never as an end, but only ever as a means.

The *first* is the morally counter-purposive, as evil proper (sin); the *second* is the physically counter-purposive, as bad (pain). But there is a purposiveness in the relation of the bad to moral evil—when the latter at some point exists and neither can nor ought to be prevented, as in the conjunction of what is bad or painful in punishments, with evil as a crime. Relative to this purposive arrangement in the world, the question arises whether in this justice be done to everyone in the world. Consequently still a

IIIrd. kind of counter-purposive in the world must be conceived, namely, the disproportion of crimes and punishments in the world.

The attributes of the supreme wisdom of the author of the world, against which those kinds of counter-purposiveness appear as objections, are likewise three:

First, his *holiness* as *lawgiver* (creator), in contradistinction to the moral evil in the world.
Secondly, his *goodness* as *governor* (preserver), contrasted with the innumerable evils and pains of the rational mundane beings.
Thirdly, his *justice* as *judge*, in comparison with the bad state in which the disproportion between the impunity of the vicious and their crimes seems to show itself in the world.[2]

2 These three attributes, of which the one can by no means be reduced to the other, as for instance justice to goodness, and so the whole to a smaller number, constitute the moral conception of God. Nor can their order be altered (as for example to make the goodness the chief condition of the creation of the world, to which the [continued]

The answer to those three impeachments must be presented in the above-mentioned manner, in these three different ways, and tested for their validity.

I. The complaint against the holiness of the divine will on account of moral evil which, it is charged, disfigures the world, as the divine work. The first vindication consists in this:

a. That there is by no means such an absolute counter-purposiveness, as the transgression of the pure laws of our reason is taken to be; rather, that it is only a fault in the eye of human wisdom and the divine judges them according to quite other rules incomprehensible to us; that what we indeed find objectionable relative to our practical reason and its vocation, may yet perhaps, in relation to divine ends and supreme wisdom, be the fittest means for our particular well-being as well as for the good of the world in general; that the ways of the supreme are not our ways (*sunt superis sua jura*[3]), and we err, when we judge what is a law only relatively for human beings in this life, to be absolutely such, and thus hold what seems to our contemplation of things from a station so low as counter-purposive, to also be so when contemplated from the highest station.—This apology, in which the defense is worse than the charge, requires no refutation, and may certainly be freely left to the detestation of every person who has the least feeling for morality.

b. The second supposed vindication indeed grants the actuality of moral evil in the world, but excuses the author of the world inasmuch as it was not possible to prevent it given that it is grounded upon the limits of human nature, as finite beings.—However, every evil would thereby be justified, and the human being would have to cease calling it a moral evil since it can no longer be imputed to men as their fault.

c. The third response—that, suppose that with respect to what we denominate moral evil it is human beings who are actually guilty, and no guilt must be imputed to God as he has, from wise causes, merely permitted it as a deed of men but by no means approved and willed or occasioned that evil—leads (if no difficulty shall be found in the concept of the mere *permitting* on the part of a being, who is the sole author of

---

holiness of law-giving is subordinated), without derogating from religion, which is founded upon just this moral conception. [...].

3 [The gods have laws peculiar to themselves (Latin); from Ovid, *Metamorphoses*, book IX.]

the world) to the same consequence as the foregoing apology (b); namely that, since it was impossible for God himself to hinder this evil, without derogating from other higher and even moral ends, the ground of this evil (for it must now be properly named thus) must unavoidably be looked for in the essence of things, namely, the necessary limits of humanity as finite nature, and consequently cannot be imputed to it.

II. The justification of the divine goodness for the bads, namely, pains, which are complained of in the world, consists

a. in this, that in the fates of men a preponderance of the bad over the pleasant enjoyment of life is falsely assumed, because everyone, however badly he may fare, chooses rather to live, than to be dead, and those few who resolve on the latter, so long as they themselves delay it, thereby continue to affirm that preponderance; and, when they are foolish enough to destroy themselves, merely pass over into a state of insensibility, in which no pain can be felt.—But the answer to this sophistry may surely be left to the decision of everyone of sound understanding, who has lived and reflected long enough on the value of life to be able to pronounce a judgment on this, when the question is proposed: whether he would wish to play the game of life over again, I will not say in the same, but in any other conditions he pleases (as long as these pertain not to a fairy-world but to this, our earthly world).

b. To the second justification, that the preponderance of the painful feelings over the agreeable cannot be separated from the nature of an animal creature, such as the human being [...]—one would reply, that, if this is so, then one wonders why the author of our existence has called us into life when, providing for the correctness of our calculation, it is not worthy of being wished for by us? Ill humour would answer here, as the Indian woman said to Genghis Khan, who could neither give her satisfaction for the violence suffered, nor afford her security against the future: "If you will not protect us, then why do you conquer us?"

c. The third solution for the knot is that out of goodness God has placed us in the world for the sake of a future felicity, but that such an exceedingly great blessedness which may be hoped for must be preceded by a state of thorough trouble and misery in the present life, where we must become worthy of that future glory through the struggle with difficulties.—Yet, that this time of probation (in which most succumb, and even the best find no proper satisfaction in their life) must for supreme wisdom be the condition without exception of the pleasure that one day or other may be enjoyed by us, and that it was not feasible to let the creature become contented with every epoch of his life, may indeed be pretended, but there can absolutely be no insight into it. In this way one can, to be sure, cut the knot by an appeal to the supreme wisdom who has so willed it, but one cannot thereby untie it, which is the task for which theodicy was engaged.

III. To the last complaint, namely, against the justice of the governor of the world,[4] it is answered:

a. That the pretext of the impunity of the vicious in the world has no ground, because every crime, according to its nature, carries with itself here the punishment suitable to it, as the internal reproaches of conscience torment the vicious more than the Furies would.—But in this judgment there is evidently a misunderstanding. For the virtuous man here lends his character of mind to the vicious, namely, conscientiousness in its whole strictness which, the more virtuous the man is, punishes the more rigorously on account of the smallest transgression that the moral law disapproves of in him. But, where this cast of mind and, with it, conscientiousness is wanting, there is likewise wanting the tormentor for crimes committed; and the vicious, if he can but escape the external chastisement for his crimes, laughs at the anxiety of the honest man to torment himself internally with his own rebukes; but the small reproaches, which he may sometimes make himself, he makes either not at all through conscience, or, if he has any, they are abundantly outweighed and requited by the sensual pleasure for which alone he has a taste. If that charge shall further

b. be refuted by this: that it is indeed not to be denied that there is absolutely to be found no proportion conformable to justice between guilt and punishment in the world, and one must often perceive with indignation in the course of it a life led with crying injustice and yet happy to the very end; that this, however, lies in nature and is not intentionally prepared; consequently, it is not moral dissonance because it

4 It is remarkable that among all the difficulties of uniting the course of the events of the world with the divinity of its author, none forces itself so strongly on the mind, as that of the appearance of justice wanting in it. If it happens (though it is but seldom) that an unjust villain, especially one possessing power, does not escape out of the world unpunished, then the impartial spectator rejoices, as it were, reconciled with heaven. No other purposiveness in nature excites, through the admiration of it, his affect to such a degree and so to speak lets the hand of God be so easily discerned. Why? The purposiveness of nature is here moral, and the only one of the sort that one may hope to perceive in some measure in the world.

belongs to virtue to struggle with adversity (to which also belongs the pain that the virtuous must suffer by the comparison of his own misfortune with the good fortune of the vicious), and sufferings serve only to enhance the value of virtue; therefore, in the eye of reason this dissonance of the undeserved bads of life is resolved into the most glorious moral concord.—This solution is opposed by this, that, though these evils, when they, as the whetstone of virtue, either *precede* or accompany it, may, it is true, be represented as in a moral harmony with it, when at least the end of life crowns the latter and punishes vice; but that, when even this end turns out nonsensically, of which experience gives many examples, suffering seems to have fallen to the lot of the virtuous not *so that* his virtue should be pure, but *because* it has been so (and on the other hand contrary to the rules of prudent self-love), which is precisely the opposite of justice as the human being is able to conceive of it. For as to the possibility that the end of this earthly life may not perhaps be the end of all life, this possibility cannot be valid as a *vindication* of providence, but is merely a decree of a morally-faithful reason, through which the sceptic is referred to patience but not satisfied.

c. If, finally, the third solution of this unharmonious proportion between the moral worth of human beings and the lot that falls to them, shall be attempted by saying that: in this world, all well-being and ill must be judged as a consequence of the use of the capacities of human beings merely according to the laws of nature, in proportion to the skill and prudence with which they are applied, at the same time to the circumstances also, into which they accidentally fall, but not according to their agreement with supersensible ends, whereas in a future world another order of things will subsist, and everyone will obtain what his deeds here below are worth according to a moral judgment—then this presupposition is arbitrary. Reason, if it does not as a morally legislative faculty render a decree conformable to its interest, must at least find it probable according to mere rules of theoretical cognition, that the course of the world according to the order of nature will determine our fate as here, so for the future. For what other clue has reason for its theoretical presumption than the law of nature? And though it allowed itself, as was required of it (no. b.), to be referred to patience and the hope of a better future world, how can it expect that, as the course of things here according to the order of nature is of itself wise, it would according to the same laws in a future world be unwise? As, according to them, there is no comprehensible relation at all between the internal determining grounds of the will (namely, the moral cast of mind) according to laws of liberty, and between the (for the most part external) causes of our well-being independent of our will according to laws of nature; so the presumption remains that the agreement of the fate of men with a divine justice, according to the conceptions we form of it, is as little to be expected there as here.

The outcome of this process before the forum of philosophy is, that all theodicy has hitherto not performed what it promises, namely, to justify the moral wisdom in the government of the world against the doubts, which are entertained of it from what experience gives to cognize in this world; though indeed these doubts as objections, as far as our insight into the nature of our reason reaches with regard to the latter, cannot prove the contrary. But whether in progress of time more proper grounds of its vindication may not be found, not to absolve the arraigned wisdom (as hitherto) merely *ab instantia*,[5] remains still undetermined, if we do not succeed in showing with certainty that our reason is absolutely incapable of insight into *the relationship in which a world, as we may always know it by experience, stands to supreme wisdom*; for then all further attempts of presumptive human wisdom at insight into the ways of divine wisdom are totally rejected. [...]

* * *

All theodicy ought, properly speaking, to be an *interpretation* of nature, so far as God makes known by it the design of his will. Now every interpretation of the declared will of a legislator is either *doctrinal* or *authentic*. The former is what infers that will from the expressions which it has used, in conjunction with the designs of the lawgiver otherwise known; the latter is given by the legislator himself.

The world, as a work of God, may be contemplated by us as a divine publication of the *purposes* of his will. In this, however, it is *often* for us a closed book; but it is *always* so when we aim to extract from it the *final end* of God (which is always moral), even though it is an object of experience. Philosophical attempts of this sort of interpretation are doctrinal, and constitute the proper theodicy which may therefore be termed the doctrinal one.—Yet the mere dismissal of all objections to the divine wisdom cannot be refused the name of a theodicy, when it is a *divine decree*,

5 [*Absolutio ab instantia* (Latin), a temporary suspension of a legal procedure until new evidence emerges.]

or (which in this case is to the same purpose) when it is a judgment of the same reason by which we form a conception of God as a moral and wise being, necessarily and before all experience. For there, God is through our reason the very interpreter of his own will announced by the creation; and this interpretation we may denominate an *authentic* theodicy. Then, however, that is not the exposition of a *rationalizing* reason, but of an *authoritative* practical reason which, since it commands absolutely without appeal to further grounds in its legislating, may be considered as the immediate declaration and voice of God, by which he gives meaning to the letter of his creation. Now I find such an authentic interpretation allegorically expressed in an ancient sacred book.

Job is presented as a man, whose enjoyment of life included everything that might possibly be conceived that would render it perfect. Healthy, opulent, free, a commander of others whom he may make happy, surrounded by a happy family, among beloved friends; and above all (what is the most essential), contented with himself in a good conscience. A heavy fate imposed on him by way of a test saw all these riches, excepting the last, suddenly torn away from him. As he gradually came to his senses after his astonishment at this unexpected overthrow, he gave vent to complaints against his disaster, which initiated a dispute between him and his friends, who were present under a pretense of consoling him, in which both parties, everyone according to his own way of thinking (but chiefly according to his situation), set forth their particular theodicy for the moral explanation of that deplorable fate. Job's friends declared themselves for the system of the interpretation of all evil in the world from divine *justice*, as so many punishments for crimes perpetrated; and though they could not name any with which they could charge the unfortunate man, they believed themselves able to judge *a priori* that he must be guilty of some, otherwise it would not be possible according to divine justice that he should be unhappy. Job, by contrast—who protests, with emotion, that his conscience does not reproach him in the least on account of his whole life, but as to inevitable human faults, God himself knows that he made him a frail creature—declares himself for the system of the *unconditional divine resolution*. "He has decided," continues Job, "He does what he wills."

In the rationalizations, or rather over-rationalizations, of both parties, there is nothing remarkable; but the character, in which they do so, merits the more attention. Job speaks as he thinks, and everyone in his situation would be of the same mind; his friends, on the other hand, speak as if the almighty, on whose affair they decide, listened to them in secret, and as if they have more at heart in seeking to gain his favour rather than the truth. These tricks of theirs, of maintaining something for the sake of appearance that they must allow they have no insight into, and to feign a conviction which in fact they have not, contrast well with Job's plain sincerity, which is so far from false flattery as almost to border on temerity, much to Job's advantage. "Will you," says he, "speak wickedly for God? Will you accept his person? Will you contend for God? He will surely reprove you, if you do secretly accept persons! For a hypocrite shall not come before him."[6]

The latter actually confirms the outcome of the story. For God deigned to set before Job's eyes the wisdom of his creation, chiefly on the side of its inscrutableness. He let him view the beautiful side of the creation where ends comprehensible to man set the wisdom and bountiful care of the author of the world in an unambiguous light; but on the other hand the frightful side too, by naming to him productions of his power, and among these even pernicious dreadful things, everyone of which, it is true, seems to be adjusted for itself and for its species purposively but which seem, with regard to others and to human beings as well, destructive, counter-purposive, and out of all harmony with a universal plan arranged by goodness and wisdom; whereby, however, he shows the disposition and preservation of the whole to proclaim the wise author of the world, even though at the same time his ways, inscrutable to us, must be hidden in the physical order of things, and how much more so then in their connection with the moral (which is yet more impenetrable to our reason)?—The conclusion is, that, as Job acknowledges to have judged, not *maliciously*, for he is conscious to himself of his probity, but only imprudently, on things which are too high for him and which he does not understand, God pronounces the condemnation of Job's friends, because they did not speak of him so well (in point of conscientiousness) as his servant Job. If now the theory, which each on both sides maintains, be taken into consideration, that of his friends may carry with it rather the appearance of more speculative reason and pious humility; and Job in all probability would have experienced a sad fate before every tribunal of dogmatical theologians, before a synod, an inquisition, a reverend congregation, or every chief consistory of our time (one only excepted). Therefore, only the sincerity of the heart, not the preference of knowledge, the honesty to acknowledge his doubts openly, and the aversion

6 [See Job 13.7–11, 16.]

to feign conviction, where it is not felt, chiefly before God (where such cunning is absurd anyhow) are the properties which in the divine judgment have decided the preference for the man of probity, in the person of Job, over the religious flatterer.

But the belief, which arose in him by so strange a solution of his doubts, namely, merely the conviction of his ignorance, could enter into the mind of none but him, who in the midst of his greatest doubts could say, "till I die I will not remove my integrity from me" (Job 27.5–6). For by this disposition he proved that he did not ground his morality upon belief, but belief upon morality: in which case this belief only, however weak it may be, is of a pure and genuine sort, that is, of that sort, which grounds a religion not of currying favour but of the good conduct of life. [...]

Unit II

EVIL WITHOUT SIN: UNDERSTANDING SUFFERING

Chapter 5

BAYLE AND HUME ON PHYSICAL EVIL

Introduction

IN THE PREVIOUS UNIT, WE CONSIDERED PHILOSOPHICAL responses to the problem of evil. Notably, while these philosophers differed concerning whether, as human beings, our intellectual capacities were up to the challenge of finding a resolution to the problem, they all agreed that the problem itself was primarily about *moral* evil. That is, these philosophers regarded the challenge as consisting in reconciling the fact of human beings' sinfulness or viciousness with the supreme goodness of the being that created them. Interestingly, for them there is no particular problem posed by the existence of (what Bayle and Leibniz term) *physical* evil, or human suffering, simply because it was assumed that if such an evil was justified it was as a consequence of moral evil; as Leibniz says at the outset of the third part of the *Theodicy*, "sorrows, sufferings, miseries will be less troublesome to explain, since these are the results of moral evil."

Yet, physical evil poses problems of its own, as some philosophers in the modern period recognized. There was, for instance, no ready moral explanation for some cases of human suffering (such as children born with painful deformities). And, aside from whatever rewards might be laid up in heaven for the virtuous, there is a question about whether we are, in this earthly life, bound to experience more pleasures than pains, that is, whether any enduring happiness is possible. Perhaps surprisingly, this is a question that many philosophers, ancient and modern, have answered in the negative. The prevalence of physical evil also prompted a number of modern philosophers to inquire into its various sources, and particularly into the way in which society and its institutions exacerbate and introduce new forms of human suffering.

In this chapter, we will look at a number of treatments of the nature of physical evil. Among the first modern philosophers to take physical evil seriously, apart from its connection with moral evil, was Pierre Bayle (see the introduction to Chapter 1, above), who turns to a consideration of physical evil in the entry in his *Dictionary* on the Greek poet and philosopher Xenophanes (late sixth–early fifth centuries BCE). Bayle uses Xenophanes' claim that "the sweets of life do not equal the bitter potions which it obliges us to swallow" as an opportunity to reflect on the nature of pleasure and pain and what this has to say about whether pains will outweigh pleasures in life. Bayle's case is developed in another reading taken from the *Dialogues concerning Natural Religion*, by David Hume (see the introduction to Chapter 3). Hume, again through his mouthpiece Philo, adds a consideration of psychological ills to Bayle's catalogue of the pains of existence, and also shows that the advent of society does not offer the human being an escape from misery. Hume also considers and rejects a number of potential objections to Bayle's (and Xenophanes') conclusion, including whether the fact that so many human beings choose to continue to exist amounts to a refutation of the alleged undesirability of life.

Pierre Bayle, *The Historical and Critical Dictionary*, from "Xenophanes"

XENOPHANES, a Greek Philosopher, born at Colophon, was a disciple of Archelaus, as some say. According to this account, he should have been contemporary with Socrates. Others will have it that he learned of himself all that he knew, and lived at the same time with Anaximander. According to this account, he must have flourished before Socrates, and about the 60th Olympiad, as Diogenes Laertius affirms. He lived very long; for some verses are cited in which he declares, (1) that his studies had been applauded in Greece sixty-seven years; (2) that he began to meet with applause at the age of twenty-five. He wrote several poems on philosophical subjects: besides two thousand on the foundation of Colophon, and on the colony of Elea. His opinion concerning the nature of God, is very little different from Spinozism. He wrote some verses against Homer and Hesiod, on the idle stories which they sung of the gods. He held a maxim which entirely overturned the Pagan religion; viz. that it is not less impious to assert that the gods were born than to affirm that they die, since in either case it would be equally true that their existence is not eternal. This maxim is very true and not at all contrary to the doctrine of the Incarnation. He believed that the Moon is an inhabited country, and that it is impossible to predict future events; and if the conjecture of a learned critic is well grounded, he asserted that there is in nature more good than evil [*D*]. He would not be singular in this opinion, but it is probable that he was of a very different sentiment; and if the question was only about evil morally considered, I do not believe he would find one opponent. Everybody owns that good and honest men are very rare, and that nothing is more common than men who depart from the rules of virtue. But, without doubt, Xenophanes intended to speak of physical evil, and his sense was that the sweets of life do not equal the bitter potions which it obliges us to swallow [*F*]. Several people are persuaded of the truth of this, and do not lack plausible reasons for it, as we shall see below. Even those who acknowledge that nature has furnished mankind with an infinite number of agreeable conveniencies, and appointed all other things for their use, consider man in another respect as an unhappy being. That kind of necessity to which so many people are reduced, of seeking a remedy for their uneasiness among forbidden pleasures, is no small part of the severity of their fate. However, we may here allege the authority of Aristotle; for that great genius who philosophized with so much application and penetration acknowledged that there was in nature more evil than good, and it was for this reason that Empedocles disliked the hypothesis of the unity of a principle, and so first supposed two principles, one of good the other of evil. The holy Scripture so emphatically represents the miseries of this life, that it is sufficient to afford a demonstrative argument on this controversy. [...] I must not forget that he was banished from his country, that he retired to Sicily, and lived at Zanche and Catana, that he founded the Eleatic sect, that Parmenides was his disciple, and that he complained of poverty. The answer he gave a man with whom he refused to play at dice, is very worthy of a philosopher: this person calling him a coward, he replied, "yes, I am extremely so with respect to shameful actions."

> [*D*] (*he asserted that there is in nature more good than evil*) Diogenes Laertius[1] reckons among the chief opinions of Xenophanes [...] that most things are worse than, or inferior to, the mind. It seems unworthy of a philosopher to speak thus; for the meanest peasant knows very well, and nobody needs to be taught, that the mind of man is better than metals, water, or air, etc. We therefore ought to believe that Xenophanes meant something greater. The following is the conjecture of Méric Casaubon.[2] He pretends that this philosopher taught that the divine mind, which made the world, endeavoured to endow all creatures with a state of perfection; but that having met with strong obstacles in matter, he could not always compass his designs and, therefore, on some occasions, he was forced to produce evil things. This is saying that in this conflict he was sometimes vanquished, but oftener vanquisher; that the greatest part of things were submitted to the desires and power of the divine mind; consequently, what is meant is not that matter is 'worse than' the mind, but 'subjected to' it and the object of its triumph. Casaubon confirms his conjecture by a passage in Plato, where it is said that necessity and the

---

1 [Diogenes Laertius (third century CE) wrote a biography of Greek philosophers entitled *Lives of Eminent Philosophers*.]

2 [Méric Casaubon (1599–1671), a classical scholar and translator.]

mind concurred in the production of the world, and that necessity was persuaded to consent that things for the most part should be governed for the best.[3] [...] Casaubon observes that Homer, having said on a particular occasion that evil exceeds good, this was converted into a general maxim as if, universally speaking, the miseries of human life overbalanced the happiness of it. The same critic observes that those who spoke of this subject with the greatest modesty excused providence on account of the fatal necessity which constrained it to open a gate to several evils. [...] He adds that Euripides[4] strenuously refuted the common opinion that evil surpasses good, and he cites the beginning of that refutation:

> "Some say that there is in nature more evil than good: but I hold a contrary opinion to others, viz. there is in nature more good than evil."

The words of Euripides that follow seemed to Casaubon to be written by an inspired pen. Pliny[5] differs from this poet's opinion; for though he does not say that it plainly appears nature behaves to us rather like a cruel stepmother than a tender indulgent parent, yet he intimates that he is of such an opinion:

> "The chief place will be justly allowed to man, for whose sake nature seems to have produced all other things. Great are the bounties of nature, but attended with many evils, and purchased with many afflictions, so that it is hard to judge whether she acts the part of a tender and indulgent parent, or that of a cruel stepmother to mankind."

She sets the presents she makes us, says he, at the price of a thousand afflictions. To this purpose he gives a long description of

3 [The reference here is to Plato's *Timaeus*.]

4 [Euripides (c. 480–c. 406 BCE) was one of the foremost tragedians of classical Athens. The following quotation is taken from his *The Supplicants*.]

5 [Pliny the Elder (23/24–79 CE) was a Roman natural scientist and philosopher, and author of the expansive *Natural History*, from which the following quotations are taken.]

human infirmities, and opposes them to the advantages of animals; nor does he forget the vices in which men exceed the brutes:

> "Of all animals man alone is subject to sorrow, to luxury, and that in numberless respects, and through all his senses; man alone is addicted to ambition, to avarice, and an immoderate and excessive desire of life; he alone is concerned for his burial, and even for what shall happen after his death. No animal is more frail, more lustful, none more liable to consternation, none more furious. In short, other animals live in a friendly way with their respective species. We see them flock and herd together, and only oppose others of a different kind. A lion, however furious, does not attack a lion. A serpent does not sting a serpent. Nor do the sea-monsters and fishes destroy any but those of a different kind from themselves. Yet men bring numberless evils upon each other."

He does not omit the reflection which several people have made: that it would be best for a man not to be born, or to die quickly.[6] He affirms elsewhere that the greatest blessing that God has bestowed upon men among so many pains and troubles of life, is the power of killing themselves. He had enumerated several of the follies of paganism, and concluded, that of all these things there is but one certainty, which is that all things are uncertain, and that man is the most miserable and vainest part of the whole creation:

> "All these things discover the weakness of our understanding; so that this alone is certain, that nothing is certain, and that MAN IS OF ALL ANIMALS THE MOST VAIN AND MISERABLE. For other living creatures take no care for their food, which is abundantly supplied to them by the voluntary produce of nature. But this advantage of theirs is greater than all the rest, that they have no thoughts of glory, riches, ambition, or even death."

---

6 [This "reflection" can be traced back to the Greek myth of Silenus, an account of which is given in the selection from Nietzsche's *The Birth of Tragedy*; see page 252, below.]

Plautus[7] has so naturally expressed an opinion contrary to Euripides's maxim, that I think myself obliged to transcribe his words:

> "How few are the pleasures in every age of life, when compared with the troubles of it? This is the fate of all men, and the will of the gods, that pain and sorrow should accompany our pleasures. But let me immediately have more pain, and more sorrow, if it is attended with any pleasure."

Diphilus,[8] the poet, thought that fortune obliges us to drink a liquor composed of three evils and only one good.

[*F*] (*his sense was that the sweets of life do not equal the bitter potions which it obliges us to swallow*) Those who hold the contrary opinion, chiefly insist upon a parallel between diseases and health. There are very few persons, whatever age they be of, but can reckon up incomparably more days of health than of sickness, and there are a great many who, in the space of twenty years, have not been afflicted with diseases that will take up fifteen days altogether. But this comparison is fallacious. For health considered alone is rather an indolence than a sense of pleasure, it is rather a bare exemption from evil than a good, while sickness is worse than a privation of pleasure: it is a positive state which plunges the mind into a sense of suffering and loads the patient with pain. Somebody judiciously says, that "when health is alone, it is a good which is not much perceived, and sometimes only serves to make us the more ardently desire all the other pleasures which we cannot have."[9] Let us make use of a comparison taken from the schoolmen: they say that *rare*, i.e., porous, bodies contain but very little matter under a great extent and that *dense* bodies contain a great quantity of matter in a small compass. According to this principle

7 [Plautus (c. 254–184 BCE) was a Roman playwright. The following quotation is from his *Amphitruo*.]

8 [Diphilus (324–291 BCE) was a poet of Greek New Comedy.]

9 I believe it is Mademoiselle Scudéry [(1607–1701), a French novelist and philosophical writer].

we must say that there is more matter in three feet of water than in two thousand five hundred feet of air. This is a lively image of sickness and health: sickness resembles the *dense* bodies, and health the *rare*. Health lasts many years successively, and yet contains but a small portion of happiness. Sickness continues but a few days, and yet comprehends a vast load of misery. If we had a scale adapted to weigh both a disease of fifteen days and the health of fifteen years, we should observe the same difference that we find in the balance between a bag of feathers and a piece of lead. In one scale we should see a body which takes up a great deal of room and, in the other, one which lies in a very small compass; and yet one of them is not heavier than the other. Let us then beware of the illusion which the extension of health may draw us into when it is paralleled with sickness. But you will say that health is valuable, not only by reason that it exempts us from a very great evil, but also by the liberty it affords us, to enjoy a thousand lively and very sensible pleasures. I grant all this, but it ought to be farther considered that, there being two sorts of evils to which we are subject, it only secures us from one and leaves us wholly exposed to the other. We are subject to pain and sorrow, two such terrible afflictions that it is not to be decided which is most dreadful. The most vigorous health does not secure us from grief. For grief flows in upon us through a thousand channels, and is of the nature of *dense* bodies: it comprises a great deal of matter in a very small compass; evil is heaped up, crowded and pressed close in it. One hour's grief contains more evil, than there is good in six or seven pleasant days. The other day I was told of a man who killed himself after an anxious melancholy of three or four weeks. Every night he had laid his sword under his bolster, in hopes that he should have courage enough to end his life when darkness should increase his grief, but his resolution failed for several nights successively. At last, not being able to resist his uneasiness, he cut the veins of his arm. I affirm, that all the pleasures which this man had enjoyed in thirty years, would not equal the evils which tormented him the last month of his life if both were weighed in the balance. Look back to my parallel of dense and rare bodies and remember this, that the good things of this life are less good, than the evil things are evil. Evils are generally more pure and unmixed than good things: the lively sense of pleasure does not continue long, it immediately grows flat and full, and is followed with disgust. [...] What appeared to us a great good when we did not possess it, hardly affects us in the enjoyment so that we acquire, with a thousand troubles and a thousand uneasinesses, what we possess with no more than a moderate pleasure, and very often the fear of losing the good we enjoy surpasses all the pleasures of the fruition of it. [...]

I have found a passage which gives a lively description of the ill side of felicities. I speak of those common to all men, in a word, I mean corporeal pleasures:

> "What need I speak of bodily pleasures, the pursuit of which is full of anxiety, and the enjoyment followed by disgust and repentance. How great diseases, how intolerable pains do they bring upon the body, as the fruits of wickedness.... But that the issue of pleasures is disagreeable and painful, whoever reflects on his own lusts, must easily understand....
>
> If pleasures ever invade the heart
> They stimulate through every part:
> But when the enjoyer's happy made,
> And when their grateful honey's shed,
> Their sweet allurements soon decay,
> They leave a sting and fly away."

Thus Boethius[10] introduces Philosophy speaking to him. It appears by this discourse that if anxiety precedes the enjoyment of pleasures, disgust and repentance follow close after it. A vast number of authors observe this unhappy concomitance, or, to speak more intelligibly, this connection of pleasure and uneasiness. The two following were cited in my first edition:

> "But mortal bliss will never come sincere;
> Pleasure may lead, but pains brings up the rear"[11]

10 [Boethius (c. 480–524 CE) was a Roman philosopher. The foregoing quotation is from his *On the Consolation of Philosophy*.]

11 [The quotation is taken from *Metamorphoses* by the Roman poet Ovid (43 BCE–17/18 CE).]

[And:]

"For still some bitter thought destroys
His fancied mirth, and poisons all his joys."[12]

Now I add a third, who is Antiphanes.

"Wherever pleasures and delights are present, pain and sorrow are at hand:

For pleasures (such is our fate!) never come alone,
But ever are with pain and toil attended."[13]

Let us also observe this circumstance: we are not only in fear of losing what we possess, but also vexed to see other people equal or surpass us, and that others will soon be able to come up to us and afterwards get before us. Observe, that in order to prove that good is not so perfectly good as evil is evil, I have made no use of this argument that it rarely happens that a good use is made of the favours of fortune, it rarely happens that they do not lead us to great miseries, and become not a grace but a snare [...]. I say, I have omitted this reason, because I do not here consider the causes and occasions of good and evil, but only good and evil in themselves. For the rest, it would be departing from the state of the question to say that man afflicts himself without cause. For it is not our business here to know whether his grief is reasonable, or the effect of his weakness; but the question is to know whether he grieves. This very thing, that a man vexes himself without reason and makes himself unhappy by his own fault, is an evil.

We must own with Seneca, when we consider the multitude of good things which nature has imparted to us, and the inexhaustible industry with which the wit of man diversifies pleasures and discovers the sources of them, that God, not contented to provide solely for our necessities, has besides furnished us the wherewithal to live deliciously:

---

12 [From *On the Nature of Things*, by Lucretius (c. 99–55 BCE), a Roman poet and philosopher.]

13 [Antiphanes (c. 408–334 BCE) was a Greek comic playwright.]

> "Whence proceed these numberless delights for the entertainment of our eyes, our ears, and mind? Whence that abundance which supplies even our luxury? For care is taken not only for our necessities, but also for our pleasures, and the gratifying of all our senses and appetites. So many pleasant trees, fruitful in various manners, so many wholesome herbs, and such a variety of meats, in every season of the year, that the casual produce of the earth might supply a lazy man with food for his maintenance. Whence all those animals, some bred on the earth, some in the waters, and others descending from the heavens, that every part of nature might pay tribute to man? [...] Whence those things which by their exquisite tastes, and delicious flavours, provoke your appetite even after it is satiated? Whence those things which awaken your pleasures when decayed? Whence that quiet and ease in which you rot and moulder away? Will you not say, if you are thankful, that you owe all this to the bounty of heaven?"

All that Seneca says in this part of his book *On Benefits* is very true; but, on the other side, does not Pliny assure us that nature makes us buy her presents at the price of so many sufferings, that it is dubious whether she deserves most the name of a parent or of a step-mother? To reconcile these two authors, we ought to consider what the Scripture teaches us concerning the economy of God, as a father, and as a judge of mankind. Those two relations require that man should feel good and evil: but the question is whether evil exceeds good? And upon this head I am apt to think that we can go no farther than opinions and conjectures. Several people say that most persons, when a little advanced in years, grow like La Mothe Le Vayer,[14] who would have refused to pass again through the same good and evil which he had felt in his life. If it be so, we must believe that, upon the whole, everyone finds the pleasures which he has enjoyed have been unequal to the uneasinesses and pains with which he has been afflicted. I do

14 [François de La Mothe Le Vayer (1588–1672) was a French libertine philosopher and historian.]

not allege that nobody is content with his condition, for this is no proof that every man believes himself less happy than unhappy. [...] Four inconveniencies mixed with twenty conveniences, would make a man wish for another condition, I mean such a one as is not charged with any inconvenience, or at least where he should find but one or two of them to forty conveniences. On the other side, it must not be alleged against me what Lactantius says, that men are so precious that they complain of the least evil, as if it absorbed all the good things they have enjoyed; for it is to no purpose to consider here what the absolute quantity of good and evil dispensed to man may be in itself—we are only to consider their relative quality or, to express myself more clearly, we ought to consider nothing but the feeling of the mind. A very great good in itself, which raises but a very moderate pleasure, ought not to pass for more than a moderate good; but an evil, though very little in itself, which gives an uneasiness, grief, or pain, that are insupportable, ought to pass for a very great evil. So, to denote a man less happy than unhappy it is sufficient that he is afflicted with three evils for thirty felicities which he enjoys, if those three evils, as little in themselves as you please, give him more disturbance than the thirty felicities, as great in their own nature as you please, afford him pleasure. The government of a province is in itself a much greater good than a ribbon; and yet if a duke and peer should feel more joy in receiving a ribbon from his mistress, than in obtaining the government of a province from his king, I affirm that a ribbon would be a greater good to him than the authority of a governor. For the same reason it would be a greater evil for him to be deprived of this ribbon, than to be deprived of his post, if he should be more grieved at the loss of the ribbon than at that of his post. On this account no man is able to judge correctly of either the misery or happiness of his neighbour. We do not know what another feels, we only know the outward causes of evil and good. Now, these causes are not always proportioned to their effects and those which seem to us very small, frequently produce a lively sensation; and those which appear to us great, very often occasion but a faint one. [...]

All this shows that none can determine positively whether his neighbour's destiny be drawn out of Homer's two vessels, in such a manner, that the dose of good be as large, or perhaps larger than that of evil.[15] All that can be said with full certainty is that no man's fate was ever drawn wholly out of the good vessel. [...]

It is certain that those who would find persons who have felt more happiness than uneasiness, will encounter them rather among the peasants or the meanest tradesmen than amongst kings and princes. [For, the source] of the unhappiness of princes [is the fact that] their being continually accustomed to the advantages of their condition renders them insensible as to good and very sensible of evil. Let them receive one piece of bad news, and three of good, they scarce feel the happiness of the latter, but are touched to the quick with the misfortune of the former. Can they then lack uneasiness? Are their prosperities not thwarted by some ill fortune? Read all that Gustavus Adolphus[16] did in Germany, and you will there find a superiority of fortune, which has very few examples; yet you will observe so great a mixture of disadvantageous events that you will easily believe him to have run through a great deal of uneasiness. Nay, suppose the victories gained in some provinces do not concur with the losses sustained in others, you will have reason to believe that the joy is not pure and unmixed but a hundred anxious reflections disturb it. People will imagine that the attack was made too soon or too late; too many men were lost, and all advantage was not taken of the disorder of the vanquished but they were permitted to recover from their fright, and they believe that by a different conduct the victory had been more complete. How many generals are there who have very uneasy nights after complete victories? They are sensible that they are beholden for them to some lucky chance, to the fault of the enemy, and sometimes even to their own faults. They are sensible they have not done all that might have been done. They are apprehensive of the comments of the experienced, and of the malicious reflections of their enemies. In a word, they cannot bear a good testimony to themselves, nor internally applaud the elogies bestowed upon them. This disturbs

15 [The reference here is to a myth in Homer's *Iliad* in which Zeus draws from two urns—one containing good and the other evil—in determining the fate of human beings.]

16 [Gustavus Adolphus (1594–1632) was king of Sweden from 1611 and enjoyed major military victories in Germany in the course of the Thirty Years' War.]

and racks them. While their consciences are sometimes asleep with regard to the law of God, they are touched to the very quick with respect to the transgression of some laws in the art of war, and the non-observance of some rules which an expert general would have followed. Observe that the most fortunate princes, either in gaining of battles or conquering of towns, are those whom the defeat of an army, or the raising of a siege, afflict the most sensibly. A long train of adversities hardens others; but these grow almost insensible as to good success, and extremely sensible of the least disgraces. Augustus is an example of this. On a thousand occasions he obtained the most important and glorious advantages over his enemies that he could have wished, and scarce experienced any of the effects of bad fortune: but the loss of three legions so prodigiously afflicted him, that the pain, we may say, he suffered on this account was greater than the pleasure which he had felt by ten victories. [...]

What I have been saying of kings, may, in proportion, be said of all those whom providence raises to eminent posts and who share in any kind of grandeur. Their lot is a mixture in which evil is for the most part predominant. Great knowledge and a sublime genius do not exempt men from this fatality. No, look rather among the most ignorant rabble than among illustrious learned men for happiness: the glory that surrounds authors and celebrated orators, does not secure them from a thousand troubles. It exposes them to envy in two ways which are very inconvenient. They have rivals who persecute them, and are jealous, in their turn, of the praises which others deserve; a typographical error gives them more disturbance than four letters full of elogies can afford them pleasure. The glory which they have acquired diminishes the pleasure they take in being praised, and increases their uneasiness for the want of praise, for censure, sharing of fame, etc. Besides, the more learning they have, the more they know that their works are imperfect. If they guard against the weakness of prejudices, and the irregularities of a hundred mean passions, and are willing to conform their language and conduct to this temper of mind, they become odious, and must renounce all external advantages. If they externally conform to the depraved taste of the world, they reproach themselves a hundred times a day with this ignominious hypocrisy, and thereby disturb their quiet. [...]

It is time to put an end to these common-places. Give me leave then to conclude with four remarks. (I) That if we consider mankind in general, it seems that Xenophanes might have said, that pain and grief prevail over pleasure. (II) That there are some private persons who, we may presume, taste in this life much more good than evil. (III) That there are others of whom we may believe that they have a much larger share of evil than good. (IV) That my second proposition is more especially probable, with respect to those who die before their declining age; and that the third appears chiefly certain in those who arrive to a decrepit old age. [...]

David Hume, *Dialogues concerning Natural Religion*, from Part X

It is my opinion, I own, replied Demea, that each man feels, in a manner, the truth of religion within his own breast; and from a consciousness of his imbecility and misery, rather than from any reasoning, is led to seek protection from that being, on whom he and all nature is dependent. So anxious or so tedious are even the best scenes of life, that futurity is still the object of all our hopes and fears. We incessantly look forward and endeavour, by prayers, adoration, and sacrifice, to appease those unknown powers whom we find, by experience, so able to afflict and oppress us. Wretched creatures that we are! What resource for us amidst the innumerable ills of life, did not religion suggest some methods of atonement, and appease those terrors with which we are incessantly agitated and tormented?

I am indeed persuaded, said Philo, that the best and indeed the only method of bringing everyone to a due sense of religion, is by just representations of the misery and wickedness of men. And for that purpose a talent of eloquence and strong imagery is more requisite than that of reasoning and argument. For is it necessary to prove what everyone feels within himself? It is only necessary to make us feel it, if possible, more intimately and sensibly.

The people, indeed, replied Demea, are sufficiently convinced of this great and melancholy truth. The miseries of life, the unhappiness of man, the general corruptions of our nature, the unsatisfactory enjoyment of pleasures, riches, honours; these phrases have become almost proverbial in all languages. And who can doubt of what all men declare from their own immediate feeling and experience?

In this point, said Philo, the learned are perfectly agreed with the vulgar; and in all letters, *sacred* and *profane*, the topic of human misery has been insisted on with the most pathetic eloquence that sorrow and melancholy could inspire. The poets, who speak from sentiment without a system, and whose testimony has therefore the more authority, abound in images of this nature. From Homer down to Dr. Young,[17] the whole

17 [Edward Young (1683–1765) was a doctor of theology and the author of a popular melancholic poem, "The Complaint: or, Night-Thoughts on Life, Death, & Immortality," published in installments beginning in 1742.]

inspired tribe have ever been sensible, that no other representation of things would suit the feeling and observation of each individual.

As to authorities, replied Demea, you need not seek them. Look round this library of Cleanthes. I shall venture to affirm that, except authors of particular sciences, such as chemistry or botany, who have no occasion to treat of human life, there is scarce one of those innumerable writers from whom the sense of human misery has not, in some passage or other, extorted a complaint and confession of it. At least, the chance is entirely on that side; and no one author has ever, so far as I can recollect, been so extravagant as to deny it.

There you must excuse me, said Philo: Leibniz has denied it; and is perhaps the first, who ventured upon so bold and paradoxical an opinion; at least, the first, who made it essential to his philosophical system.

And by being the first, replied Demea, might he not have been sensible of his error? For is this a subject, in which philosophers can propose to make discoveries, especially in so late an age? And can any man hope by a simple denial (for the subject scarcely admits of reasoning) to bear down the united testimony of mankind, founded on sense and consciousness?

And why should man, added he, pretend to an exemption from the lot of all other animals? The whole earth, believe me Philo, is cursed and polluted. A perpetual war is kindled amongst all living creatures. Necessity, hunger, want, stimulate the strong and courageous. Fear, anxiety, terror, agitate the weak and infirm. The first entrance into life gives anguish to the new-born infant and to its wretched parent. Weakness, impotence, distress, attend each stage of that life, and it is at last finished in agony and horror.

Observe too, says Philo, the curious artifices of nature, in order to embitter the life of every living being. The stronger prey upon the weaker, and keep them in perpetual terror and anxiety. The weaker too, in their turn, often prey upon the stronger, and vex and molest them without relaxation. Consider that innumerable race of insects, which either are bred on the body of each animal or flying about infix their stings in him. These insects have others still less than themselves which torment them. And thus on each hand, before and behind, above and below, every animal is surrounded with enemies, which incessantly seek its misery and destruction.

Man alone, said Demea, seems to be, in part, an exception to this rule. For by combination in society, he can easily master lions, tigers, and bears, whose greater strength and agility naturally enable them to prey upon him.

On the contrary, it is here chiefly, cried Philo, that the uniform and equal maxims of nature are most apparent. Man, it is true, can, by combination, surmount all his *real* enemies, and become master of the whole animal creation: but does he not immediately raise up to himself *imaginary* enemies, the demons of his fancy, who haunt him with superstitious terrors, and blast every enjoyment of life? His pleasure, as he imagines, becomes, in their eyes, a crime: his food and repose give them umbrage and offence: his very sleep and dreams furnish new materials to anxious fear: and even death, his refuge from every other ill, presents only the dread of endless and innumerable woes. Nor does the wolf molest more the timid flock, than superstition does the anxious breast of wretched mortals.

Besides, consider, Demea, this very society, by which we surmount those wild beasts, our natural enemies; what new enemies does it not raise to us? What woe and misery does it not occasion? Man is the greatest enemy of man. Oppression, injustice, contempt, contumely, violence, sedition, war, calumny, treachery, fraud; by these they mutually torment each other: and they would soon dissolve that society which they had formed, were it not for the dread of still greater ills, which must attend their separation.

But though these external insults, said Demea, from animals, from men, from all the elements, which assault us, form a frightful catalogue of woes, they are nothing in comparison of those, which arise within ourselves, from the distempered condition of our mind and body. How many lie under the lingering torment of diseases? Hear the pathetic enumeration of the great poet.

> Intestine stone and ulcer, colic-pangs,
> Dæmoniac frenzy, moping melancholy,
> And moon-struck madness, pining atrophy,
> Marasmus, and wide-wasting pestilence.
> Dire was the tossing, deep the groans: DESPAIR
> Tended the sick, busiest from couch to couch.
> And over them triumphant DEATH his dart
> Shook: but delay'd to strike, tho' oft invok'd
> With vows, as their chief good and final hope.[18]

The disorders of the mind, continued Demea, though more secret, are not perhaps less dismal and vexatious. Remorse, shame, anguish, rage, disappointment, anxiety, fear, dejection, despair; who has ever passed

18 [The passage is from *Paradise Lost*, by the English Puritan poet John Milton (1608–74).]

through life without cruel inroads from these tormentors? How many have scarcely ever felt any better sensations? Labour and poverty, so abhorred by everyone, are the certain lot of the far greater number: and those few privileged persons who enjoy ease and opulence never reach contentment or true felicity. All the goods of life united would not make a very happy man: but all the ills united would make a wretch indeed; and any one of them almost (and who can be free from everyone) nay often the absence of one good (and who can possess all) is sufficient to render life ineligible.

Were a stranger to drop on a sudden into this world, I would show him, as a specimen of its ills, a hospital full of diseases, a prison crowded with malefactors and debtors, a field of battle strewn with carcasses, a fleet foundering in the ocean, a nation languishing under tyranny, famine, or pestilence. To turn the gay side of life to him, and give him a notion of its pleasures; whither should I conduct him? to a ball, to an opera, to court? He might justly think, that I was only showing him a diversity of distress and sorrow.

There is no evading such striking instances, said Philo, but by apologies, which still farther aggravate the charge. Why have all men, I ask, in all ages, complained incessantly of the miseries of life? - - - They have no just reason, says one: these complaints proceed only from their discontented, repining, anxious disposition. - - - And can there possibly, I reply, be a more certain foundation of misery, than such a wretched temper?

But if they were really as unhappy as they pretend, says my antagonist, why do they remain in life? - - -

> Not satisfied with life, afraid of death.[19]

This is the secret chain, say I, that holds us. We are terrified, not bribed to the continuance of our existence.

It is only a false delicacy, he may insist, which a few refined spirits indulge, and which has spread these complaints among the whole race of mankind. - - - And what is this delicacy, I ask, which you blame? Is it anything but a greater sensibility to all the pleasures and pains of life? And if the man of a delicate, refined temper, by being so much more alive than the rest of the world, is only so much more unhappy, what judgement must we form in general of human life?

19 [This is a line from the poem "Solomon on the Vanity of the World" by the English poet Matthew Prior (1664–1721).]

Let men remain at rest, says our adversary, and they will be easy. They are willing artificers of their own misery. - - - No! reply I; an anxious languor follows their repose: disappointment, vexation, trouble, their activity and ambition.

I can observe something like what you mention in some others, replied Cleanthes: but I confess, I feel little or nothing of it in myself; and hope that it is not so common as you represent it.

If you feel not human misery yourself, cried Demea, I congratulate you on so happy a singularity. Others, seemingly the most prosperous, have not been ashamed to vent their complaints in the most melancholy strains. Let us attend to the great, the fortunate Emperor, Charles V, when, tired with human grandeur, he resigned all his extensive dominions into the hands of his son. In the last harangue, which he made on that memorable occasion, he publicly avowed, *that the greatest prosperities which he had ever enjoyed, had been mixed with so many adversities, that he might truly say he had never enjoyed any satisfaction or contentment.* But did the retired life, in which he sought for shelter, afford him any greater happiness? If we may credit his son's account, his repentance commenced the very day of his resignation.

Cicero's fortune, from small beginnings, rose to the greatest lustre and renown; yet what pathetic complaints of the ills of life do his familiar letters, as well as philosophical discourses, contain? And suitably to his own experience, he introduces Cato, the great, the fortunate Cato, protesting in his old age that, had he a new life in his offer, he would reject the present.

Ask yourself, ask any of your acquaintance, whether they would live over again the last ten or twenty years of their life. No! but the next twenty, they say, will be better:

And from the dregs of life, hope to receive
What the first sprightly running could not give.[20]

Thus at last they find (such is the greatness of human misery; it reconciles even contradictions) that they complain, at once, of the shortness of life, and of its vanity and sorrow. [...]

20 [Quoted from the play *Aureng-Zebe*, written by the English poet John Dryden (1631–1700).]

Chapter 6

SOURCES OF SUFFERING: ROUSSEAU AND ASTELL

Introduction

AS WE HAVE SEEN, BAYLE'S "XENOPHANES" AND PART X OF Hume's *Dialogues* offer a fairly detailed treatment as to the *nature* of pleasure and pain; however, both have rather less to say about the *sources* of suffering, or what the natural and human-made circumstances are that cause and exacerbate suffering. For the most part, Bayle thinks that many of our sufferings (outside of those caused by moral evil) are due to our *natural* desires and wants, the pursuit and satisfaction of which is intertwined with painful sensations. One notable exception here are the harms that result from *religious intolerance*—as a member of a persecuted religious minority himself, Bayle was well aware of the needless suffering that such intolerance causes (and a number of his articles on religions and religious figures, including the Manichaean articles, can be understood as an effort to undermine any claim to privileged access to the truth on the part of any religion). Hume does consider the sorts of "new enemies," imagined and real, that are introduced through our society with others, but these are largely extensions of the sorts of suffering we are naturally subject to (the threat of violence through conflict with others, the influence of the passions). In the end, both give little attention to other sophisticated, human-made causes of unjustified suffering—the sort of suffering that has its roots in social or cultural practices, or in corrupted institutions.

It was Jean-Jacques Rousseau (introduced in Chapter 3 above), in his *Discours sur l'origine et les fondements de l'inégalité parmi les hommes* (*Discourse on the Origin and the Foundation of the Inequality of Mankind*) of 1751, who would offer a systematic account of one of the principal sources of widespread suffering, namely, the inequality among human beings. For Rousseau, artificial inequality—the invented distinctions in terms of wealth, power, and status—is one of the principal sources of suffering among modern human beings. Rousseau contends, however, that this condition of inequality is a direct result of modern society and of the changes that regular concourse with other human beings have wrought in human nature. By way of illustrating this, he offers a conjectural account of how human nature might have been constituted in the primitive state of nature, before socialization with other humans produced jealous love, and the artificial desires for esteem and for mastery over others that characterize the modern human being. This unsparing criticism of modern society, and the modern human being within it, is what led Voltaire to mockingly characterize Rousseau's *Discourse* as a "book written against mankind." Yet Rousseau would maintain that his overall outlook remains optimistic since, as he documents in his account of the natural human being's transition to the social condition, human nature was not corrupted in itself, or by God, or (entirely) by circumstances outside of our control, but through our own choices, meaning that it might still be possible for human choices to change the course of human history.

One sort of inequality that Rousseau was (notoriously) less interested in is the inequality between the sexes. Indeed, sexual inequality seems to be a kind of inequality which Rousseau concedes already exists before the advent of society. Interestingly, what Rousseau overlooks is the focus of an earlier piece by Mary Astell (1666–1731), an English philosopher and writer. In her *Some Reflections upon Marriage* of 1700, she develops an incisive account of the institution of marriage as a profound source of suffering for women, rooted in sexual inequality. She argues that prevailing inequality between men and women corrupts an institution that was originally intended to be a friendly partnership between equals. Astell's analysis is striking for her time and context (and certainly not without relevance to our own), as is her conclusion that, given the inequality of the sexes, and the harm that proceeds from unjust unions, women are better advised not to marry.

Jean-Jacques Rousseau, from *Discourse on the Origin and the Foundation of the Inequality of Mankind*

Preface

The most useful and least improved of all human studies is, in my opinion, that of man, and I dare say, that the inscription on the Temple of *Delphos* did alone contain a more important and difficult precept than all the huge volumes of the moralists.[1] I therefore consider the subject of this *Discourse*, as one of the most interesting questions philosophy can propose, and, unhappily for us, one of the most knotty philosophers can labour to solve: for how is it *possible* to know the source of the inequality among men without knowing men themselves? And how shall man be able to see himself, such as nature formed him, in spite of all the alterations which a long succession of years and events must have produced in his original constitution, and to distinguish what is of his own essence, from what the circumstances he has been in, and the progresses he has made, have added to, or changed in, his primitive condition. The human soul, like the statue of *Glaucus*[2] which time, the sea and storms had so much disfigured that it resembled a wild beast more than a god, the human soul, I say, altered in the bosom of society by the perpetual succession of a thousand causes, by the accession of numberless discoveries and errors, by the changes that have happened in the constitution of surrounding bodies, by the perpetual jarring of its own passions, has in a manner lost so much of its original appearance as to be scarcely distinguishable; and now, instead of a being always acting from certain and invariable principles, instead of that heavenly and majestic simplicity which its author had impressed upon it, we perceive in it nothing but the shocking contrast of passion that thinks it reasons and a delirious understanding.

1 [A reference to the famous injunction to "know thyself."]

2 [A Greek sea-god.]

But what is still more cruel, as every improvement made by the human species serves only to remove it still further from its primitive condition, the more we accumulate new information the more we deprive ourselves of the means of acquiring the most important of all; and it is, in a manner, a result of studying man that we have lost the power of knowing him.

We need not be very clear-sighted to perceive that it is in these successive alterations of the human frame that we must look out for the first origin of those differences that distinguish men who, it is universally allowed, are naturally as equal among themselves as were the animals of every species before various physical causes had introduced those varieties we now observe among some of them. In fact, it is not possible to conceive how these first changes, whatever causes may have produced them, could have altered all at once and in the same manner, all the individuals of the species. It seems obvious, that while some improved or impaired their condition, or acquired diverse good or bad qualities not inherent in their nature, the rest continued a longer time in their primitive posture; and such was among men the first source of inequality, which it is much easier thus to point out in general, than to trace back with precision to its true causes.

Let not then my readers imagine, that I dare flatter myself with having seen what I think is so difficult to discover. I have opened some arguments; I have risked some conjectures; but not so much from any hopes of being able to solve the question, as with a view of throwing upon it some light and giving a true state of it. [...]

Introduction

It is of man I am to speak; and the very question, in answer to which I am to speak of him, sufficiently informs me that I am going to speak to men; for to those alone who are not afraid of honouring truth it belongs to propose discussions of this kind. I shall therefore maintain with confidence the cause of mankind before the sages, who invite me to stand up in its defense; and I shall think myself happy if I can but behave in a manner not unworthy of my subject and of my judges.

I conceive two species of inequality among men; one which I call natural, or physical inequality, because it is established by nature, and consists in the difference of age, health, bodily strength, and the qualities of the mind, or of the soul; the other which may be termed moral, or political inequality, because it depends on a kind of convention, and is established, or at least authorized, by the common consent of mankind. This species of inequality consists in the different privileges which some men enjoy, to the prejudice of others, such as that of being richer, more honoured, more powerful, and even that of exacting obedience from them.

It were absurd to ask what is the cause of natural inequality, seeing as the bare definition of natural inequality answers the question: it would be more absurd still to enquire if there might not be some essential connection between the two species of inequality, as it would be asking, in other words, if those who command are necessarily better men than those who obey; and if strength of body or of mind, wisdom or virtue are always to be found in individuals in the same proportion with power or riches: a question, fit perhaps to be discussed by slaves in the hearing of their masters, but unbecoming free and reasonable beings in search of truth.

What therefore is precisely the subject of this *Discourse*? It is to point out, in the progress of things, that moment, when, right taking place of violence, nature became subject to law; to display that chain of surprising events in consequence of which the strong submitted to serve the weak, and the people to purchase imaginary ease at the expense of real happiness. [...]

First Part

However important it may be, in order to form a proper judgment of the natural state of man, to consider him from his origin, and to examine him, as it were, in the first embryo of the species, I shall not attempt to trace his organization through its successive approaches to perfection. I shall not stop to examine in the animal system what he might have been in the beginning, to become at last what he actually is. I shall not inquire whether, as Aristotle thinks, his neglected nails were no better at first than crooked talons; whether his whole body was not, bear-like, thick covered with rough hair; and whether, walking upon all-fours, his eyes, directed to the earth, and confined to a horizon of a few paces extent, did not at once point out the nature and limits of his ideas. [...] I shall suppose his conformation to have always been what we now behold it: that he always walked on two feet, made the same use of his hands that we do of ours, extended his looks over the whole face of nature, and measured with his eyes the vast extent of the heavens.

If I strip this being, thus constituted, of all the supernatural gifts which he may have received and of all the artificial faculties which we could not have acquired but by slow degrees, if I consider him, in a word, such as he must have issued from the hands of nature, I see an animal less strong than some, and less active than others but, upon the whole, the most advantageously organized of any. I see him satisfying the calls of hunger under the first oak, and those of thirst at the first rivulet. I see him laying himself down to sleep at the foot of the same tree that afforded him his meal, and behold, this done, all his wants are completely supplied.

The earth left to its own natural fertility and covered with immense woods that no hatchet ever disfigured offers at every step food and shelter to every species of animals. Men, dispersed among them, observe and imitate their industry and thus rise to the instinct of beasts, with this advantage that, whereas every species of beasts is confined to one peculiar instinct, man, who perhaps has not any that particularly belongs to him, appropriates to himself those of all other animals and lives equally upon most of the different aliments which they only divide among themselves; a circumstance which qualifies him to find his subsistence, with more ease than any of them.

Men, accustomed from their infancy to the inclemency of the weather and to the rigour of the different seasons, inured to fatigue and obliged to defend, naked and without arms, their life and their prey against the other wild inhabitants of the forest, or at least to avoid their fury by flight, acquire a robust and almost unalterable habit of body. The children, bringing with them into the world the excellent constitution of their parents, and strengthening it by the same exercises that first produced it, attain by this means all the vigour that the human frame is capable of. Nature treats them exactly in the same manner that Sparta treated the children of her citizens as those who come well formed into the world she renders strong and robust, and destroys all the rest; differing in this respect from our societies, in which the state, by permitting children to become burdensome to their parents, murders them all without distinction, even in the wombs of their mothers.

The body being the only instrument that savage man is acquainted with, he employs it to different uses, of which ours, for want of practice, are incapable; and we may thank our industry for the loss of that strength and agility which necessity obliges him to acquire. Had he a hatchet, would his hand so easily snap off from an oak so stout a branch? Had he a sling, would it dart a stone to so great a distance? Had he a ladder, would he run so nimbly up a tree? Had he a horse, would he with such swiftness shoot along the plain? Give civilized man but time to gather about him all his machines, and no doubt he will be an overmatch for the savage: but if you have a mind to see a contest still more unequal, place them naked and unarmed one opposite to the other, and you will soon discover the advantage there is in perpetually having all our forces at our disposal, in being constantly prepared against all events, and in always carrying ourselves, as it were, whole and entire about us. [...]

Turn out a bear or a wolf against a sturdy, active, resolute savage (and this they all are) provided with stones and a good stick, and you will soon find that the danger is at least equal on both sides, and that after several trials of this kind wild beasts, who are not fond of attacking each other, will not be very fond of attacking man whom they have found every whit as wild as themselves. As to animals who have really more strength than man has address, he is, in regard to them, what other weaker species are who find means to subsist notwithstanding; he has even this great advantage over such weaker species, that being equally fleet with them, and finding on every tree an almost inviolable asylum, he is always at liberty to take it or leave it, as he likes best, and of course to fight or to fly, whichever is most agreeable to him. To this we may add that no animal naturally makes war upon man, except in the case of self-defense or extreme hunger, nor ever expresses against him any of these violent antipathies which seem to indicate that some particular species are intended by nature for the food of others.

But there are other more formidable enemies and against which man is not provided with the same means of defense. I mean natural infirmities, infancy, old age, and sickness of every kind, melancholy proofs of our weakness, whereof the two first are common to all animals, and the last chiefly attends man living in a state of society. It is even observable in regard to infancy that the mother being able to carry her child about with her, wherever she goes, can perform the duty of a nurse with a great deal less trouble than the females of many other animals, who are obliged to be constantly going and coming with no small labour and fatigue, one way to look out for their own subsistence and another to suckle and feed their young ones.

True it is that, if the woman happens to perish her child is exposed to the greatest danger of perishing with her; but this danger is common to a hundred other species, whose young ones require a great deal of time to be able to provide for themselves. And if our infancy is longer than theirs, our life is longer likewise so that, in this respect too, all things are in a manner equal; not but that there are other rules concerning the duration of the first age of life, and the number of the young of man and other animals, but they do not belong to my subject. With old men, who stir and perspire but little, the demand for food diminishes with their abilities to provide it; and as a savage life would exempt them from the gout and the rheumatism, and old age is of all ills that which human assistance is least capable of alleviating, they would at last go off without its being perceived by others that they ceased to exist, and almost without perceiving it themselves.

In regard to sickness, I shall not repeat the vain and false declamations made use of to discredit medicine by most men while they enjoy their health; I shall only ask if there are any solid observations from which we may conclude that in those countries where the healing art is most neglected, the mean duration of man's life is shorter than in those where it is most cultivated? And how is it possible this should be the case, unless we inflict more diseases upon ourselves than medicine can supply us with remedies! [...]

Man therefore, in a state of nature where there are so few sources of sickness, can have no great occasion for physic and still less for physicians; neither is the human species more to be pitied in this respect than any other species of animals. Ask those who make hunting their recreation or business, if in their excursions they meet with many sick or feeble animals. They meet with many carrying the marks of considerable wounds, that have been perfectly well healed and closed up; with many, whose bones formerly broken, and whose limbs almost torn off, have completely knit and united, without any other surgeon but time, any other regimen but their usual way of living, and whose cures were not the less perfect for their not having been tortured with incisions, poisoned with drugs, or worn out by diet and abstinence. In a word, however useful medicine well administered may be to us who live in a state of society, it is still past doubt that if, on the one hand, the sick savage, destitute of help, has nothing to hope from nature, on the other, he has nothing to fear but from his disease; a circumstance, which often renders his situation preferable to ours.

Let us therefore beware of confounding savage man with the men whom we daily see and converse with. Nature behaves towards all animals left to her care with a predilection, that seems to prove how jealous she is of that prerogative. The horse, the cat, the bull, even the ass itself, have generally a higher stature and always a more robust constitution, more vigour, more strength and courage in their forests than in our houses; they lose half these advantages by becoming domestic animals, and it looks as if all our attention to treat them kindly and to feed them well served only to bastardize them. It is thus with man himself. In proportion as he becomes sociable and a slave to others, he becomes weak, fearful, mean-spirited, and his soft and effeminate way of living at once completes the enervation of his strength and of his courage. We may add, that there must be still a wider difference between man in a savage and a domestic condition than between beasts in such conditions; for as men and beasts have been treated alike by nature, all the conveniences with which men indulge themselves more than they do the beasts tamed by them are so many particular causes which make them degenerate more sensibly.

Nakedness therefore, the want of houses, and of all these unnecessaries which we consider as so very necessary are not such mighty evils in respect to these primitive men, and much less still any obstacle to their preservation. Their skins, it is true, are destitute of hair, but then they have no occasion for any such covering in warm climates, and in cold climates they soon learn to apply to that use those of the animals they have conquered. They have but two feet to run with, but they have two hands to defend themselves with, and provide for all their wants. It costs them perhaps a great deal of time and trouble to make their children walk, but the mothers carry them with ease, an advantage not granted to other species of animals with whom the mother, when pursued, is obliged to abandon her young ones or regulate her steps by theirs. In short, unless we admit those singular and fortuitous concurrences of circumstances, which I shall speak of hereafter, and which, it is very possible, may never have existed, it is evident, in every state of the question, that the man who first made himself clothes and built himself a cabin, supplied himself with things which he did not much want, since he had lived without them till then; and why should he not have been able to support in his riper years, the same kind of life, which he had supported from his infancy? [...]

As yet I have considered man merely in his physical capacity; let us now endeavour to examine him in a metaphysical and moral light.

I can discover nothing in any mere animal but an ingenious machine to which nature has given senses to wind itself up and guard, to a certain degree, against everything that might destroy or disorder it. I perceive the very same things in the human machine, with this difference that nature alone operates in all the operations of the beast, whereas man, as a free agent, has a share in his. One chooses by instinct, the other by an act of liberty for which reason the beast cannot deviate from the rules that have been prescribed to it, even in cases where such deviation might be useful, and man often deviates from the rules laid down for him to his prejudice. Thus a pigeon would starve near a dish of the best meat, and a cat on a heap of fruit or corn, though both might very well support life with the food which they thus disdain, did they but bethink themselves to make a trial of it. It is in this manner dissolute men run into excesses, which bring on fevers and death itself, because the mind depraves the senses and when nature ceases to speak, the will still continues to dictate. [...]

But though the difficulties in which all these questions are involved should leave some room to dispute on this difference between man and beast, there is another very specific quality that distinguishes them, and a quality which will admit of no dispute. This is the faculty of improvement, a faculty which, as circumstances offer, successively unfolds all the other faculties, and resides among us not only in the species, but in the individuals that compose it; whereas a beast is, at the end of some months, all he ever will be during the rest of his life; and his species, at the end of a thousand years, precisely what it was the first year of that long period. [...]

Savage man, abandoned by nature to pure instinct, or rather indemnified for that which has perhaps been denied to him by faculties capable of immediately supplying the place of it and of raising him afterwards a great deal higher, would therefore begin with functions that were merely animal: to see and to feel would be his first condition, which he would enjoy in common with other animals. To will and not to will, to wish and to fear, would be the first, and in a manner, the only operations of his soul, till new circumstances occasioned new developments.

Let moralists say what they will, the human understanding is greatly indebted to the passions, which on their side are likewise universally allowed to be greatly indebted to the human understanding. It is by the activity of our passions, that our reason improves: we covet knowledge merely because we covet enjoyment, and it is impossible to conceive why a man exempt from fears and desires should take the trouble to reason. The passions, in their turn, owe their origin to our wants, and their increase to our progress in science; for we cannot desire or fear anything, but in consequence of the ideas we have of it, or of the simple impulses of nature; and savage man, destitute of every species of knowledge, experiences no passions but those of this last kind. His desires never extend beyond his physical wants; he knows no goods but food, a female, and rest; he fears no evil but pain, and hunger—I say pain, and not death, for no animal merely as such will ever know what it is to die, and the knowledge of death and of its terrors is one of the first acquisitions made by man, in consequence of his deviating from the animal state. [...]

In fact, it is impossible to conceive, why in this primitive state one man should have more occasion for the assistance of another, than one monkey, or one wolf for that of another animal of the same species; or supposing that he had, what motive could induce another to assist him; or even, in this last case, how he, who wanted assistance, and he from whom it was wanted, could agree among themselves upon the conditions. Authors, I know, are continually telling us, that in this state man would have been a most miserable creature; and if it is true, as I fancy I have proved it, that he must have continued many ages without either the desire or the opportunity of emerging from such a state, this their assertion could only serve to justify a charge against nature and not any against the being which nature had thus constituted. But, if I thoroughly understand this term *miserable*, it is a word that either has no meaning, or signifies nothing but a privation attended with pain, and a suffering state of body or soul. Now I would eagerly know what kind of misery can be that of a free being, whose heart enjoys perfect peace, and body perfect health? And which is aptest to become insupportable to those who enjoy it, a civil or a natural life? In civil life we can scarcely meet a single person who does not complain of his existence; many even throw away as much of it as they can, and the united force of divine and human laws can hardly put bounds to this disorder. Was ever any free savage known to have been so much as tempted to complain of life and lay violent hands on himself? Let us therefore judge with less pride on which side real misery is to be placed. Nothing, on the contrary, would have been so unhappy as a savage man dazzled by flashes of knowledge, racked by passions, and reasoning on a state different from that in which he saw himself placed. It was in consequence of a very wise providence, that the faculties which he potentially enjoyed were not to develop themselves but in proportion as there offered occasions to exercise them, lest they should be superfluous or troublesome to him when he did not want them, or tardy and useless when he did. He had in his instinct alone everything requisite to live in a state of nature; in his cultivated reason he has barely what is necessary to live in a state of society.

It appears at first sight that, as there was no kind of moral relations between men in this state, nor any known duties, they could not be either good or bad and had neither vices nor virtues, unless we take these words in a physical sense and call vices in the individual the qualities which may prove detrimental to his own preservation, and virtues those which may contribute to it; in which case we should be obliged to consider him as most virtuous who made least resistance against the simple impulses of nature. But without deviating from the usual meaning of these terms, it is proper to suspend the judgment we might form of such a situation, and be on our guard against prejudice until, the balance in hand, we have examined whether there are more virtues or vices among civilized men, or whether the improvement of their understanding is sufficient to compensate for the damage which they mutually do to each other, in proportion as they become better informed of the services which they ought to do; or whether, upon the whole, they would not be much happier in a condition where they had nothing to fear or to hope from each other, than in that where they had submitted to an universal subservience and have obliged themselves to depend for everything upon the good will of those who do not think themselves obliged to give anything in return.

But above all things let us beware of concluding with Hobbes,[3] that man, as having no idea of goodness, must be naturally bad; that he is vicious because he does not know what virtue is; that he always refuses to do any service to those of his own species, because he believes that none is due to them; that, in virtue of that right which he justly claims to everything he wants, he foolishly looks upon himself as proprietor of the whole universe. Hobbes very plainly saw the flaws in all the modern definitions of natural right: but the consequences which he draws from his own definition show that it is, in the sense he understands it, equally objectionable. This author, to argue from his own principles, should say that the state of nature, being that where the care of our own preservation interferes least with the preservation of others, was of course the most favourable to peace and most suitable to mankind; whereas he advances the very reverse in consequence of his having injudiciously admitted, as objects of that care which savage man should take of his preservation, the satisfaction of numberless passions which are the work of society and have rendered laws necessary. A bad man, says he, is a robust child.

3 [Thomas Hobbes (1588–1679) was an English political philosopher. Rousseau is here referring to Hobbes's infamous characterization, in his *Leviathan* (1651), of the primitive state of nature as a state of widespread scarcity of resources and insecurity, hence a state of "war of all against all."]

But this is not proving that savage man is a robust child; and even if we were to grant that he was, what could this philosopher infer from such a concession? That if this man, when robust, depended on others as much as when feeble then there is no excess that he would not be guilty of. He would make nothing of striking his mother when she delayed ever so little to give him the breast; he would claw, and bite, and strangle without remorse the first of his younger brothers that ever so accidentally jostled or otherwise disturbed him. But these are two contradictory suppositions in the state of nature: to be robust and dependent. Man is weak when dependent, and his own master before he grows robust. Hobbes did not consider that the same cause which hinders savages from making use of their reason, as our jurisconsults pretend, hinders them at the same time from making an ill use of their faculties, as he himself pretends; so that we may say that savages are not bad, precisely because they don't know what it is to be good; for it is neither the development of the understanding, nor the curb of the law, but the calmness of their passions and their ignorance of vice that hinders them from doing ill [...].

There is besides another principle that has escaped Hobbes, and which having been given to man to moderate, on certain occasions, the blind and impetuous sallies of self-love, or the desire of self-preservation previous to the appearance of that passion, allays the ardour with which he naturally pursues his private welfare by an innate abhorrence to see beings suffer that resemble him. I shall not surely be contradicted in granting to man the only natural virtue which the most passionate detractor of human virtues could not deny him, I mean that of pity, a disposition suitable to creatures weak as we are and liable to so many evils; a virtue so much the more universal, and so useful to man, as it takes place in him of all manner of reflection; and so natural, that the beasts themselves sometimes give evident signs of it. Not to speak of the tenderness of mothers for their young, and of the dangers they face to screen them from danger; with what reluctance are horses known to trample upon living bodies; one animal never passes unmoved by the dead carcass of another animal of the same species: there are even some who bestow a kind of sepulture upon their dead fellows; and the mournful lowings of cattle, on their entering the slaughter-house, publish the impression made upon them by the horrible spectacle they are there struck with. [...]

Such is the pure motion of nature, anterior to all manner of reflection; such is the force of natural pity, which the most dissolute manners have as yet found it so difficult to extinguish, since we every day see, in our theatrical representation, those men sympathize with the unfortunate and weep at their sufferings who, if in the tyrant's place, would aggravate the torments of their enemies. [...] Though it were true that commiseration is no more than a sentiment which puts us in the place of him who suffers, a sentiment obscure but active in the savage, developed but dormant in civilized man, how could this notion affect the truth of what I advance but to make it more evident. In fact, commiseration must be so much the more energetic, the more intimately the animal that beholds any kind of distress identifies himself with the animal that labours under it. Now it is evident that this identification must have been infinitely more perfect in the state of nature than in the state of reason. It is reason that engenders self-love and reflection that strengthens it; it is reason that makes man shrink into himself; it is reason that makes him keep aloof from everything that can trouble or afflict him: it is philosophy that destroys his connections with other men; it is in consequence of her dictates that he mutters to himself at the sight of another in distress, You may perish for aught I care, nothing can hurt me. Nothing less than those evils, which threaten the whole species, can disturb the calm sleep of the philosopher and force him from his bed. One man may with impunity murder another under his windows; he has nothing to do but clap his hands to his ears, argue a little with himself to hinder nature that startles within him from identifying him with the unhappy sufferer. Savage man lacks this admirable talent and, for want of wisdom and reason, is always ready foolishly to obey the first whispers of humanity. In riots and street-brawls the populace flock together, the prudent man sneaks off. It is the dregs of the people, the poor basket- and barrow-women, that part the combatants, and hinder gentle folks from cutting one another's throats.

It is therefore certain that pity is a natural sentiment, which, by moderating in every individual the activity of self-love, contributes to the mutual preservation of the whole species. It is this pity which hurries us without reflection to the assistance of those we see in distress; it is this pity which, in a state of nature, stands in for laws, for manners, for virtue, with this advantage, that no one is tempted to disobey her sweet and gentle voice; it is this pity which will always hinder a robust savage from plundering a feeble child, or infirm old man, of the subsistence they have acquired with pain and difficulty, if he has but the least prospect of providing for himself by any other means; it is this pity which, instead of that sublime maxim of argumentative justice, *Do to others as you would have others do to you*, inspires all men with that other maxim of natural goodness a great deal less perfect, but perhaps more useful, *Consult your own happiness with as little prejudice as you can to that of others.* It is in a word, in this natural sentiment, rather than in fine-spun arguments, that we must look for the cause of that reluctance which every man would experience to do evil, even independently of the maxims of education. Though it may be the peculiar happiness of Socrates and other geniuses of his stamp, to reason themselves into virtue, the human species would long ago have ceased to exist had it depended entirely for its preservation on the reasonings of the individuals that compose it.

With passions so tame, and so salutary a curb, men, more wild than wicked, and more attentive to guard against mischief than to do any to other animals, were not exposed to any dangerous dissensions. As they kept up no manner of correspondence with each other, and were of course strangers to vanity, to respect, to esteem, to contempt; as they had no notion of what we call *Meum* and *Tuum*,[4] nor any true idea of justice; as they considered any violence they were liable to, as an evil that could be easily repaired, and not as an injury that deserved punishment; and as they never so much as dreamed of revenge, unless perhaps mechanically and unpremeditatedly, as a dog who bites the stone that has been thrown at him, their disputes could seldom be attended with bloodshed, were they never occasioned by a more considerable stake than that of subsistence: but there is a more dangerous subject of contention, which I must not leave unnoticed.

Among the passions which ruffle the heart of man, there is one of a hot and impetuous nature, which renders the sexes necessary to each other; a terrible passion which despises all dangers, bears down all obstacles, and to which in its transports it seems proper to destroy the human species which it is destined to preserve. What must become of men abandoned to this lawless and brutal rage, without modesty, without shame, and every day disputing the objects of their passion at the expense of their blood?

We must in the first place allow that the more violent the passions, the more necessary are laws to restrain them. But, besides that the disorders and the crimes to which these passions daily give rise among us, sufficiently prove the insufficiency of laws for that purpose, we would do well to look back a little further and examine whether these evils did not spring up with the laws themselves; for at this rate, though the laws were

4 [Mine and thine (Latin).]

capable of repressing these evils, it is the least that might be expected from them, seeing it is no more than stopping the progress of a mischief which they themselves have produced.

Let us begin by distinguishing between what is moral and what is physical in the passion called love. The physical part of it is that general desire which prompts the sexes to unite with each other; the moral part is that which determines that desire and fixes it upon a particular object to the exclusion of all others, or at least gives it a greater degree of energy for this preferred object. Now it is easy to perceive that the moral part of love is a factitious sentiment, engendered by society, and cried up by the women with great care and address in order to establish their empire and secure command to that sex which ought to obey. This sentiment, being founded on certain notions of beauty and merit which a savage is not capable of having, and upon comparisons which he is not capable of making, can scarcely exist in him: for as his mind was never in a condition to form abstract ideas of regularity and proportion, neither is his heart susceptible of sentiments of admiration and love which, even without our perceiving it, are produced by our application of these ideas. He listens solely to the dispositions implanted in him by nature, and not to taste which he never was in a way of acquiring; every woman answers his purpose.

Confined entirely to what is physical in love, and happy enough not to know these preferences which sharpen the appetite for it, at the same time that they increase the difficulty of satisfying such appetite, men, in a state of nature, must be subject to fewer and less violent fits of that passion, and of course there must be fewer and less violent disputes among them in consequence of it. The imagination which causes so many ravages among us, never speaks to the heart of savages, who peaceably wait for the impulses of nature, yield to these impulses without choice and with more pleasure than fury; and whose desires never outlive their necessity for the thing desired.

Nothing therefore can be more evident, than that it is society alone, which has added even to love itself as well as to all the other passions, that impetuous ardour which so often renders it fatal to mankind; and it is so much the more ridiculous to represent savages constantly murdering each other to glut their brutality, as this opinion is diametrically opposite to experience. The Caribbeans, the people in the world who have as yet deviated least from the state of nature, are to all intents and purposes the most peaceable in their amours, and the least subject to jealousy, though they live in a burning climate which seems always to add considerably to the activity of these passions. [...]

Let us conclude that savage man, wandering about in the forests, without industry, without speech, without any fixed residence, an equal stranger to war and every social connection, without standing in any shape in need of his fellows, as well as without any desire of hurting them, and perhaps even without ever distinguishing them individually one from the other, subject to few passions, and finding in himself all he wants, let us, I say, conclude that savage man thus circumstanced had no knowledge or sentiment but such as are proper to that condition, that he alone was sensible of his real necessities, took notice of nothing but what it was his interest to see, and that his understanding made as little progress as his vanity. If he happened to make any discovery, he could the less communicate it as he did not even know his children. The art perished with the inventor; there was neither education nor improvement; generations succeeded generations to no purpose; and as all constantly set out from the same point, whole centuries rolled on in the rudeness and barbarity of the first age; the species was grown old, while the individual still remained in a state of childhood.

If I have enlarged so much upon the supposition of this primitive condition, it is because I thought it my duty, considering what ancient errors and inveterate prejudices I have to extirpate, to dig to the very roots, and show in a true picture of the state of nature, how much even natural inequality falls short in this state of that reality and influence which our writers ascribe to it.

In fact, we may easily perceive that among the differences which distinguish men, several pass for natural, which are merely the work of habit and the different kinds of life adopted by men living in a social way. [...]

But though nature in the distribution of her gifts should really affect all the preferences that are ascribed to her, what advantage could the most favoured derive from her partiality, to the prejudice of others, in a state of things, which scarce admitted any kind of relation between her pupils? Of what service can beauty be, where there is no love? What will wit avail people who do not speak, or craft those who have no affairs to transact? Authors are constantly crying out, that the strongest would oppress the weakest; but let them explain what they mean by the word oppression. One man will rule with violence, another will groan under a constant subjection to all his caprices: this is indeed precisely what I observe among us, but I do not see how it can be said of savage men, into whose heads it would be a harder matter to drive even the meaning of the words *domination* and *servitude*. One man might, indeed, seize on the fruits which another had gathered, on the game which another had killed, on the cavern which another had occupied for shelter; but how is it possible he should ever exact obedience from him, and what chains of dependence can there be among men who possess nothing? If I am driven from one tree, I have nothing to do but look out for another; if one place is made uneasy to me, what can hinder me from taking up my quarters elsewhere? But suppose I should meet a man so much superior to me in strength, and withal so wicked, so lazy and so barbarous as to oblige me to provide for his subsistence while he remains idle; he must resolve not to take his eyes from me a single moment, to bind me fast before he can take the least nap, lest I should kill him or give him the slip during his sleep: that is to say, he must expose himself voluntarily to much greater troubles than what he seeks to avoid, than any he gives me. And after all, let him abate ever so little of his vigilance; let him at some sudden noise but turn his head another way; I am already buried in the forest, my fetters are broke, and he never sees me again.

But without insisting any longer upon these details, everyone must see that, as the bonds of servitude are formed merely by the mutual dependence of men one upon another and the reciprocal necessities which unite them, it is impossible for one man to enslave another, without having first reduced him to a condition in which he cannot live without the enslaver's assistance; a condition which, as it does not exist in a state of nature, must leave every man his own master, and render the law of the strongest altogether vain and useless.

Having proved that the inequality which may subsist between man and man in a state of nature is almost imperceivable, and that it has very little influence, I must now proceed to show its origin, and trace its progress, in the successive developments of the human mind. After having showed, that perfectibility, the social virtues, and the other faculties, which natural man had received *in potentia*, could never be developed of themselves, that for that purpose there was a necessity for the fortuitous concurrence of several foreign causes, which might never have happened, and without which he must have eternally remained in his primitive condition; I must proceed to consider and bring together the different accidents which may have perfected the human understanding by debasing the species, render a being wicked by rendering him sociable, and from so remote a term bring man at last and the world to the point in which we now see them.

I must own that, as the events I am about to describe might have happened many different ways, my choice of these I shall assign can be grounded on nothing but mere conjecture; but besides these conjectures becoming reasons, when they are not only the most probable that can be drawn from the nature of things but the only means we can have of discovering truth, the consequences I mean to deduce from mine will not be merely conjectural since, on the principles I have just established, it is impossible to form any other system, that would not supply me with the same results, and from which I might not draw the same conclusions. [...]

Second Part

The first man, who, after enclosing a piece of ground, took it into his head to say, "This is mine," and found people simple enough to believe him, was the true founder of civil society. How many crimes, how many wars, how many murders, how many misfortunes and horrors would that man have saved the human species who, pulling up the stakes or filling up the ditches should have cried to his fellows: "Be sure not to listen to this imposter; you are lost, if you forget that the fruits of the earth belong equally to us all, and the earth itself to nobody!" But it is highly probable that things, having now come to such a pass, could not continue much longer in the same way; for as this idea of property depends on several prior ideas which could only spring up gradually one after another, it was not formed all at once in the human mind. Men must have made great progress, they must have acquired a great stock of industry and knowledge, and transmitted and increased it from age to age before they could arrive at this final stage of the state of nature. Let us therefore take up things a little higher, and collect into one point of view, and in their most natural order, this slow succession of events and mental improvements.

The first sentiment of man was that of his existence, his first care that of preserving it. The productions of the earth yielded him all the assistance he required; instinct prompted him to make use of them. Among the various appetites, which made him at different times experience different modes of existence, there was one that excited him to perpetuate his species; and this blind propensity, quite void of anything like pure love or affection, produced nothing but an act that was merely animal. The present heat once allayed, the sexes took no further notice of each other, and even the child ceased to have any tie with his mother the moment he ceased to want her assistance.

Such was the condition of infant man. Such was the life of an animal confined at first to pure sensations. And so far from harbouring any thought of forcing her gifts from nature was he that he scarcely availed himself of those which she offered to him of her own accord. But difficulties soon arose, and there was a necessity for learning how to surmount them: the height of some trees, which prevented his reaching their fruits; the competition of other animals equally fond of the same fruits; the fierceness of many that even aimed at his life; these were so many circumstances, which obliged him to apply to bodily exercise. There was a necessity for becoming active, swift-footed, and sturdy in battle. The natural arms, which are stones and the branches of trees, soon offered themselves to his assistance. He learned to surmount the obstacles of nature, to contend in case of necessity with other animals, to dispute his subsistence even with other men, or indemnify himself for the loss of whatever he found himself obliged to part with to the strongest.

In proportion as the human species grew more numerous and extended itself, its pains likewise multiplied and increased. The difference of soils, climates, and seasons might have forced men to observe some difference in their way of living. Bad harvests, long and severe winters, and scorching summers which parched up all the fruits of the earth, required extraordinary exertions of industry. On the sea shore and the banks of rivers they invented the line and the hook and became fishermen and fish-eaters. In the forests they made themselves bows and arrows and became huntsmen and warriors. In the cold countries they covered themselves with the skins of the beasts they had killed; thunder, a volcano, or some happy accident made them acquainted with fire, a new resource against the rigours of winter: they discovered the method of preserving this element, then that of reproducing it, and lastly the way of preparing with it the flesh of animals, which heretofore they devoured raw from the carcass.

This reiterated application of various beings to himself and to one another must have naturally engendered in the mind of man the idea of certain relations. These relations, which we express by the words, great, little, strong, weak, swift, slow, fearful, bold, and the like, compared occasionally and almost without thinking of it, produced in him some kind of reflection, or rather a mechanical prudence, which pointed out to him the precautions most essential to his preservation and safety.

The new lights resulting from this development increased his superiority over other animals by making him sensible of it. He laid himself out to ensnare them, he played them a thousand tricks, and though several surpassed him in strength or in swiftness he in time became the master of those that could be of any service to him, and a sore enemy to those that could do him any mischief. It is thus that the first look he gave into himself produced the first emotion of pride in him; it is thus that at a time he scarcely knew how to distinguish between the different ranks of existence, by attributing to his species the first rank among animals in general, he prepared himself at a distance to pretend to it as an individual among those of his own species in particular.

Though other men were not to him what they are to us, and he had hardly more intercourse with them than with other animals, they were not overlooked in his observations. The conformities which in time he might discover between them, and between himself and his female, made him judge of those he did not perceive; and seeing that they all behaved as himself would have done in similar circumstances, he concluded that their manner of thinking and willing was quite conformable to his own. This important truth, when once engraved deeply on his mind, made him follow, by a presentiment as sure as any logic and altogether much quicker, the best rules of conduct which for the sake of his own safety and advantage it was proper he should observe towards them.

Instructed by experience that the love of happiness is the sole principle of all human actions, he found himself in a condition to distinguish the few cases in which common interest might authorize him to build upon the assistance of his fellows, and those still fewer in which a competition of interests might justly render it suspected. In the first case he united with them in the same flock, or at most by some kind of free association which obliged none of its members, and lasted no longer than the transitory necessity that had given birth to it. In the second case everyone aimed at his own private advantage, either by open force if he found himself strong enough, or by cunning and address if he thought himself too weak to use violence.

Such was the manner in which men might have insensibly acquired some gross idea of their mutual engagements and the advantage of fulfilling them, but this only as far as their present and sensible interest required; for as to foresight they were utter strangers to it, and far from troubling their heads about a distant futurity, they scarcely thought of the day following. Was a deer to be taken? Everyone saw that to succeed he must faithfully stand to his post; but suppose a hare to have slipped by within reach of any one of them, it is not to be doubted but he pursued it without scruple and when he had seized his prey never reproached himself with having made his companions miss theirs.

We may easily conceive that such an intercourse scarce required a more refined language than that of crows and monkeys, which flock together almost in the same manner. Inarticulate exclamations, a great many gestures, and some imitative sounds, must have been for a long time the universal language of mankind, and by joining to these in every country some articulate and conventional sounds, of which, as I have already hinted, it is not very easy to explain the institution, there arose particular languages, but rude, imperfect, and such nearly as are to be found at this day among several savage nations. My pen straightened by the rapidity of time, the abundance of things I have to say, and the almost insensible progress of the first improvements, flies like an arrow over numberless ages, for the slower the succession of events, the quicker I may allow myself to be in relating them.

At length, these first improvements enabled man to improve at a greater rate. Industry grew perfect in proportion as the mind became more enlightened. Men, soon ceasing to fall asleep under the first tree or take shelter in the first cavern, lit upon some hard and sharp kinds of stone resembling spades or hatchets and employed them to dig the ground, cut down trees, and with the branches build huts, which they afterwards bethought themselves of plastering over with clay or dirt. This was the epoch of a first revolution, which produced the establishment and distinction of families and which introduced a species of property, and along with it perhaps a thousand quarrels and battles. As the strongest however were probably the first to make themselves cabins, which they knew they were able to defend, we may conclude that the weak found it much shorter and safer to imitate than to attempt to dislodge them: and as to those who were already provided with cabins, no one could have any great temptation to seize upon that of his neighbour, not so much because it did not belong to him as because it could be of no service to him; and as besides to make himself master of it, he must expose himself to a very sharp conflict with the present occupiers.

The first developments of the heart were the effects of a new situation which united husbands and wives, parents, and children under one roof; the habit of living together gave birth to the sweetest sentiments the human species is acquainted with, conjugal and paternal love. Every family became a little society, so much the more firmly united as a mutual attachment and liberty were the only bonds of it; and it was now that the sexes, whose way of life had been hitherto the same, began to adopt different manners and customs. The women became more sedentary, and accustomed themselves to stay at home and look after the children, while the men rambled abroad in quest of subsistence for the whole family. The two sexes likewise by living a little more at their ease began to lose somewhat of their usual ferocity and sturdiness. But if on the one hand individuals became less able to engage separately with wild beasts, they on the other were more easily got together to make a common resistance against them.

In this new state of things, the simplicity and solitariness of man's life, the limitedness of his wants and the instruments which he had invented to satisfy them, leaving him a great deal of leisure, he employed it to supply himself with several conveniences unknown to his ancestors; and this was the first yoke he inadvertently imposed upon himself and the first source of mischief which he prepared for his children. For besides continuing in this manner to soften both body and mind, these conveniences having through use lost almost all their aptness to please and even degenerated into real wants, the privation of them became far more intolerable than the possession of them had been agreeable; to lose them was a misfortune, to possess them no happiness. [...]

Everything now begins to wear a new aspect. Those who heretofore wandered through the woods, by taking to a more settled way of life, gradually flock together, coalesce into several separate bodies, and at length form in every country distinct nations united in character and manners, not by any laws or regulations but by an uniform manner of life, a sameness of provisions, and the common influence of the climate. A permanent neighbourhood must at last infallibly create some connection between different families. The transitory commerce required by nature soon produced, among the youth of both sexes living in contiguous cabins, another kind of commerce, which besides being equally agreeable is rendered more durable by mutual intercourse. Men begin to consider different objects and to make comparisons; they insensibly acquire ideas of merit and beauty, and these soon produce sentiments of preference. By seeing each other often they contract a habit which makes it painful not to see each other always. Tender and agreeable sentiments steal into the soul and are by the smallest opposition wound up into the most impetuous fury. Jealousy kindles with love; discord triumphs; and the gentlest of passions requires sacrifices of human blood to appease it.

In proportion as ideas and sentiments succeed each other and the head and the heart exercise themselves, men continue to shake off their original wildness and their connections become more intimate and extensive. They now begin to assemble round a great tree: singing and dancing, the genuine offspring of love and leisure, become the amusement or rather the occupation of the men and women, free from care, thus gathered together. Everyone begins to survey the rest and wishes to be surveyed himself, and public esteem acquires a value. He who sings or dances best; the handsomest, the strongest, the most dexterous, the most eloquent, comes to be the most respected. This was the first step towards inequality and at the same time towards vice. From these first preferences there proceeded on one side vanity and contempt, on the other envy and shame, and the fermentation raised by these new leavens at length produced combinations fatal to happiness and innocence.

Men no sooner began to set a value upon each other and know what esteem was than each laid claim to it, and it was no longer safe for any man to refuse it to another. Hence the first duties of civility and politeness, even among savages; and hence every voluntary injury became an affront, as besides the mischief, which resulted from it as an injury, the party offended was sure to find in it a contempt for his person more intolerable than the mischief itself. It was thus that every man, punishing the contempt expressed for him by others in proportion to the value he set upon himself, the effects of revenge became terrible and men learned to be sanguinary and cruel. Such precisely was the degree attained by most of the savage nations with whom we are acquainted. And it is for want of sufficiently distinguishing ideas and observing at how great a distance these people were from the first state of nature that so many authors have hastily concluded that man is naturally cruel and requires a regular system of police to be reclaimed, whereas nothing can be more gentle than he in his primitive state when placed by nature at an equal distance from the stupidity of brutes and the pernicious good sense of civilized man. Equally confined by instinct and reason to the care of providing against the mischief which threatens him, he is withheld by natural compassion from doing any injury to others, so far from being ever so little prone even to return that which he has received. [...]

As long as men remained satisfied with their rustic cabins; as long as they confined themselves to the use of clothes made of the skins of other animals and the use of thorns and fish-bones in putting these skins together; as long as they continued to consider feathers and shells as sufficient ornaments, and to paint their bodies different colours, to improve or ornament their bows and arrows, to form and scoop out with sharp-edged stones some little fishing boats or clumsy instruments of music; in a word, as long as they undertook such works only as a single person could finish, and stuck to such arts as did not require the joint endeavours of several hands, they lived free, healthy, honest, and happy as much as their nature would admit and continued to enjoy with each other all the pleasures of an independent intercourse. But from the moment one man began to stand in need of another's assistance, from the moment it appeared an advantage for one man to possess the quantity of provisions requisite for two all equality vanished, property started up, labour became necessary, and boundless forests became smiling fields which it was found necessary to water with human sweat and in which servitude and misery were soon seen to sprout out and grow with the fruits of the earth. [...]

For this reason the invention of other arts must have been necessary to oblige mankind to apply to that of agriculture. As soon as men were wanted to fuse and forge iron, others were wanted to maintain them. The more hands were employed in manufactures, the fewer hands were left to provide subsistence for all, though the number of mouths to be supplied with food continued the same. And as some required commodities in exchange for their iron, the rest at last found out the method of making iron subservient to the multiplication of commodities. Hence on the one hand husbandry and agriculture, and on the other the art of working metals and of multiplying the uses of them.

To the tilling of the earth the distribution of it necessarily succeeded, and to property once acknowledged, the first rules of justice: for to secure every man his own, every man must have something. Moreover, as men began to extend their views to futurity, and all found themselves in possession of more or less goods capable of being lost, everyone in particular had reason to fear lest reprisals should be made on him for any injury he might do to others. This origin is so much the more natural, as it is impossible to conceive how property can flow from any other source but industry; for what can a man add but his labour to things which he has not made, in order to acquire a property in them? It is the labour of the hands alone which, giving the husbandman a title to the produce of the land he has tilled gives him a title to the land itself, at least till he has gathered in the fruits of it, and so on from year to year; and this enjoyment forming a continued possession is easily transformed into a property. [...]

Things thus circumstanced might have remained equal, if men's talents had been equal, and if, for instance, the use of iron, and the consumption of commodities had always held an exact proportion to each other. But as this proportion had no support, it was soon broken. The man that had most strength performed most labour, the most dexterous turned his labour to best account, the most ingenious found out methods of lessening his labour, the husbandman required more iron, or the smith more corn, and while both worked equally, one earned a great deal by his labour while the other could scarce live by his. It is thus that natural inequality insensibly unfolds itself with that arising from a variety of combinations, and that the difference among men, developed by the difference of their circumstances becomes more sensible, more permanent in its effects, and begins to influence in the same proportion the condition of private persons.

Things once arrived at this period, it is an easy matter to imagine the rest. I shall not stop to describe the successive inventions of other arts, the progress of language, the trial and employments of talents, the inequality of fortunes, the use or abuse of riches, nor all the details which follow these, and which everyone may easily supply. I shall just give a glance at mankind placed in this new order of things.

Behold then all our faculties developed, our memory and imagination at work, self-love interested, reason rendered active, and the mind almost arrived at the utmost bounds of that perfection it is capable of. Behold all our natural qualities put in motion, the rank and condition of every man established, not only as to the quantum of property and the power of serving or hurting others, but likewise as to genius, beauty, strength or address, merit or talents; and as these were the only qualities which could command respect, it was found necessary to have or at least to affect them. It was requisite for men to be thought what they really were not. To be and to appear became two very different things, and from this distinction sprang pomp and knavery and all the vices which form their train. On the other hand, man, heretofore free and independent, was now in consequence of a multitude of new wants brought under subjection, as it were, to all nature, and especially to his fellows, whose slave in some sense he became even by becoming their master. If rich, he stood in need of their services, if poor, of their assistance; even mediocrity itself could not enable him to do without them. He must therefore have been continually at work to interest them in his happiness, and make them, if not really, at least apparently find their advantage in labouring for his. This rendered him sly and artful in his dealings with some, imperious and cruel in his dealings with others, and laid him under the necessity of using ill all those whom he stood in need of, as often as he could not awe them into a compliance with his will, and did not find it his interest to purchase it at the expense of real services. In fine, an insatiable ambition, the rage of raising their relative fortunes, not so much through real necessity, as to over-top others, inspire all men with a wicked inclination to injure each other, and with a secret jealousy so much the more dangerous, as to carry its point with the greater security, it often puts on the face of benevolence. [...]

Mary Astell, from *Some Reflections upon Marriage*

Men may be very happy in a married state; it is their own fault if they are at any time otherwise. The wise institutor of matrimony never did anything in vain; we are the sots and fools if what he designed for our good, be to us an occasion of falling. For marriage, notwithstanding all the loose talk of the town, the satires of ancient or modern pretenders to wit, will never lose its due praise from judicious persons. Though much may be said against this or that match, though the ridiculousness of some, the wickedness of others and imprudence of too many, too often provoke our wonder or scorn, our indignation or pity, yet marriage in general is too sacred to be treated with disrespect, too venerable to be the subject of raillery and buffoonery. It is the institution of Heaven, the only honourable way of continuing mankind, and far be it from us to think there could have been a better than infinite wisdom has found out for us.

But upon what are the satires against marriage grounded? Not upon the state itself, if they are just, but upon the ill choice, or the foolish conduct of those who are in it, and what has marriage, considered in itself, to do with these? Let every man bear his own burden: If through inordinate passion, rashness, humour, pride, covetousness, or any the like folly, a man makes an imprudent choice, why should marriage be exclaimed against? Let him blame himself for entering into an unequal yoke, and making choice of one who perhaps may prove a burden, a disgrace and plague, instead of a help and comfort to him. Could there be no such thing as an happy marriage, arguments against marriage would hold good, but since the thing is not only possible, but even very probable, provided we take but competent care, act like wise men and Christians, and acquit ourselves as we ought, all we have to say against it serves only to show the levity or impiety of our own minds; we only make some flourishes of wit, though scarcely without injustice; and though we talk prettily it is but very little to the purpose.

Is it the being tied to *one* that offends us? Why this ought rather to recommend marriage to us, and would really do so, were we guided by reason, and not by humour or brutish passion. He who does not make friendship the chief inducement to his choice, and prefer it before any other consideration, does not deserve a good wife, and therefore should not complain if he goes without one. Now we can never grow weary of our friends; the longer we have had them the more they are endeared to us; and if we have one well assured, we need seek no further but are sufficiently happy in her. The love of variety in this and in other cases, shows only the ill temper of our own minds, in that we seek for settled happiness in this present world where it is not to be found, instead of being content with a competent share, cheerfully enjoying and being thankful for the good that is afforded us, and patiently bearing with the inconveniences that attend it.

The Christian institution of marriage provides the best that may be for domestic quiet and content, and for the education of children; so that if we were not under the tie of religion, even the good of society and civil duty would oblige us to what that requires at our hands. And since the very best of us are but poor, frail creatures, full of ignorance and infirmity, so that in justice we ought to tolerate each other, and exercise that patience towards our companions today, which we shall give them occasion to show towards us tomorrow, the more we are accustomed to anyone's conversation, the better shall we understand their humour, be more able to comply with their weakness and be less offended at it. For he who would have everyone submit to his humours and will not in his turn comply with them, though we should suppose him always in the right, whereas a man of this temper very seldom is so, he's not fit for a husband, scarcely fit for society, but ought to be turned out of the herd to live by himself.

There may indeed be inconveniencies in a married life, but is there any condition without them? And he who lives single that he may indulge licentiousness and give up himself to the conduct of wild and ungoverned desires, or indeed out of any other inducement than the glory of God and the good of his soul, through the prospect he has of doing more good, or because his frame and disposition of mind are fitted for it, may rail as he pleases against matrimony, but can never justify his own conduct, nor clear it from the imputation of wickedness and folly.

But if marriage be such a blessed state how comes it, may you say, that there are so few happy marriages? Now in answer to this, it is not to be wondered that so few succeed, we should rather be surprised to find so many do, considering how imprudently men engage, the motives they act by, and the very strange conduct they observe throughout.

For pray, what do men propose to themselves in marriage? What qualifications do they look after in a spouse? What will she bring is the first enquiry? How many acres? Or how much ready coin? Not that this is altogether an unnecessary question, for marriage without a competency, that is, not only a bare subsistence but even a handsome and plentiful provision, according to the quality and circumstances of the parties, is no very comfortable condition. They who marry for love as they call it, find time enough to repent of their rash folly, and are not long in being convinced that whatever fine speeches might be made in the heat of passion, there could be no *real kindness* between those who can agree to make each other miserable. But as an estate is to be considered, so it should not be the *main*, much less the *only* consideration, for happiness does not depend on wealth, *that* may be wanting, and too often is, where *this* abounds. He who marries himself to a fortune only, must expect no other satisfaction than that can bring him, but let him not say that marriage, but that his own covetous or prodigal temper, has made him unhappy. What joy has that man in all his plenty, who must either run from home to possess it, contrary to all the rules of justice, to the laws of God and man, nay, even in opposition to good nature, and good breeding too, which some men make more account of than all the rest; or else be forced to share it with a woman whose person or temper is disagreeable, whose presence is sufficient to sour all his enjoyments of religion or good manners, he must suffer the uneasiness of a continual watch, to force himself to a constrained civility!

Few men have so much goodness as to bring themselves to a liking of what they loathed, merely because it is their duty to like; on the contrary, when they marry with an indifference to please their friends or increase their fortune, the indifference proceeds to an aversion, and perhaps even the kindness and complaisance of the poor abused wife shall only serve to increase it. What follows then? There is no content at home, so it is sought elsewhere, and the fortune so unjustly got, is as carelessly squandered. The man takes a loose,[5] what should hinder him? He has all in his hands, and custom has almost taken off that small restraint reputation used to lay. The wife finds too late what was the idol the man adored, which her vanity perhaps, or it may be the commands and importunities of relations, would not let her see before; and now he has got that into his possession, she must make court to him for a little sorry alimony out

5 [That is, he acts without any inhibitions.]

of her own estate. If discretion and piety prevails upon her passions she sits down quietly, contented with her lot, seeks no consolation in the multitude of adorers, since he whom only she desired to please, because it was her duty to do so, will take no delight in her wit or beauty: she follows no diversion to allay her grief, uses no cordials to support her spirit, that may sully her virtue or bring a cloud upon her reputation, she makes no appeals to the mis-judging crowd, hardly mentions her misfortunes to her most intimate acquaintance, nor lays a load on her husband to ease her self, but would if it were possible conceal his crimes, though her prudence and virtue give him a thousand reproaches without her intention or knowledge; and retiring from the world, she seeks a more solid comfort than it can give her, taking care to do nothing that censoriousness or even malice itself can misconstrue to her prejudice. Now she puts on all her reserves, and thinks even innocent liberties scarcely allowable in her disconsolate state; she has other business to mind: nor does she in her retirements reflect so much upon the hand that administers this bitter cup, as consider what is the best use she can make of it. And thus indeed marriage, however unfortunate in other respects, becomes a very great blessing to her. She might have been exposed to all the temptations of a plentiful fortune, have given up herself to sloth and luxury, and gone on at the common rate even of the better sort, in doing no hurt, and as little good: but now her kind husband obliges her to *consider*, and gives opportunity to exercise her virtue; he makes it necessary to withdraw from those gaieties and pleasures of life, which do more mischief under the show of innocence, than they could if they appeared attended with a crime, discomposing and dissolving the mind, and making it incapable of any manner of good, to be sure of anything great and excellent. Silence and solitude, the being forced from the ordinary entertainments of her station, may perhaps seem a desolate condition at first, and we may allow her, poor weak woman! to be somewhat shocked at it, since even a wise and courageous man perhaps would not keep his ground. We would conceal if we could for the honour of the sex, men's being baffled and dispirited by a smaller matter, were not the instances too frequent and too notorious.

But a little time wears off all the uneasiness, and puts her in possession of pleasures, which till now she has unkindly been kept a stranger to. Affliction, the sincerest friend, the frankest monitor, the best instructor, and indeed the only useful school that women are ever put to, rouses her understanding, opens her eyes, fixes her attention, and diffuses such a light, such a joy into her mind, as not only informs her better, but entertains her more than ever her *Ruel*[6] did though crowded by the men of wit. She now distinguishes between truth and appearances, between solid and apparent good; has found out the instability of all earthly things, and won't any more be deceived by relying on them; can discern who are the flatterers of her fortune, and who the admirers and encouragers of her virtue; accounting it no little blessing to be rid of those leeches, who only hung upon her for their own advantage. Now sober thoughts succeed to hurry and impertinence, to forms and ceremony, she can secure her time, and knows how to improve it; never truly a happy woman till she came in the eye of the world to be reckoned miserable.

Thus the husband's vices may become an occasion of the wife's virtues, and his neglect do her a more real good than his kindness could. But all injured wives don't behave themselves after this fashion, nor can their husbands justly expect it. With what face can he blame her for following his example, and being as extravagant on the one hand, as he is on the other? Though she cannot justify her excesses to God, to the world, nor to herself, yet surely in respect of him they may admit of an excuse. For to all the rest of his absurdities (for vice is always unreasonable) he adds one more, who expects that virtue from another which he won't practice himself. [...]

If therefore it is a woman's hard fate to meet with a disagreeable temper, and of all other the haughty, imperious and self-conceited are the most so, she is as unhappy as anything in this world can make her. For when a wife's temper does not please, if she makes her husband uneasy, he can find entertainments abroad, he has a hundred ways of relieving himself, but neither prudence nor duty will allow a woman to fly out, her business and entertainment are at home, though he makes it ever so uneasy to her she must be content and make her best of it. She who elects a monarch for life, who gives him an authority she cannot recall however he misapply it, who puts her fortune and person entirely in his power, nay even the very desires of her heart according to some learned casuists, so as that it is not lawful to will or desire anything but what he approves and allows, had need be very sure that she does not make a fool her head, nor a vicious man her guide and pattern; she had best stay till she can meet with one who has the government of his own passions, and has duly

6 [Possibly a reference to the Château de Ruel, a famous pleasure garden owned at one point by Cardinal Richelieu.]

regulated his own desires, since he is to have such an absolute power over hers. But he who dotes on a face, he who makes money his idol, he who is charmed with vain and empty wit, gives no such evidence, either of wisdom or goodness, that a woman of any tolerable sense should care to venture her self to his conduct.

Indeed, your fine gentleman's actions are nowadays such, that did not custom and the dignity of his sex give weight and authority to them, a woman that thinks twice might bless herself, and say, is this the lord and master to whom I am to promise love, honour and obedience? What can be the object of love but amiable qualities, the image of the Deity impressed upon a generous and God-like mind, a mind that is above this world, to be sure above all the vices, the tricks and baseness of it; a mind that is not full of itself, nor contracted to little private interests, but which in imitation of that glorious pattern it endeavours to copy after, expands and diffuses itself to its utmost capacity in doing good? But this fine gentleman is quite of another strain, he is the reverse of this in every instance. He is I confess very fond of his own dear person, he sees very much in it to admire; his air and mien, his words and actions, every motion he makes declares it; but they must have a judgment of his size, every whit as shallow, and a partiality as great as his own, who can be of his mind. How then can I love? And if not love, much less honour. Love may arise from pity or a generous desire to make that lovely which as yet is not so, when we see any hopes of success in our endeavours of improving it; but honour supposes some excellent qualities already, something worth our esteem, but alas there is nothing more contemptible than this trifle of a man, this mere outside, whose mind is as base and mean as his external pomp is glittering. His office or title apart, to which some ceremonious observance must be paid for order's sake, there's nothing in him that can command our respect. Strip him of equipage and fortune, and such things as only dazzle our eyes and imaginations but don't in any measure affect our reason, or cause a reverence in our hearts, and the poor creature sinks beneath our notice, because not supported by real worth. And if a woman can neither love nor honour, she does ill in promising to obey, since she is like to have but a crooked rule to regulate her actions.

A mere obedience, such as is paid only to authority, and not out of love and a sense of justice and reasonableness of the command, will be of an uncertain tenure. As it can't but be uneasy to the person who pays it, so he who receives it will be sometimes disappointed when he expects to find it; for that woman must be endowed with a wisdom and goodness much above what we suppose the sex capable of, I fear much greater than any man can pretend to, who can so constantly conquer her passions, and divest herself even of innocent self-love as to give up the cause when she is in the right, and to submit her enlightened reason to the imperious dictates of a blind will and wild imagination, even when she clearly perceives the ill consequences of it, the imprudence, nay folly and madness of such a conduct.

And if a woman runs such a risk when she marries prudently according to the opinion of the world, that is, when she permits herself to be disposed of to a man equal to her in birth, education and fortune, and as good as the most of his neighbours (for if none were to marry but men of strict virtue and honour, I doubt the world would be but thinly peopled) if at the very best her lot is hard, what can she expect who is sold, or any other wife betrayed into mercenary hands, to one who is in all, or most respects unequal to her? A lover who comes upon what is called equal terms, makes no very advantageous proposal to the lady he courts, and to whom he seems to be an humble servant. For under many founding compliments, words that have nothing in them, this is his true meaning, he wants one to manage his family, a house-keeper, a necessary evil, one whose interest it will be not to wrong him, and in whom therefore he can put greater confidence than in any he can hire for money. One who may breed his children, taking all the care and trouble of their education, to preserve his name and family. One whose beauty, wit, or good humour and agreeable conversation, will entertain him at home when he has been contradicted and disappointed abroad; who will do him that justice the ill-natured world denies him, that is, in anyone's language but his own, sooth his pride and flatter his vanity, by having always so much good sense as to be on his side, to conclude him in the right, when others are so ignorant or so rude as to deny it. Who will not be blind to his merit nor contradict his will and pleasure, but make it her business, her very ambition to content him; whose softness and gentle compliance will calm his passions, to whom he may safely disclose his troublesome thoughts, and in her breast discharge his cares; whose duty, submission, and observance, will heal those wounds other people's opposition or neglect have given him. In a word, one whom he can entirely govern, and consequently may form her to his will and liking, who must be his of life, and therefore cannot quit his service let him treat her how he will. [...]

It is the hardest thing in the world for a woman to know that a man is not mercenary, that he does not act on base and ungenerous principles, even when he is her equal, because being absolute master, she and all the grants he makes her are in his power, and there have been but too many instances of husbands that by wheedling or threatening their wives, by seeming kindness or cruel usage, have persuaded or forced them out of what has been settled on them. So that the woman has in truth no security but the man's honours and good nature, a security that in this present age no wise person would venture much upon. A man enters into articles very readily before marriage, and so he may, for he performs no more of them afterwards than he thinks fit. A wife must never dispute with her husband, his reasons are now no doubt on it better than hers, whatever they were before; he is sure to persuade her out of her agreement, and bring her, it must be supposed, willingly, to give up what she did vainly hope to obtain, and what she thought had been made sure to her. And if she shows any refractoriness, there are ways enough to humble her; so that by right or wrong the husband gains his will. For covenants betwixt husband and wife, like laws in an arbitrary government, are of little force, the will of the sovereign is all in all. Thus it is in matter of fact, I will not answer for the right of it; for if the woman's reasons upon which those agreements are grounded are not just and good, why did he consent to them? Was it because there was no other way to obtain his suit, and with an intention to annul them when it shall be in his power? Where then is his sincerity? But if her reasons are good, where is his justice in obliging her to quit them? He neither way acts like an equitable or honest man. [...]

But how can a man respect his wife when he has a contemptible opinion of her and her sex? When from his own elevation he looks down on them as void of understanding, and full of ignorance and passion, so that 'folly' and 'a woman' are equivalent terms with him? Can he think there is any gratitude due to her whose utmost services he exacts as strict duty? Because she was made to be a slave to his will, and has no higher end than to serve and obey him! Perhaps we arrogate too much to ourselves when we say this material world was made for our sakes; that its glorious maker has given us the use of it is certain, but when we suppose a thing to be made purely for our sakes, because we have dominion over it, we draw a false conclusion, as he who should say the people were made for the prince who is set over them, would be thought to be out of his senses as well as his politics. Yet even allowing that God who made everything in number, weight, and measure, who never acts but for some great and glorious end, an end agreeable to his majesty, allowing that he created such a number of rational spirits merely to serve their fellow creatures, yet how are these lords and masters helped by the contempt they show of their poor humble vassals? Is it not rather a hindrance to that service they expect, as being an undeniable and constant proof how unworthy they are to receive it?

None of God's creatures absolutely considered are in their own nature contemptible; the meanest fly, the poorest insect has its use and virtue. Contempt is scarcely a human passion, one may venture to say it was not in innocent man, for till sin came into the world, there was nothing in it to be condemned. But pride which makes everything serve its purposes, wrested this passion from its only use, so that instead of being an antidote against sin, it is become a grand promoter of it, nothing making us more worthy of that contempt we show, than when poor, weak, dependent creatures as we are, we look down with scorn and disdain on others.

There is not a surer sign of a noble mind, a mind very far advanced towards perfection, than being able to bear contempt and an unjust treatment from one's superiors evenly and patiently. For inward worth and real excellency are the true ground of superiority, and one person is not in reality better than another, but as he is more wise and good. But this world being a place of trial and governed by general laws, just retribution being reserved for hereafter, respect and obedience many times become due for order's sake to those who don't otherwise deserve them. Now though humility keeps us from over-valuing ourselves or viewing our merit through a false and magnifying *medium*, yet it does not put out our eyes; it does not, it ought not to deprive us of that pleasing sentiment which attends our acting as we ought to act, which is as it were a fore-taste of heaven, our present reward for doing what is just and fit. And when a superior does a mean and unjust thing, as all contempt of one's neighbour is, and yet this does not provoke his inferiors to refuse that observance which their stations in the world require, they cannot but have an inward sense of their own real superiority, the other having no pretense to it, at the same time that they pay him an outward respect and deference, which is such a flagrant testimony of the sincerest love of order as proves their souls to be of the highest and noble rank.

A man therefore for his own sake, and to give evidence that he has a right to those prerogatives he assumes, should treat women with a little more humanity and regard than is usually paid them. Your whiffling wits may scoff at them, and what then? It matters not, for they rally everything though ever so sacred, and rail at the women commonly in very good company. Religion, its priests, and those its most constant and regular professors, are the usual subjects of their manly, mannerly, and surprising jests. Surprising indeed! Not for the newness of the thought, the brightness of the fancy, or nobleness of expression, but for the good assurance with which such threadbare jests are again and again repeated. But that your grave dons, your learned men, and which is more, your men of sense as they would be thought, should stoop so low as to make invectives against the women, forget themselves so much as to jest with their slaves, who have neither liberty nor ingenuity to make reprisals! That they should waste their time, and debase their good sense, which fits them for the most weighty affairs, such as are suitable to their profound wisdoms and exalted understandings! To render those poor wretches more ridiculous and odious who are already in their opinion sufficiently contemptible, and find no better exercise of their wit and satire than such as are not worth their pains, though it were possible to reform them, this, this indeed may justly be wondered at! [...]

To wind up this matter, if a woman were duly principled and taught to know the world, especially the true sentiments that men have of her, and the traps they lay for her under so many gilded compliments, and such a seemingly great respect, that disgrace would be prevented which is brought upon too many families, women would marry more discreetly, and demean themselves better in a married state than some people say they do. The foundation indeed ought to be laid deep and strong, she should be made a good Christian, and understand why she is so, and then she will be everything else that is good. Men need keep no spies on a woman's conduct, need have no fear of her virtue, or so much as of her prudence and caution, were but a due sense of true honour and virtue awakened in her, were her reason excited and prepared to consider the sophistry of those temptations which would persuade her from her duty; and were she put in a way to know that it is both her wisdom and interest to observe it, she would then duly examine and weigh all the circumstances, the good and evil of a married state, and not be surprised with unforeseen inconveniences, and either never consent to be a wife, or make a good one when she does. This would show her what human nature *is*, as well as what it *ought to be*, and teach her not only what she may justly expect, but what she must be content with; would enable her to cure some faults, and patiently to suffer what she cannot cure.

Indeed nothing can assure obedience and render it what it ought to be, but the conscience of duty, the paying it for God's sake. Superiors don't rightly understand their own interest when they attempt to put out their subjects eyes to keep them obedient. A blind obedience is what a rational creature should never pay, nor would such a one receive it did he rightly understand its nature. For human actions are no otherwise valuable than as they are conformable to reason, but a blind obedience is an obeying *without reason*, for ought we know *against it*. God himself does not require our obedience at this rate, he lays before us the goodness and reasonableness of his laws, and were there anything in them whose equity we could not readily comprehend, yet we have this clear sufficient reason on which to found our obedience, that nothing but what's just and fit, can be enjoyed by a just, a wise, and gracious God, but this is a reason will never hold in respect of men's commands, unless they can prove themselves infallible, and consequently impeccable too. [...]

Again, it may be said, if a wife's case be as it is here represented, it is not good for a woman to marry and so there's an end of human race. But this is no fair consequence, for all that can justly be inferred from hence is that a woman has no mighty obligations to the man who makes love to her, she has no reason to be fond of being a wife, or to reckon it a piece of preferment when she is taken to be a man's upper-servant; it is no advantage to her in this world, if rightly managed it may prove one as to the next. For she who marries purely to do good, to educate souls for heaven, who can be so truly mortified as to lay aside her own will and desires to pay such an entire submission for life to one whom she cannot be sure will always deserve it, does certainly perform a more heroic action than all the famous masculine heroes can boast of, she suffers a continual martyrdom to bring glory to God and benefit to mankind, which consideration indeed may carry her through all difficulties, I know not what else can, and engage her to love him who proves perhaps so much worse than a brute, as to make this condition yet more grievous than it needed to be. She has need of a strong reason, of a truly Christian and well-tempered spirit, of all the assistance the best education can give her, and ought to have some good assurance of her own firmness and virtue, who ventures on such a trial; and for this reason it is less to be wondered at that women marry off in haste, for perhaps if they took time to consider and reflect upon it, they seldom would marry.

Unit III

THE WORST OF ALL POSSIBLE WORLDS: THE CHALLENGE OF PESSIMISM

Chapter 7

SCHOPENHAUER ON THE CASE FOR PESSIMISM

Introduction

IN THIS UNIT, WE TURN TO PHILOSOPHICAL PESSIMISM. The term 'pessimism' was deliberately coined as a counterpart to the term '*optimism*'—so, where the latter derives from *optimus*, meaning the best, so the former derives from *pessimus*, meaning the worst. As such, pessimism as a philosophical position denotes first and foremost the view that this world is the *worst* of all possible. However, pessimistic thinkers were not united in supporting this very strong claim. As we will see, some thought it sufficed to show that the world (or life within it) is, on the whole, bad; that is, that the balance of suffering and joy is tilted towards suffering, and so that non-existence was preferable to existence. Understood in these broader terms, a number of philosophers from previous chapters might be counted among pessimistic thinkers. Bayle, for instance, argued in favor of Xenophanes' claim that, on the whole, the bitters in life outweigh the sweets (and is followed by Hume in this); Kant also memorably claimed that no one would choose to live life again, in any form, testifying to its undesirability; and Rousseau contended that modern human beings are corrupted in their natures and in a state of utter servitude.

While these thinkers certainly stake out unhappy positions, their views do not constitute pessimistic outlooks, at least not by the standards of the philosophers we will turn to in this unit. For these thinkers, true pessimism consists not only in upholding the general undesirability of life but also in endorsing the following two claims. First, they contend that the badness of life is not a *contingent* matter, or something that holds only on the whole or for the most part; rather, that life is bad, that suffering prevails over happiness, that existence is undesirable altogether, is something that holds with metaphysical certainty and for every human being. Second, the terribleness of existence is not something that we can escape from (at least not for more than a few moments), nor is it mitigated by any other redemptive possibility, such as the possibility of a better political order or of an afterlife, such as that in the Christian picture, where the just who suffer in this life find their reward (and the vicious who prosper suffer the wages of sin).

The first philosopher to argue systematically for the truth of pessimism was the nineteenth-century German philosopher Arthur Schopenhauer (1788–1860). He does this in his *magnum opus*, *Die Welt als Wille und Vorstellung* (*The World as Will and Representation*), which he published originally in 1818, and then supplemented with a second volume in 1844. In this work, Schopenhauer elaborates a complete philosophical outlook, including a distinctive metaphysical view (informed by Kant and Plato but also by non-Western philosophical traditions), a novel ethical perspective, and an innovative aesthetic theory (which will be taken up in Chapter 9). But Schopenhauer's philosophy is informed by, and in the service of, his broader pessimism, and his arguments for this are presented in the selections of this chapter. Schopenhauer offers two sorts of arguments for his pessimism: *a priori*, or on the basis of purely conceptual considerations, and *a posteriori*, or on the basis of what we know of the world through experience. There are two *a priori* arguments contained in §§57–58 in the first volume, and these turn on the claim that suffering is essential to life and on Schopenhauer's "negative" conception of pleasure or satisfaction, respectively; the *a posteriori* argument, which simply relies upon our direct and indirect knowledge of the miseries of existence to support the claim that life is suffering, follows in §59. Schopenhauer would later add to these his notorious argument that this is, in fact, the "worst of all possible worlds" in §46 of the second volume of his work.

Arthur Schopenhauer, from *The World as Will and Representation*, Volume I

§57. At every grade that is enlightened by knowledge, the will appears as an individual. The human individual finds himself as finite in infinite space and time, and consequently as a vanishing quantity compared with them. He is projected into them, and, on account of their unlimited nature, he has always a merely relative, never an absolute when and where of his existence; for his place and duration are finite parts of what is infinite and boundless. His real existence is only in the present, whose unchecked flight into the past is a constant transition into death, a constant dying. For his past life, apart from its possible consequences for the present, and the testimony regarding the will that is expressed in it, is now entirely done with, dead, and no longer anything; and, therefore, it must be, as a matter of reason, indifferent to him whether the content of that past was pain or pleasure. But the present is always passing through his hands into the past; the future is quite uncertain and always short. Thus his existence, even when we consider only its formal side, is a constant hurrying of the present into the dead past, a constant dying. But if we look at it from the physical side, it is clear that, as our walking is admittedly merely a constantly prevented falling, the life of our body is only a constantly prevented dying, an ever-postponed death; finally, in the same way, the activity of our mind is a constantly deferred *ennui*. Every breath we draw wards off the death that is constantly intruding upon us. In this way we fight with it every moment, and again, at longer intervals, through every meal we eat, every sleep we take, every time we warm ourselves, etc. In the end, death must conquer, for we became subject to him through birth, and he only plays for a little while with his prey before he swallows it up. We pursue our life, however, with great interest and much solicitude as long as possible, as we blow out a soap-bubble as long and as large as possible, although we know perfectly well that it will burst.

We saw that the inner being of unconscious nature is a constant striving without end and without rest. And this appears to us much more distinctly when we consider the nature of brutes and man. Willing and striving is its whole being, which may be very well compared to an unquenchable thirst. But the basis of all willing is need, deficiency, and thus pain. Consequently, the nature of brutes and man is subject to pain originally and through its very being. If, on the other hand, it lacks objects of desire, because it is at once deprived of them by a too easy satisfaction, a terrible void and *ennui* comes over it, i.e., its being and existence itself becomes an unbearable burden to it. Thus its life swings like a pendulum backwards and forwards between pain and *ennui*. This has also had to express itself very oddly in this way; after man had transferred all pain and torments to hell, there then remained nothing over for heaven but *ennui*.

But the constant striving which constitutes the inner nature of every manifestation of will obtains its primary and most general foundation at the higher grades of objectification, from the fact that here the will manifests itself as a living body, with the iron command to nourish it; and what gives strength to this command is just that this body is nothing but the objectified will to live itself. Man, as the most complete objectification of that will, is in like measure also the most necessitous of all beings: he is through and through concrete willing and needing; he is a concretion of a thousand necessities. With these he stands upon the earth, left to himself, uncertain about everything except his own need and misery. Consequently the care for the maintenance of that existence under exacting demands, which are renewed every day, occupies, as a rule, the whole of human life. To this is directly related the second claim, that of the propagation of the species. At the same time he is threatened from all sides by the most different kinds of dangers, from which it requires constant watchfulness to escape. With cautious steps and casting anxious glances round him he pursues his path, for a thousand accidents and a thousand enemies lie in wait for him. Thus he went while yet a savage, thus he goes in civilised life; there is no security for him. [...] The life of the great majority is only a constant struggle for this existence itself, with the certainty of losing it at last. But what enables them to endure this wearisome battle is not so much the love of life as the fear of death, which yet stands in the background as inevitable, and may come upon them at any moment. Life itself is a sea, full of rocks and whirlpools, which man avoids with the greatest care and solicitude, although he knows that even if he succeeds in getting through with all his efforts and skill, he yet by doing so comes nearer at every step to the greatest, the total, inevitable, and irremediable shipwreck, death; nay, even steers right upon it: this is the final goal of the laborious voyage, and worse for him than all the rocks from which he has escaped.

Now it is well worth observing that, on the one hand, the suffering and misery of life may easily increase to such an extent that death itself, in the flight from which the whole of life consists, becomes desirable, and we hasten towards it voluntarily; and again, on the other hand, that as soon as want and suffering permit rest to a man, *ennui* is at once so near that he necessarily requires diversion. The striving after existence is what occupies all living things and maintains them in motion. But when existence is assured, then they know not what to do with it; thus the second thing that sets them in motion is the effort to get free from the burden of existence, to make it cease to be felt, "to kill time," i.e., to escape from *ennui*. Accordingly we see that almost all men who are secure from want and care, now that at last they have thrown off all other burdens, become a burden to themselves, and regard as a gain every hour they succeed in getting through, and thus every diminution of the very life which, until then, they have employed all their powers to maintain as long as possible. *Ennui* is by no means an evil to be lightly esteemed; in the end it depicts on the countenance real despair. It makes beings who love each other so little as men do, seek each other eagerly, and thus becomes the source of social intercourse. Moreover, even from motives of policy, public precautions are everywhere taken against it, as against other universal calamities. For this evil may drive men to the greatest excesses, just as much as its opposite extreme, famine: the people require *panem et circenses*.[1] The strict penitentiary system of Philadelphia makes use of *ennui* alone as a means of punishment, through solitary confinement and idleness, and it is found so terrible that it has even led prisoners to commit suicide. As want is the constant scourge of the people, so *ennui* is that of the fashionable world. In middle-class life *ennui* is represented by the Sunday, and want by the six week-days.

Thus between desiring and attaining all human life flows on throughout. The wish is, in its nature, pain; the attainment soon begets satiety: the end was only apparent; possession takes away the charm; the wish, the need, presents itself under a new form; when it does not, then follows desolateness, emptiness, *ennui*, against which the conflict is just as painful as against want. That wish and satisfaction should follow each other neither too quickly nor too slowly reduces the suffering, which both occasion to the smallest amount, and constitutes the happiest life. For that which we might otherwise call the most beautiful part of life,

1 [Bread and circuses (Latin), or superficial amusements.]

its purest joy, if it were only because it lifts us out of real existence and transforms us into disinterested spectators of it—that is, pure knowledge, which is foreign to all willing, the pleasure of the beautiful, the true delight in art—this is granted only to a very few, because it demands rare talents, and to these few only as a passing dream. And then, even these few, on account of their higher intellectual power, are made susceptible of far greater suffering than duller minds can ever feel, and are also placed in lonely isolation by a nature which is obviously different from that of others; thus here also accounts are squared. [...]

The ceaseless efforts to banish suffering accomplish no more than to make it change its form. It is essentially deficiency, want, care for the maintenance of life. If we succeed, which is very difficult, in removing pain in this form, it immediately assumes a thousand others, varying according to age and circumstances, such as lust, passionate love, jealousy, envy, hatred, anxiety, ambition, covetousness, sickness, etc., etc. If at last it can find entrance in no other form, it comes in the sad, grey garments of tediousness and *ennui*, against which we then strive in various ways. If finally we succeed in driving this away, we shall hardly do so without letting pain enter in one of its earlier forms, and the dance begin again from the beginning; for all human life is tossed backwards and forwards between pain and *ennui*. Depressing as this view of life is, I will draw attention, by the way, to an aspect of it from which consolation may be drawn, and perhaps even a stoical indifference to one's own present ills may be attained. For our impatience at these arises for the most part from the fact that we regard them as brought about by a chain of causes which might easily be different. We do not generally grieve over ills which are directly necessary and quite universal; for example, the necessity of age and of death, and many daily inconveniences. It is rather the consideration of the accidental nature of the circumstances that brought some sorrow just to us, that gives it its sting. But if we have recognised that pain, as such, is inevitable and essential to life, and that nothing depends upon chance but its mere fashion, the form under which it presents itself, that thus our present sorrow fills a place that, without it, would at once be occupied by another which now is excluded by it, and that therefore fate can affect us little in what is essential; such a reflection, if it were to become a living conviction, might produce a considerable degree of stoical equanimity, and very much lessen the anxious care for our own well-being. But, in fact, such a powerful control of reason over directly felt suffering seldom or never occurs. [...]

For the most part, however, we close our minds against the knowledge, which may be compared to a bitter medicine, that suffering is essential to life, and therefore does not flow in upon us from without, but that everyone carries about with him its perennial source in his own heart. We rather seek constantly for an external particular cause, as it were, a pretext for the pain which never leaves us, just as the free man makes himself an idol, in order to have a master. For we unweariedly strive from wish to wish; and although every satisfaction, however much it promised, when attained fails to satisfy us, but for the most part comes presently to be an error of which we are ashamed, yet we do not see that we draw water with the sieve of the Danaides, but ever hasten to new desires. [...] Thus it either goes on forever, or, what is more rare and presupposes a certain strength of character, until we reach a wish which is not satisfied and yet cannot be given up. In that case we have, as it were, found what we sought, something that we can always blame, instead of our own nature, as the source of our suffering. And thus, although we are now at variance with our fate, we are reconciled to our existence, for the knowledge is again put far from us that suffering is essential to this existence itself, and true satisfaction impossible. The result of this form of development is a somewhat melancholy disposition, the constant endurance of a single great pain, and the contempt for all lesser sorrows or joys that proceeds from it; consequently an already nobler phenomenon than that constant seizing upon ever-new forms of illusion, which is much more common.

§58. All satisfaction, or what is commonly called happiness, is always really and essentially only negative, and never positive. It is not an original gratification coming to us of itself, but must always be the satisfaction of a wish. The wish, i.e., some want, is the condition which precedes every pleasure. But with the satisfaction the wish and therefore the pleasure cease. Thus the satisfaction or the pleasing can never be more than the deliverance from a pain, from a want; for such is not only every actual, open sorrow, but every desire, the importunity of which disturbs our peace, and, indeed, the deadening *ennui* also that makes life a burden to us. It is, however, so hard to attain or achieve anything; difficulties and troubles without end are opposed to every purpose, and at every step hindrances accumulate. But when finally everything is overcome and attained, nothing can ever be gained but deliverance from some sorrow or desire, so that we find ourselves just in the same position as we occupied before this sorrow or desire appeared. All that is even directly given us is merely the want, i.e., the pain. The satisfaction and the pleasure we can only know indirectly through the remembrance of the preceding suffering and want, which ceases with its appearance. Hence it arises that we are not properly conscious of the blessings and advantages we actually possess, nor do we prize them, but think of them merely as a matter of course, for they gratify us only negatively by restraining suffering. Only when we have lost them do we become sensible of their value; for the want, the privation, the sorrow, is the positive, communicating itself directly to us. Thus also we are pleased by the remembrance of past need, sickness, want, and such like, because this is the only means of enjoying the present blessings. [...]

That all happiness is only of a negative not a positive nature, that just on this account it cannot be lasting satisfaction and gratification, but merely delivers us from some pain or want which must be followed either by a new pain, or by languor, empty longing, and *ennui*; this finds support in art, that true mirror of the world and life, and especially in poetry. Every epic and dramatic poem can only represent a struggle, an effort, and fight for happiness, never enduring and complete happiness itself. It conducts its heroes through a thousand difficulties and dangers to the goal; as soon as this is reached, it hastens to let the curtain fall; for now there would remain nothing for it to do but to show that the glittering goal in which the hero expected to find happiness had only disappointed him, and that after its attainment he was no better off than before. Because a genuine enduring happiness is not possible, it cannot be the subject of art. [...]

It is really incredible how meaningless and void of significance when looked at from without, how dull and unenlightened by intellect when felt from within, is the course of the life of the great majority of men. It is a weary longing and complaining, a dreamlike staggering through the four ages of life to death, accompanied by a series of trivial thoughts. Such men are like clockwork, which is wound up and goes it knows not why; and every time a man is begotten and born, the clock of human life is wound up anew, to repeat the same old piece it has played innumerable times before, passage after passage, measure after measure, with insignificant variations. Every individual, every human being and his course of life, is but another short dream of the endless spirit of nature, of the persistent will to live; is only another fleeting form, which it carelessly sketches on its infinite page, space and time; allows to remain for a time so short that it vanishes into nothing in comparison with these, and then obliterates to make new room. And yet, and here lies the serious side of life, everyone of these fleeting forms, these empty fancies, must be paid for by the whole will to live, in all its activity, with many and deep sufferings, and finally with a bitter death, long feared and coming at last. This is why the sight of a corpse makes us suddenly so serious.

The life of every individual, if we survey it as a whole and in general, and only lay stress upon its most significant features, is really always a tragedy, but gone through in detail, it has the character of a comedy. For the deeds and vexations of the day, the restless irritation of the moment, the desires and fears of the week, the mishaps of every hour, are all through chance, which is ever bent upon some jest, scenes of a comedy. But the never-satisfied wishes, the frustrated efforts, the hopes unmercifully crushed by fate, the unfortunate errors of the whole life, with increasing suffering and death at the end, are always a tragedy. Thus, as if fate would add derision to the misery of our existence, our life must contain all the woes of tragedy, and yet we cannot even assert the dignity of tragic characters, but in the broad detail of life must inevitably be the foolish characters of a comedy.

But however much great and small trials may fill human life, they are not able to conceal its insufficiency to satisfy the spirit; they cannot hide the emptiness and superficiality of existence, nor exclude *ennui*, which is always ready to fill up every pause that care may allow. Hence it arises that the human mind, not content with the cares, anxieties, and occupations which the actual world lays upon it, creates for itself an imaginary world also in the form of a thousand different superstitions, then finds all manner of employment with this, and wastes time and strength upon it, as soon as the real world is willing to grant it the rest which it is quite incapable of enjoying. This is accordingly most markedly the case with nations for which life is made easy by the congenial nature of the climate and the soil, most of all with the Hindus, then with the Greeks, the Romans, and later with the Italians, the Spaniards, etc. Demons, gods, and saints man creates in his own image; and to them he must then unceasingly bring offerings, prayers, temple decorations, vows and their fulfilment, pilgrimages, salutations, ornaments for their images, etc. Their service mingles everywhere with the real, and, indeed, obscures it. Every event of life is regarded as the work of these beings; the intercourse with them occupies half the time of life, constantly sustains hope, and by the charm of illusion often becomes more interesting than intercourse with real beings. It is the expression and symptom of the actual need of mankind, partly for help and support, partly for occupation and diversion; and if it often works in direct opposition to the first need because, when accidents and dangers arise, valuable time and strength, instead of being directed to warding them off, are uselessly wasted on prayers and offerings; it serves the second end all the better by this imaginary converse with a visionary spirit world, and this is the by no means contemptible gain of all superstitions.

§ 59. If we have so far convinced ourselves *a priori*, by the most general consideration, by investigation of the primary and elemental features of human life, that in its whole plan it is capable of no true blessedness, but is in its very nature suffering in various forms, and throughout a state of misery, we might now awaken this conviction much more vividly within us if, proceeding more *a posteriori*, we were to turn to more definite instances, call up pictures to the fancy, and illustrate by examples the unspeakable misery which experience and history present, wherever one may look and in whatever direction one may seek. But the chapter would have no end, and would carry us far from the standpoint of the universal, which is essential to philosophy; and, moreover, such a description might easily be taken for a mere declamation on human misery, such as has often been given, and, as such, might be charged with one-sidedness, because it started from particular facts. From such a reproach and suspicion our perfectly cold and philosophical investigation of the inevitable suffering which is founded in the nature of life is free, for it starts from the universal and is conducted *a priori*. But confirmation *a posteriori* is everywhere easily obtained. Everyone who has awakened from the first dream of youth, who has considered his own experience and that of others, who has studied himself in life, in the history of the past and of his own time, and finally in the works of the great poets, will, if his judgment is not paralysed by some indelibly imprinted prejudice, certainly arrive at the conclusion that this human world is the kingdom of chance and error, which rule without mercy in great things and in small, and along with which folly and wickedness also wield the scourge. Hence it arises that everything better only struggles through with difficulty; what is noble and wise seldom attains to expression, becomes effective and claims attention, but the absurd and the perverse in the sphere of thought, the dull and tasteless in the sphere of art, the wicked and deceitful in the sphere of action, really assert a supremacy, only disturbed by short interruptions. On the other hand, everything that is excellent is always a mere exception, one case in millions, and therefore, if it presents itself in a lasting work, this, when it has outlived the enmity of its contemporaries, exists in isolation, is preserved like a meteoric stone, sprung from an order of things different from that which prevails here. But as far as the life of the individual is concerned, every biography is the history of suffering, for every life is, as a rule, a continual series of great and small misfortunes, which each one conceals as much as possible, because he knows that others can seldom feel sympathy or compassion, but almost always satisfaction at the sight of the woes from which they are themselves for the moment exempt. But perhaps at the end of life, if a man is sincere and in full possession of his faculties, he will never wish to have it to live over again, but rather than this, he will much prefer absolute annihilation. The essential content of the famous soliloquy in *Hamlet* is briefly this: our state is so wretched that absolute annihilation would be decidedly preferable. If suicide really offered us this, so that the alternative "to be or not to be," in the full sense of the word, was placed before us, then it would be unconditionally to be chosen as "a consummation devoutly to be wished." But there is something in us which tells us that this is not the case: suicide is not the end; death is not absolute annihilation. In like manner, what was said by the father of history has not since him been contradicted, that no man has ever lived who has not wished more than once that he had not to live the following day.[2] According to this, the brevity of life, which is so constantly lamented, may be the best quality it possesses. If, finally, we should bring clearly to a man's sight the terrible sufferings and miseries to which his life is constantly exposed, he would be seized with horror; and if we were to conduct the confirmed optimist through the hospitals, infirmaries, and surgical operating-rooms, through the prisons, torture-chambers, and slave-kennels, over battlefields and places of execution; if we were to open to him all the dark abodes of misery, where it hides itself from the glance of cold curiosity, and, finally, allow him to glance into the starving dungeon of Ugolino, he, too, would understand at last the nature of this "best of possible worlds." For whence did Dante

2 [Herodotus (c. 484–c. 425), often called the father of history due to his *Histories*. The quote referenced here is taken from book VII, chapter 46.]

take the materials for his hell but from this our actual world?[3] And yet he made a very proper hell of it. And when, on the other hand, he came to the task of describing heaven and its delights, he had an insurmountable difficulty before him, for our world affords no materials at all for this. Therefore there remained nothing for him to do but, instead of describing the joys of paradise, to repeat to us the instruction given him there by his ancestor, by Beatrice,[4] and by various saints. But from this it is sufficiently clear what manner of world it is. Certainly human life, like all bad ware, is covered over with a false lustre: what suffers always conceals itself; on the other hand, whatever pomp or splendour anyone can get, he makes a show of openly, and the more inner contentment deserts him, the more he desires to exist as fortunate in the opinion of others: to such an extent does folly go, and the opinion of others is a chief aim of the efforts of everyone, although the utter nothingness of it is expressed in the fact that in almost all languages vanity, *vanitas*, originally signifies emptiness and nothingness. But under all this false show, the miseries of life can so increase—and this happens every day—that the death which hitherto has been feared above all things is eagerly seized upon. Indeed, if fate will show its whole malice, even this refuge is denied to the sufferer, and, in the hands of enraged enemies, he may remain exposed to terrible and slow tortures without remedy. In vain the sufferer then calls on his gods for help; he remains exposed to his fate without grace. [...] For the rest, I cannot here avoid the statement that, to me, optimism, when it is not merely the thoughtless talk of such as harbour nothing but words under their low foreheads, appears not merely as an absurd, but also as a really wicked way of thinking, as a bitter mockery of the unspeakable suffering of humanity. Let no one think that Christianity is favourable to optimism; for, on the contrary, in the Gospels world and evil are used as almost synonymous.

---

3 [A reference to the Inferno of the *Divine Comedy* by Dante Alighieri (1265–1321). Ugolino della Gherardesca (c. 1214–89) was a nobleman of Pisa who allegedly betrayed his town, for which he was condemned and died of starvation along with his children in a dungeon. Dante depicts him in the ninth circle of hell, reserved for the treasonous.]

4 [Beatrice Portinari (1265–90) was Dante's muse and likely the inspiration for the Beatrice in Dante's poem.]

Arthur Schopenhauer, from *The World as Will and Representation*, Volume II

§46. (*On the Vanity and Suffering of Life.*) Awakened to life out of the night of unconsciousness, the will finds itself an individual in an endless and boundless world, among innumerable individuals, all striving, suffering, erring; and as if through a troubled dream it hurries back to its old unconsciousness. Yet until then its desires are limitless, its claims inexhaustible, and every satisfied desire gives rise to a new one. No possible satisfaction in the world could suffice to still its longings, set a goal to its infinite cravings, and fill the bottomless abyss of its heart. Then let one consider what as a rule are the satisfactions of any kind that a man obtains. For the most part nothing more than the bare maintenance of this existence itself, extorted day by day with unceasing trouble and constant care in the conflict with want, and with death in prospect. Everything in life shows that earthly happiness is destined to be frustrated or recognised as an illusion. The grounds of this lie deep in the nature of things. Accordingly the life of most men is troubled and short. Those who are comparatively happy are so, for the most part, only apparently, or else, like men of long life, they are the rare exceptions, a possibility of which there had to be—as decoy-birds. Life presents itself as a continual deception in small things as in great. If it has promised, it does not keep its word, unless to show how little worth desiring were the things desired: thus we are deluded now by hope, now by what was hoped for. If it has given, it did so in order to take. The enchantment of distance shows us paradises which vanish like optical illusions when we have allowed ourselves to be mocked by them. Happiness accordingly always lies in the future, or else in the past, and the present may be compared to a small dark cloud which the wind drives over the sunny plain before and behind it all is bright, only it itself always casts a shadow. The present is therefore always insufficient; but the future is uncertain, and the past irrevocable. Life with its hourly, daily, weekly, yearly, little, greater, and great misfortunes, with its deluded hopes and its accidents destroying all our calculations, bears so distinctly the impression of something with which we must become disgusted, that it is hard to conceive how one has been able to mistake this and allow oneself to be persuaded that life is there in order to be thankfully enjoyed, and that man exists in order to be happy. Rather that continual illusion and disillusion, and also the nature of life throughout, presents itself to us as intended and calculated to awaken the conviction that nothing at all is worth our striving, our efforts and struggles, that all good things are vanity, the world in all its ends bankrupt, and life a business which does not cover its expenses; so that our will may turn away from it. [...]

We shall, however, enter into the details of the matter, for it is in these views that I have met with most contradiction. First of all, I have to confirm by the following remarks the proof given in [§58, above] of the negative nature of all satisfaction, thus of all pleasure and all happiness, in opposition to the positive nature of pain. We feel pain, but not painlessness; we feel care, but not the absence of care; fear, but not security. We feel the wish as we feel hunger and thirst; but as soon as it has been fulfilled, it is like the mouthful that has been taken, which ceases to exist for our feeling the moment it is swallowed. Pleasures and joys we miss painfully whenever they are wanting; but pains, even when they cease after having long been present, are not directly missed, but at most are intentionally thought of by means of reflection. For only pain and want can be felt positively, and therefore announce themselves; well-being, on the other hand, is merely negative. Therefore we do not become conscious of the three greatest blessings of life—health, youth, and freedom—so long as we possess them, but only after we have lost them, for they also are negations. We only observe that days of our life were happy after they have given place to unhappy ones. In proportion as pleasures increase, the susceptibility for them decreases; what is customary is no longer felt as a pleasure. Just in this way, however, is the susceptibility for suffering increased, for the loss of what we are accustomed to is painfully felt. Thus the measure of what is necessary increases through possession, and thereby the capacity for feeling pain. The hours pass the quicker the more agreeably they are spent, and the slower the more painfully they are spent; because pain, not pleasure, is the positive, the presence of which makes itself felt. In the same way we become conscious of time when we are bored, not when we are diverted. Both these cases prove that our existence is most happy when we perceive it least, from which it follows that it would be better not to have it. Great and lively joy can only be conceived as the consequence of great misery, which has preceded it; for nothing can be added to a state of permanent satisfaction but some amusement, or the satisfaction of vanity. [...]

Before so confidently affirming that life is a blessing worth desiring or giving thanks for, let one compare calmly the sum of the possible pleasures which a man can enjoy in his life with the sum of the possible sorrows which may come to him in his life. I believe the balance will not be hard to strike. At bottom, however, it is quite superfluous to dispute whether there is more good or evil in the world: for the mere existence of evil decides the matter. For the evil can never be annulled, and consequently can never be balanced by the good which may exist along with it or after it. [...] For that a thousand had lived in happiness and pleasure would never do away with the anguish and death-agony of a single one; and just as little does my present well-being undo my past suffering. If, therefore, the evils in the world were a hundred times less than is the case, yet their mere existence would be sufficient to establish a truth which may be expressed in different ways, though always somewhat indirectly, the truth that we have not to rejoice but rather to mourn at the existence of the world—that its non-existence would be preferable to its existence; that it is something which at bottom ought not to be [...].

The truth is, we ought to be wretched, and we are so. The chief source of the serious evils which affect men is man himself: *homo homini lupus*.[5] Whoever keeps this last fact clearly in view beholds the world as a hell, which surpasses that of Dante in this respect, that one man must be the devil of another. For this, one is certainly more fitted than another; an arch-fiend, indeed, more fitted than all others, appearing in the form of a conqueror, who places several hundred thousand men opposite each other, and says to them: "To suffer and die is your destiny; now shoot each other with guns and cannons," and they do so.

In general, however, the conduct of men towards each other is characterised as a rule by injustice, extreme unfairness, hardness, nay, cruelty: an opposite course of conduct appears only as an exception. Upon this depends the necessity of the state and legislation, and upon none of your false pretenses. But in all cases which do not lie within the reach of the law, that regardlessness of his like peculiar to man shows itself at once; a regardlessness which springs from his boundless egoism, and sometimes also from wickedness. How man deals with man is shown, for example, by negro slavery, the final end of which is sugar and coffee. But we do not need to go so far: at the age of five years to enter a cotton-spinning or other factory, and from that time forth to sit there daily, first ten, then

5 [Man is a wolf to man (Latin).]

twelve, and ultimately fourteen hours, performing the same mechanical labour, is to purchase dearly the satisfaction of drawing breath. But this is the fate of millions, and that of millions more is analogous to it.

We others, however, can be made perfectly miserable by trifling misfortunes; perfectly happy, not by the world. Whatever one may say, the happiest moment of the happy man is the moment of his falling asleep, and the unhappiest moment of the unhappy that of his awaking. An indirect but certain proof of the fact that men feel themselves unhappy, and consequently are so, is also abundantly afforded by the fearful envy which dwells in us all, and which in all relations of life, on the occasion of any superiority, of whatever kind it may be, is excited, and cannot contain its poison. Because they feel themselves unhappy, men cannot endure the sight of one whom they imagine happy; he who for the moment feels himself happy would like to make all around him happy also [...]. If life were in itself a blessing to be prized, and decidedly to be preferred to non-existence, the exit from it would not need to be guarded by such fearful sentinels as death and its terrors. But who would continue in life as it is if death were less terrible? And again, who could even endure the thought of death if life were a pleasure! But thus the former has still always this good, that it is the end of life, and we console ourselves with regard to the suffering of life with death, and with regard to death with the suffering of life. The truth is, that the two inseparably belong to each other, for together they constitute a deviation from the right path, to return to which is as difficult as it is desirable. [...]

And to this world, to this scene of tormented and agonised beings, who only continue to exist by devouring each other, in which, therefore, every ravenous beast is the living grave of thousands of others, and its self-maintenance is a chain of painful deaths, and in which the capacity for feeling pain increases with knowledge, and therefore reaches its highest degree in man, a degree which is the higher the more intelligent the man is; to this world it has been sought to apply the system of optimism, and demonstrate to us that it is the best of all possible worlds. The absurdity is glaring. But an optimist bids me open my eyes and look at the world, how beautiful it is in the sunshine, with its mountains and valleys, streams, plants, animals, etc. etc. Is the world, then, a kind of penny theatre? These things are certainly beautiful to look at, but to be them is something quite different. Then comes a teleologist, and praises to me the wise arrangement by virtue of which it is taken care that the planets do not run their heads together, that land and sea do not get mixed into a pulp, but are held so beautifully apart, also that everything is neither rigid with continual frost nor roasted with heat; in the same way, that in consequence of the obliquity of the ecliptic there is no eternal spring, in which nothing could attain to ripeness, etc. etc. But this and all like it are mere *conditiones sine quibus non*.[6] If in general there is to be a world at all, if its planets are to exist at least as long as the light of a distant fixed star requires to reach them, and are not [...] to depart again immediately after birth, then certainly it must not be so clumsily constructed that its very framework threatens to fall to pieces. But if one goes on to the results of this applauded work, considers the players who act upon the stage which is so durably constructed, and now sees how with sensibility pain appears, and increases in proportion as the sensibility develops to intelligence, and then how, keeping pace with this, desire and suffering come out ever more strongly, and increase until at last human life affords no other material than this for tragedies and comedies, then whoever is honest will scarcely be disposed to set up hallelujahs. David Hume [...] explains clearly in the tenth and eleventh books of his *Dialogues concerning Natural Religion*, with very pertinent arguments, which are yet of quite a different kind from mine, the miserable nature of this world and the untenableness of all optimism; in doing which he attacks this in its origin. [...]

The founder of systematic optimism, again, is Leibniz, whose philosophical merit I have no intention of denying [...]. But indeed to the palpably sophistical proofs of Leibniz that this is the best of all possible worlds, we may seriously and honestly oppose the proof that it is the worst of all possible worlds. For *possible* means, not what one may construct in imagination, but what can actually exist and continue. Now this world is so arranged as to be able to maintain itself with great difficulty; but if it were a little worse, it could no longer maintain itself. Consequently a worse world, since it could not continue to exist, is absolutely impossible: thus this world itself is the worst of all possible worlds. For not only if the planets were to run their heads together, but even if any one of the actually appearing perturbations of their course, instead of being gradually balanced by others, continued to increase, the world would soon reach its end. Astronomers know upon what accidental

6 [Conditions without which not (Latin), or necessary conditions, here, for the existence of a world at all rather than features that make our world particularly worthy of admiration.]

circumstances—principally the irrational relation to each other of the periods of revolution—this depends, and have carefully calculated that it will always go on well; consequently the world also can continue and go on. We will hope that, although Newton was of an opposite opinion, they have not miscalculated, and consequently that the mechanical perpetual motion realised in such a planetary system will not also, like the rest, ultimately come to a standstill. Again, under the firm crust of the planet dwell the powerful forces of nature, which, as soon as some accident affords them free play, must necessarily destroy that crust, with everything living upon it, as has already taken place at least three times upon our planet, and will probably take place oftener still. The earthquake of Lisbon, the earthquake of Haiti, the destruction of Pompeii, are only small, playful hints of what is possible. A small alteration of the atmosphere, which cannot even be chemically proved, causes cholera, yellow fever, black death, etc., which carry off millions of men; a somewhat greater alteration would extinguish all life. A very moderate increase of heat would dry up all the rivers and springs. The brutes have received just barely so much in the way of organs and powers as enables them to procure with the greatest exertion sustenance for their own lives and food for their offspring; therefore if a brute loses a limb, or even the full use of one, it must generally perish. Even of the human race, powerful as are the weapons it possesses in understanding and reason, nine-tenths live in constant conflict with want, always balancing themselves with difficulty and effort upon the brink of destruction. Thus throughout, as for the continuance of the whole, so also for that of each individual being the conditions are barely and scantily given, but nothing over. The individual life is a ceaseless battle for existence itself; while at every step destruction threatens it. Just because this threat is so often fulfilled provision had to be made, by means of the enormous excess of the germs, that the destruction of the individuals should not involve that of the species, for which alone nature really cares. The world is therefore as bad as it possibly can be if it is to continue to be at all. Q.E.D.[7] The fossils of the entirely different kinds of animal species which formerly inhabited the planet afford us, as a proof of our calculation, the records of worlds the continuance of which was no longer possible, and which consequently were somewhat worse than the worst of possible worlds.

---

7 [*Quod erat demonstrandum* (Latin), or "that which was to be demonstrated," which typically concluded a scholastic proof.]

Optimism is at bottom the unmerited self-praise of the real originator of the world, the will to live, which views itself complacently in its works; and accordingly it is not only a false, but also a pernicious doctrine. For it presents life to us as a desirable condition, and the happiness of man as the end of it. Starting from this, everyone then believes that he has the most just claim to happiness and pleasure; and if, as is wont to happen, these do not fall to his lot, then he believes that he is wronged, nay, that he loses the end of his existence; while it is far more correct to regard work, privation, misery, and suffering, crowned by death, as the end of our life (as Brahmanism and Buddhism, and also genuine Christianity do); for it is these which lead to the denial of the will to live. In the New Testament the world is represented as a valley of tears, life as a process of purifying or refining, and the symbol of Christianity is an instrument of torture. Therefore, when Leibniz [...] and Pope brought forward optimism, the general offence which it gave depended principally upon the fact that optimism is irreconcilable with Christianity; as Voltaire states and explains in the preface to his excellent poem, "On the Lisbon Disaster," which is also expressly directed against optimism. This great man, whom I so gladly praise, in opposition to the abuse of venal German ink-slingers, is placed decidedly higher than Rousseau by the insight to which he attained in three respects, and which prove the greater depth of his thinking: (1) the recognition of the preponderating magnitude of the evil and misery of existence with which he is deeply penetrated; (2) that of the strict necessity of the acts of will; (3) that of the truth of [the] principle that what thinks may also be material: while Rousseau opposes [...] the beautiful poem of Voltaire which has just been referred to with ill-founded, shallow, and logically false reasoning, in the interests of optimism, in his long letter to Voltaire of 18th August 1756, which is devoted simply to this purpose. Indeed, the fundamental characteristic and the original mistake of Rousseau's whole philosophy is this, that in the place of the Christian doctrine of original sin, and the original depravity of the human race, he puts an original goodness and unlimited perfectibility of it, which has only been led astray by civilisation and its consequences, and then founds upon this his optimism and humanism. [...]

Chapter 8

DEFENDING PESSIMISM: VON HARTMANN AND PLUMACHER

Introduction

SCHOPENHAUER'S IDEAS PROVED QUITE INFLUENTIAL, especially in the second half of the nineteenth century during the so-called *pessimism controversy*. This was a period in which pessimistic ideas were vigorously debated and refined beyond their original Schopenhauerian formulations. Among the major figures involved in this controversy was Eduard von Hartmann (1842–1906), a German philosopher who defended pessimism but sought a foundation for it outside of Schopenhauer's treatment. His principal work was *Die Philosophie des Unbewußten* (*The Philosophy of the Unconscious*), which was first published in 1869 and went through many editions in his lifetime. In it, von Hartmann rejects Schopenhauer's characterization of pessimism (in §46 of volume II of *The World as Will and Representation*) as upholding that this is the *worst* of all possible worlds; instead, what von Hartmann identifies as the central tenet of pessimism is the claim that happiness is unattainable, which he elsewhere refers to as "eudaemonological pessimism." Von Hartmann also disputes the negative conception of pleasure on which Schopenhauer relies for his *a priori* proof (in §58 of volume I of *The World as Will and Representation*), claiming that even if one allows for a positive sort of pleasure (that is, one that is not conditioned by a painful stimulus), a number of other factors conspire to rule out the attainability of happiness.

Von Hartmann goes further than this and contends that the view that happiness is, in fact, attainable, is little more than an illusion that has taken progressively different forms throughout human history. The first form of this illusion consisted in the simple view that happiness was attainable by the individual in this life. The second form, grounded on the evident falsehood of the first, projected individual happiness into a (Christian) afterlife or (Buddhistic) transcendent state. The third form proceeds from the rejection of these religious myths and accepts that happiness is not attainable for the individual but takes it to be achievable for future generations through collective action and scientific advancement. Von Hartmann likewise identifies this third form of the illusion as deceptive, contending for instance that technology creates new needs even as it satisfies old ones, and that disease and hunger systematically elude our efforts to eradicate them. With this exposure of the third and final form of the illusion, von Hartmann thinks that the path is cleared for humanity as a whole to recognize that it is not external obstacles that prevent us from attaining happiness but the world and life itself that stand in the way.

Von Hartmann's pessimism found a strident defender in the Russian-born Swiss thinker Olga Plumacher (also Plümacher, 1839–95). Although lacking a formal university education, she was introduced to Schopenhauer's works by a friend and quickly took to von Hartmann's pessimism. Her books played an important role in the pessimism controversy, and inspired later thinkers like Friedrich Nietzsche and even Samuel Beckett. The piece included below is from an English-language essay, simply titled "Pessimism," that was published in the philosophy journal *Mind* in 1879 (a testament to the international interest in the topic at the height of the controversy). Plumacher's essay is a response to a book written by the English psychologist James Sully (1842–1923) entitled *Pessimism: A History and a Criticism* published in 1877. Unsurprisingly, Sully offers a reductive take on philosophical pessimism, tracing it back to a "pre-philosophical" attitude or disposition to negative thinking. Plumacher disputes this and defends the philosophical character of pessimism. Significantly, she also charges Sully with having missed the true "pessimistic question." Sully makes much of the fact that human beings naturally desire to continue existing, and so that securing the means to do so provides us with a measure of happiness, but Plumacher contends that this is just to overlook entirely the question as to whether continuing to exist is itself desirable, or, in her memorable formulation, *whether life is something that ought to be.*

Eduard von Hartmann, from *The Philosophy of the Unconscious*

Chapter XIII: The Irrationality of Volition and the Misery of Existence

The object of this chapter is to inquire whether the *being* or the *non-being* of this present world deserves the preference. And here, more than at any other stage of our inquiry, must we crave the reader's indulgence, since a tolerably exhaustive treatment of the subject would require a book to itself. [...]

Imagine someone who is no genius, but a man with the best general culture of his time, endowed with all the other good things of an enviable lot, in the most vigorous years of manhood, who is fully conscious of the advantage which he enjoys over the lower orders in the uncivilised nations and over his fellows of ruder ages, and who by no means envies those above him who are tormented by all sorts of discomforts spared to himself; a man who is neither exhausted and rendered *blasé* by immoderate pleasure, nor has ever been crushed by exceptional strokes of fate.

Let us imagine Death to draw nigh this man and say, "Thy life-period is run out, and at this hour thou art on the brink of annihilation; but it depends on thy present voluntary decision, once again, precisely in the same way, to go through thy now closed life with complete oblivion of all that has passed. Now choose!"

I question whether the man would prefer the repetition of the past performance to non-existence, if his mind be free from fear, and calm, and if he has not altogether lived so thoughtlessly, without all self-reflection, that, in his inability to offer a summary criticism of the experiences of his life, he does but give expression in his answer merely to the instinct of the desire of living at all cost, or allows his judgment to be thereby too much biassed. How much more, however, now must this man prefer non-being to a re-entrance into life, which offers him not the favourable conditions his past life offered, but, on the contrary, leaves it perfectly to chance into what new life-conditions he enters, which thus offers him, with a possibility bordering on certainty, worse conditions than those which he first disdained! [...]

It must now be inquired here, in respect of the different impulses and aims of life, how far instinct and passion themselves cause a corruption of the judgment with regard to the total enjoyment or pain endured through the particular aim; but this would be a very difficult problem, because the assent of every reader would depend on this, that in judging of his previous judgment he perfectly emancipate himself in each of these directions from the corrupting influence of impulse and passion, which is hardly to be expected; for a conscientious life-long self-observation is scarcely able to effect that. Apart from the small prospect of success which this effort by its very nature would offer, there would be also an external inconvenience connected with it. This consideration, namely, would by no means dispense us from the task of afterwards subjecting all those feelings to a criticism which, in spite of their complete reality, rest on illusions, and *which therefore are destroyed along with the destruction of these illusions with advancing conscious intelligence.* [...]

The question as to how far the feelings rest on illusions is thus of the highest importance for the decision of our problem, since what will *become* of the world, whither it is tending, is manifestly of far greater importance for the estimation of its value than the provisional stage of development at which it may accidentally happen to be.

In many cases where the reader might be disinclined to admit that the ordinary theoretical *assumption* of a preponderating enjoyment rests on an *error*, i.e., on a corruption of the *judgment* by impulse or by other sources of error, he would hardly refuse to allow that the preponderating *enjoyment itself* supposed by him, *if* it really exists, still depends on an *illusion*, and is accordingly rendered questionable by the thorough destruction of the illusion. Both, however, come, for the object of our inquiry, almost to the same thing; for if it is true that with the progressive intelligence of the world the illusions of existence also must be more and more undermined, until finally all is recognised as "vanity of vanities,"[1] the condition of the world would become ever more unhappy the more it approaches the goal of its evolution, whence we should conclude that it would have been more rational to prevent the development of the world the earlier the better, best of all to suppress its arising at the moment of its origin. [...]

1 [See Ecclesiastes 1.1–8.]

FIRST STAGE OF THE ILLUSION

Happiness is considered as having been actually attained at the present stage of the world's development, accordingly attainable by the individual of today in his earthly life.

I must in this inquiry presuppose an acquaintance with the so-called pessimism of Schopenhauer, and entreat the perusal of the sections indicated in the above order,[2] a request for which the reader hitherto unacquainted with Schopenhauer's piquant style will certainly be obliged to me. How far I differ from the views there expounded will be sufficiently evident from what has been previously said. The attempted proof [...] that this world is the worst of all possible ones is a manifest sophism; everywhere else Schopenhauer himself tries to maintain and prove nothing further than that the existence of this world is worse than its non-existence, and this assertion I hold to be correct. The word 'pessimism' is thus an *inappropriate* imitation of the word 'optimism.' Further, futile as I must regard the attempts of Leibniz to demonstrate out of existence the misery of the world in order to save the supreme wisdom and the best of all possible worlds, as little can I approve that Schopenhauer overlooks so much the wisdom of the world's arrangements in dwelling on its misery, and, although he cannot quite deny it, that he leaves it as far as possible unnoticed and makes light of it. Then I keep clear of the notion of guilt which Schopenhauer imports into the creation. I have frequently expressed myself against a transcendent use of ethical conceptions, because these have a meaning only for conscious individuals in their intercourse with one another. Only this can I conclude with Schopenhauer from the misery of existence, that the creation owes its first origin to an *irrational* act, i.e., to such an act in which reason has had no part, therefore to the *mere groundless will*. Lastly, however, I have still to signalise Schopenhauer's wrong use of the concept of negation. As Leibniz endeavours to attribute to pain an exclusively negative character, so Schopenhauer to pleasure; not, indeed, altogether in the privative sense of Leibniz, but in such a way that pain alone is said to arise *directly*, but pleasure *only* to become possible *indirectly*, through abolition or diminution of pain. Now I do not in the least intend to dispute that every removal or diminution of a pain is a pleasure, but not every pleasure is a removal or diminution of pain, and,

2 [Here von Hartmann refers to the texts by Schopenhauer included in Chapter 7, above.]

conversely, it just as much holds good that the removal or diminution of pleasure is a displeasure. [...]

It has, again, been very clearly shown how infinitely more fruitful than mere criticism is reflection on the reasons by which great men have been led to frame false hypotheses. While, namely, we [find] the hypothesis of the negative character of pleasure just as incorrect as that of Leibniz on the negativity of evil, [at the same time we apprehend] three moments, each of which falls into one scale in favour of pain, and which in combination practically yield almost the same result as the theory of Schopenhauer [i.e., of the negative character of pleasure]. They are (1.) the stimulation and fatigue of the nerves, and the need thence arising of the cessation of enjoyment, as of pain; (2.) the necessity of regarding all pleasure as *indirect* which only arises through cessation or remission of a displeasure, but not through instantaneous satisfaction of a will at the moment of the excitation of the same; (3.) the difficulties which oppose the apperception of the satisfaction of will, while displeasure *eo ipso*[3] produces consciousness; we may add: (4) the brief duration of the satisfaction, which is little more than a passing moment, while the non-satisfaction lasts as long as the actual will, thus, as there is hardly an instant when an actual will was not present, is, so to speak, eternal, and only always limited by the satisfaction which hope affords.

The first point depends on the nature of organic life, in particular of the nervous functions, as foundation of consciousness; the last three points follow immediately from the nature of the will itself. The latter undoubtedly hold good, therefore, not merely for our world, but for every world that is at all possible as objective form of the will. But the first point will also hold good wherever there is question of a balance between pleasure and displeasure; for since pleasure can only be obtained through the contrast with displeasure in a consciousness already highly developed, but a consciousness again presupposes individuation with the help of matter or its analogue, so also in every other world conceivable as objectified will the law of fatigue and the dulling of pleasure thence arising will hold good in this analogue of matter. We may accordingly regard all *four* points as necessary consequences of the nature of the will in respect to pleasure and pain [...].

We must still pay some attention to the second of the four points. If we look for examples of such pleasure-sensations as only consist in a

3 [By that very fact itself (Latin).]

cessation or remission of pain, we must carefully beware lest we do not introduce at the same time cases in which pleasure is enhanced by an additional satisfaction of will, as, *e.g.*, the relish of food and the cooling refreshment of drink add to the satisfaction of hunger and thirst, the physical sexual enjoyment to the stilling of the longings of love. Pure examples in the sensuous sphere are a subsiding toothache; in the intellectual, the recovery of a friend from a dangerous illness. When we consider such pure examples, no one will any longer doubt that the pleasure arising through cessation of pain is very much less than was that pain, just as conversely pain arising through the cessation of a pleasure is far less than that pleasure.

This phenomenon might at the first blush surprise us, since we regard the intensity of feeling as dependent only on the degree of change, but not on the relation of the beginning or end of the change to the indifference-point of the sensation. However, in my opinion, it is explained in the case of the ceasing displeasure by the subsequent vexation, detracting from the pleasure, that one has had so long to endure the pain; one feels less bound to return thanks, as it were, to one's fate for the liberation from the pain than entitled to grumble and demand satisfaction for the infliction of the pain, because the whole movement took place below the point of indifference, whereas in the ceasing pleasure the blunting effect of fatigue renders more indifferent to the termination of the enjoyment. According to this explanation, that lessening of the pleasure in proportion to the pain, in whose cessation it consists, only occurs if the circumstance that the whole movement has taken place below the zero of sensation also actually falls into consciousness. The less the consciousness of the interested person places the movement below the zero-point of sensation, the more as a matter of fact does the pleasure become equal in degree to the displeasure in the cessation of which it consists. This is least possible with sensuous pain; hence nobody would consent to be stretched on the rack in order to enjoy the pleasure of the cessation of the pain. In the intellectual sphere, however, the contest with distress and the rejoicing over every attained victory securing the immediate future is the proof of it. As soon as mankind makes clear to itself that this delight is similarly related to the preceding uneasiness as the remission of pains to the tortures of the rack, and that this movement, equally with that, falls wholly below the zero-point of sensation, so soon will it too enjoy those victories over want as little as the racked enjoy the relaxation of the cords.

What nowadays is called the spectre of the poverty of the masses is nothing but this dawning consciousness that the struggle with want, care and its alleviation lies entirely on the negative (pain) side of the zero-point of sensation, while formerly, when the poverty of the masses was ten times greater, this consciousness was wanting, and the people endured their poverty as sent from God. Another proof how progressive intelligence makes man unhappy. This contest of man with want is, however, only one example; if we look round at the possible joys of the world, we shall very soon become aware that, with the exception of the physically sensuous, the aesthetic and the scientific enjoyments, there is hardly a happiness to be perceived which did not depend on the liberation from a preceding displeasure. Quite especially, however, does this hold for great and vivid joys. [...]

Closely connected with this is the interesting question whether in general pleasure can be a countervailing equivalent for pain, and what *coefficient* or exponent must be assigned to a degree of pleasure to counterbalance for consciousness an equal degree of pain. Schopenhauer, citing the verse of Petrarch, *Mille placer non vagliono un tormento* ("A thousand pleasures are not worth one pain"), makes the eccentric assertion that altogether a pain can never be balanced by any degree of pleasure; that therefore a world in which pain can occur at all is, under all circumstances, with ever so much preponderating happiness, worse than none. This view could hardly be supported; whether, however, there does not lie in it a core of truth so far as the co-efficient necessary for equivalence does not at all need to be =1, as is usually assumed, that were well worthy of consideration.

If I have the choice either of not at all hearing, or of hearing first for five minutes discords and then for five minutes a fine piece of music; if I have the choice either not to smell at all, or to smell first a stench and then a perfume; if I have the choice either not to taste, or to taste first something disagreeable and then something agreeable, I shall in all the cases decide for the non-hearing, non-smelling, and non-tasting, even if the successive homogeneous painful and pleasurable sensations appear to me to be equal in degree, although it would certainly be very difficult to ascertain the equality of the degree.

Hence I conclude that the pleasure must be *perceptibly greater* in degree than a pain of like kind, if they are to be equivalent in consciousness, so that one determines their combination as equal to the zero of sensation and prefers it to the latter on a small enhancement of the pleasure or lowering of the pain. For the rest, this coefficient probably fluctuates with different individuals within certain limits, and only its *mean* amount should be greater than 1.

On the causes underlying this remarkable phenomenon, I venture to make no supposition. This much is certain, that, if the fact is correct, this circumstance also tells against a preponderance of happiness in the world, for suppose the case that even the sum of pleasure and pain objectively taken were equal, yet their combination subjectively would stand *below* the zero-point, as the combination of a stench and a fragrance is below zero. The world accordingly resembles a money-lottery: the appointed pains one must pay in full, but the gains one receives only with a deduction, which answers to the difference between the constant coefficient of the pleasure-and-pain equation and 1. Were this remarkable inequality in value of pleasure and pain, which seems to me highly probable, confirmed on other sides, it should be added to the above four points as a fifth. [...]

Resumé of the First Stage of Illusion.—Suppose it lay in the nature of the will to produce, as it were, in gross an equal amount of pleasure as of pain, yet the net result of pleasure and pain would in general be modified unfavourably to pleasure by the following five factors:

(a.) Nervous fatigue increases the repugnance to pain, diminishes the effort to retain pleasure; thus increases the pain of pain, diminishes the pleasure in pleasure.
(b.) The pleasure which arises through the cessation or remission of a pain cannot by a long way balance this pain, and of this kind is the largest part of existing pleasure.
(c.) Pain thrusts itself on consciousness, which must feel it; not so pleasure, which must, as it were, be discovered and inferred by consciousness, and is therefore very often lost to consciousness where the motive for its discovery is wanting.
(d.) Satisfaction is short and quickly fades; pain endures, so far as it is not limited by hope, so long as desire exists without satisfaction (and when does not such exist?).
(e.) Equal quantities of pleasure and pain united in a consciousness are not of equal value; they do not compensate one another, but pain remains in excess, or the exclusion of every sensation is preferred to the questionable union.

These five items produce by their co-operation approximately the same result as if pleasure, as Schopenhauer deems, were something negative, unreal, and pain alone the positive and real.

If one considers the several phases of life, the various desires, impulses, ambitions, passions, and states of mind, they fall, according to their importance as conducive to real happiness, into the following groups:

(a.) Such as bring *only* pain, or as good as no pleasure at all [...].
(b.) Such as represent only the zero-mark of sensation, or the level of life, the privation of certain kinds of pain, as health, youth, liberty, a competence, comfort, and in largest part also communion with one's fellows, or sociality.
(c.) Such as have a real importance only as means to ends lying beyond them, whose value therefore can only be measured by the value of these ends, which, however, regarded as ends in themselves, are illusory, *e.g.*, striving after possessions, power, and honour, partly also sociality and friendship.
(d.) Such as bring indeed a certain pleasure to the actor, but to him or the sufferers a pain far outweighing this pleasure, so that their total effect, and reciprocity being supposed, also the effect for all concerned is pain, *e.g.*, wrong-doing, lust of power, choler, hate and vindictiveness (even so far as they keep within the bounds of right), sexual seduction, and the food-instinct of flesh-eaters.
(e.) Such as, on the average, cause those experiencing them far more pain than pleasure, *e.g.*, hunger, sexual love, love of children, compassion, vanity, ambition, lust of fame, lust of power, hope.
(f.) Such as rest on illusions, which must be seen through in the progress of mental development, whereupon then indeed the pain arising through them is just as much diminished as the pleasure, but the latter far more speedily, so that hardly anything remains of it, *e.g.*, love, vanity, ambition, lust of fame, religious edification, hope.
(g.) Such as are perceived with clear consciousness as evils, and yet are voluntarily undertaken in order to avoid other evils that are regarded as still greater (no matter whether they are so or not), *e.g.*, work (instead of want and *ennui*), marriage, adopted children, and also the surrendering oneself to those impulses, of which one has perceived that they bring preponderating pain, the suppression of which, however, is regarded as still more tormenting.

(h.) Such as bring preponderating pleasure, although a pleasure purchased by more or less pain, *e.g.*, art and science, which, however, fall to the lot of relatively few, and with still fewer meet with a genuine love for and capacity of enjoying them; which few, again, are just those individuals who feel more acutely the other sorrows and pains of life.

In all this one should bear constantly in mind the assertion of Spinoza,[4] "that we neither endeavour after, will, yearn for, nor desire anything because we hold it to be good, but rather that we hold it to be good because we endeavour after, will, yearn for, and desire it" *(Ethics,* Book III, Proposition 9), and always and everywhere apply this truth as corrective to one's emotional judgment rebelling against the results of rational reflection.

If, then, we put together the general and special considerations, there emerges the undoubted result that at present pain not only preponderates in the world in general to a high decree, *but also in each single individual, even him who is placed in the most favourable circumstances conceivable.* It further follows that the less sensitive individuals, and those endowed with a more obtuse nervous system, are better off than the more sensitive natures, because with the less amount of the perceived pleasure and pain the difference in favour of pain also becomes less. This thoroughly agrees with empirical observation in the case of man, and has, however, universal validity on account of its deductive character, so that it may be extended also to animals and plants. [...]

SECOND STAGE OF THE ILLUSION

Happiness is conceived as attainable by the individual in a transcendent life after death.

On this extreme weariness of life of the ancient world falls the kindling ray of the Christian Idea. The founder of Christianity completely adopts the contempt and weariness of earthly life, and draws from them their last and most repulsive consequences [...].

Only to those who feel the misery of existence, sinners, outcasts (Samaritans and publicans), oppressed (slaves and women), poor, sick,

4 [Benedict de Spinoza (1632–77) was a Dutch philosopher, whose principal work the *Ethics* notoriously argued for metaphysical monism and the necessity of all events.]

and suffering, but not to those who feel themselves well off and comfortable in the earthly life, does he bring his gospel (Matt. 11. 5; Luke 6.20–23; Matt. 19.23–24; Matt. 11.28). He rejects everything natural, not even laws of nature does he acknowledge (Matt. 17.20); he speaks slightingly of the ties of family (Matt. 10.35–37; Matt. 19.29; Matt. 11.47–50); he requires sexual continence (Matt. 19.11–12); he condemns the world and its goods (Luke 12.15; Matt. 6.25–34; 1 John 1.15–16; Luke 16.15); declares it to be impossible simultaneously to attain earthly and heavenly bliss (Matt. 6.19–21, and 24; John 12.25; Matt. 19.23–24), and demands, therefore, voluntary poverty (Matt. 19.21–22; Luke 12.33; Matt. 6.25, and 31–34). Nowhere and in no respect does Christ prescribe asceticism, although he does prescribe voluntary restraint and the fewest possible wants, whence it is clear that he assumes pain to increase with the number of wants and desires. He regards his age as so corrupt (Matt., 23.27; Matt. 16.2–3) that the day of judgment must be near at hand (Matt. 24.33–34), and the quintessence of his teaching is, patiently to bear this life of affliction in the terrestrial vale of tears as one's cross (Matt. 10.38), and to follow him in worthy preparation and cheerful hope of the blessedness of a future eternal life (Matt. 10.38–39). "These things I have spoken unto you, that in *me* ye might have *peace. In the world ye shall have tribulation: but be of good cheer; I have overcome the world*" (John 26.33).

This is the fundamental difference between the older Judaism and Christianity; the promises of the former have reference to the life here ("that it may be well with thee, and thou mayest live long on the earth"), those of the latter to the life beyond; and this earthly vale of tears has only a meaning as preparation and trial for the life hereafter (1 Peter 1.5–7); in itself, however, of no value whatever; on the contrary, the earthly life is composed of tribulation (John 16.33) and daily torment and evil (Matt. 6.34: "Sufficient unto the day is the evil thereof"). Love makes this limbo more bearable, and is also the test of worthiness (Rom. 13.8–10; Matt. 22.37–39); faith and hope of the hereafter enable us to "overcome the world" or "to be delivered from the world," *i.e.*, from evil and sin.

The redemption of the world through Christ comes to pass, therefore, through this, that all men follow him in despising the world, and in living in faith and hope of a hereafter; but not through his death with the subsequent Judaical conception of the same as a purifying sin-offering, of which Christ himself assuredly would not have heard for a moment.

This is the historical and only important content of the doctrine preached by Jesus, to which, at the most, the rejection of an outward ritual and all priestly mediation in worship is to be added. Christian virtue also follows on its negative side from contempt of the flesh, whence all sin arises, on its positive side from the supreme commandment of love.

All that relates to earthly relations themselves is so unimportant and indifferent to him, that he either fits himself to the existing order with smiling contempt (Matt. 22.21; Matt. 27.24–27), or only gently hints at what is desirable, *e.g.*, self-government and independent jurisdiction (Matt. 18.15–17) of the communistic society. All other ideas, which we are accustomed to regard as Christian, were already current in the ancient world, but outside India the combination of contempt of the world and intense belief in an eternal transcendent blessedness was new. It was the peculiar world-redeeming idea which saved the dying antiquity from its despair and world-weariness, in that it condemned the flesh and enthroned the spirit, conceived the natural world as the kingdom of the devil (John 14.30, and 17.9), and only this transcendent world of the spirit as the kingdom of God (1 John 4.4, and 5.19), which latter certainly, according to Christ himself, could even here have its commencement in the hearts of believers; as Paul (Rom. 8.24) very truly says, "For we are saved by *hope*."

Contempt for the world combined with a transcendent life of the spirit had, indeed, in India already found a place in the esoteric doctrine of Buddhism; had, however, in the first place, not become known to the Western mind; in the second place, in India itself was only within the reach of a narrow circle of celibate adepts; and, thirdly, had soon been submerged in exoteric frenzy, so that the thought only attained realisation in the eccentric phenomena of hermits and penitents; fourthly, it did not originally spring up in a soil so fertile by reason of previous corruption; fifthly, it did not possess in the same degree the cosmopolitan side, the idea of the universal human brotherhood and the divine fatherhood (Matt. 23.8–9); sixthly and lastly, what is most important, it knows indeed an eternal transcendent blessedness for those finally released from terrestrial existence, but no *individual* immortality. Christianity, however, which promises a resurrection (of the flesh), and, accordingly, an *individual* everlasting life in the transcendent kingdom of God, thereby appeals more directly to human egoism, and consequently inspires the believer with a far more felicific hope. In this satisfying hope the Christian world has hitherto lived, and still for the most part continues to live. [...]

Thus, then, also, the hope of an individual duration of the soul turns out to be an *illusion*, and therewith the main nerve of the Christian promises is cut, the Christian idea outgrown. The draft on the life hereafter, which is to compensate for the miseries of the life here, has only one fault: place and date of discharge are forged. *Egoism* finds this result *cheerless*; *to it* indeed immortality was a postulate of the heart; and with the observation that postulates of the heart can establish no metaphysical verities [...], *its* comfortable condition ceases. But the sterling soul that puts its trust in self-renunciation and love does not find this result cheerless. To the unselfish the guarantee of an endless self-affirmation appears not merely worthless, but disquieting and abhorrent, and all the attempts to demonstrate immortality as an emotional postulate on any other basis than that of the grossest self-love utterly fail [...]. Even the humblest form of the desire for immortality, the wish to live on in one's works, deeds, and achievements, is egoistic; for one may indeed rightly desire the continued production of good deeds and the continued influence of useful and admirable works, but the insertion of the dear self into this wish, the demand that it shall be just my deeds and works that shall bear fruit for the future of the world, is, if, humanly speaking, excusable, yet always an ethically unjustified *selfishness*, which becomes even vanity when it requires the grateful preservation of the *name* and its memory among the men who derive a benefit from the deeds and works.

Since *all* longing for immortality is egoism, it would seem to be of small importance to all who have been "saved by hope" in the immortality dogma whether, after the destruction of the hope in *individual* immortality, Christianity, with its transcendent optimism as regards the truth of an eternal blessedness in general, in contrast to the originally purely negative Buddhism, is right or wrong; for he to whom immortality is a postulate of the heart is also always so far egoist as to say, "What is the greatest future blessedness *to me*, if *I* do not feel and enjoy it?" [...]

But now, if, on the one hand, the Christian hope of blessedness rests on an illusion, that necessarily disappears in the further course of the development of consciousness; if, on the other hand, the mission of the gospel through Jesus, and its eager reception by the nations, in spite of Greek philosophy, that had long risen above this childish standpoint, can certainly only be understood as [...] the genius of the founders and the popular instinct of the rage for conversion, the question arises, *what* then was the object of this illusion? The answer is simply this, that this second stage is the necessary link between the first and the third, because through despair of the first stage of the illusion, *Egoism* is not yet so far broken as not to cling with both arms to the only egoistic hope still remaining to it. Not till this anchor too breaks, and the complete despair of attaining happiness for one's dear self has taken possession of the soul, not till then does it become receptive for the self-denying thought, to work *only* for the weal of future generations, to lose itself in the universal movement for the future good of the whole. [...]

Apart from all this, there is exhibited, however, a decided *advance* from the first to the second stage of the illusion, namely, in the acquired conviction that happiness is *not* to be found in the present phase of the evolution, just as in the transition from the second to the third stage the advance consists in the attained perception, that the way to redemption from the misery of the present, in the first place, is *not* to be sought outside the *world-process*, but lies *in the world-process itself*; that thus the future redemption of the world is not to be found in *abstention from life*, but in *devotion to life*; that, however, again this devotion to life, which for its own sake would be an absurdity, has only a meaning for the sake of the future of the process of the whole.

This passage from the second to the third stage is certainly with human weakness hardly otherwise to be conceived than through a partial mistaking of the latter truth, *i.e.*, than through a partial relapse into the first stage of the illusion; for how is man to attain to a sufficiently strong faith in a future happiness on earth if he regards the present state as miserable in every respect, and all attainable happiness in the life of the present as vain? [...]

THIRD STAGE OF THE ILLUSION

Happiness relegated to the future of the world.

This hope of a future positive happiness of humanity, and the *co-operation for its sake* in the process of the whole, forms the *third stage of the illusion*, whose examination is now our task. [...]

When we were occupied with the criticism of the first stage of the illusion, it was not possible to avoid occasional glimpses into the future shaping of the world; nay, we may go so far as to assert that the attentive reader must have already found in that criticism of the first stage the criticism of the third.

To save repetition, I therefore beg that the *Resumé* of the critique of the first stage may be re-read in this sense, and the reader will be convinced of the truth of my assertion that those results contain far more than was then concluded from them for the refutation of the first stage of the illusion. Thus, *e.g.*, the proof of the proposition that the pain of non-satisfaction is always and fully felt, but the pleasure of satisfaction only under favourable circumstances, and, with considerable deductions, holds good not merely for the present, but *quite universally*.

However great the progress of mankind, it will never get rid of, or even only diminish, the greatest of sufferings sickness, age, dependence on the will and power of others, want, and discontent. However many the remedies found against diseases, diseases, especially the tormenting slighter chronic ills, always increase in quicker progression than medical science. Cheerful youth will always form only a fraction of mankind, and the other part be composed of morose age. The hunger due to the indefinite increase of the human race will always be the portion of a large stratum of the population, which has more hunger than it can satisfy, which, by reason of deficient nutriment, shows a long bill of mortality; in short, which continually succumbs to a considerable percentage in the bitter struggle with want [...]. The most contented peoples are the rude peoples living in a state of nature, and the uneducated classes of civilised peoples; with the increasing cultivation of the people grows, as experience shows, its discontent.

That stratum of the population living on the borders of hunger felt formerly, and in part now feels, its misery only as long as the stomach gnawed; but the farther the world gets the more threatening becomes the spectre of the poverty of the masses, the more fearful does the whole consciousness of their wretchedness take possession of those wretched ones. The social question of the present day rests in the last resort upon a heightened consciousness of the working classes of the wretchedness of their situation, while actually this situation is truly golden in comparison with that of two hundred years ago, when nothing was known of a social question.

Immorality, if one measures by the standard of the disposition, has not grown less since the establishment of a primitive human society to the present day, only the form in which the criminal character expresses itself is changed. Apart from variations of the ethical character of nations on the large scale, everywhere we see the same proportion of egoism and charity, and when the atrocities and barbarities of former times are pointed to, we should also not forget to take into account, on the one hand, the probity and honesty, the clear feeling of equity, and the reverence for consecrated custom of ancient peoples living in a state of nature, and, on the other, the growing deceit, falsehood, cunning, chicane, non-regardance of property and of the well-founded, but no longer understood, instinctive morality accompanying civilisation. [...] Theft, fraud, and forgery increase, despite the penalties annexed to them, more rapidly than the gross and serious crimes (such as robbery, murder, rape, etc.) decrease; the basest self-interest shamelessly rends asunder the most sacred bonds of the family and friendship wherever it comes into collision with them, and only the infallible execution of the punishments assigned by the state and society prevents the brutal cruelty of ruder times, which *immediately* breaks forth again and reveals human bestiality in all its hideousness, when the bonds of law and of order are loosened or rent, as in the Polish Revolution, the last year of the American Civil War, or the horrors of the Paris Commune in the spring of 1871. No; thus far the wickedness and the all-devouring selfishness of man has *not lessened*; it is only artificially *dammed in* by the dikes of the law and of civil society; it knows, however, in place of the open overflow how to find a thousand secret paths by which it percolates the dams. The degree of the immoral disposition has remained the same, but it has discarded the cloven foot and walks about in conventional costume; the thing and its consequences remain the same, the form alone becomes more elegant. [...]

The two other factors, to which we had accorded a positive excess of pleasure, science and art, will also alter their position in the future of the world. [...] The more we approach the present day, the more numerous become the scientific workers, the more co-operative their work. While the geniuses of former times resembled magicians who cause an edifice to spring up out of nothing, the spiritual works of modern times may be compared to the construction of an industrious body of builders, in which each adds his stone to the great building, a larger or smaller, according to his strength. The method of the future will become more exclusively inductive, and the fundamental character of scientific work be not depth but breadth. [...] As society is levelled by the civilian's black coat, so also in spiritual reference we are steering more and more towards a level of respectable mediocrity. It follows from this that the pleasure in scientific production is becoming ever less, and the world is limited more and more to the receptive enjoyment of science. This, however, is only considerable where the wrestling and struggling after truth has been personally experienced, not, however, where truth is presented to one like a baked pastry. Then often the pleasure of knowing hardly balances the effort of acquiring, and the practical utility of the acquisition or ambition must yield the proper motives of learning.

A similar state of things takes place in art, although this has a more favourable outlook than science. In it, too, the productive men of genius will become ever rarer the more humanity leaves behind it the spontaneous life of childhood and the transcendent ideals of its enthusiastic youth, and is careful for the comfortable furnishing of its earthly home, the more in manhood the social, economical, and practical scientific interests gain the upper hand. Art is then no longer what it was to the youth, the sublime beatific goddess; it is only a distraction enjoyed with half-attention as a refreshment from the toils of the day, an opiate for *ennui*, or an amusement after the seriousness of business. Hence an ever-extending dilettante superficiality, and a neglect of all earnest tendencies of art to be enjoyed only with strenuous application. The artistic *production* of the manhood of humanity estranged from the ideal naturally reflects the same facile dilettante superficiality, skillfully mastering the form and living on the treasures of the past, and no longer produces men of genius, because they are no longer needs of the time, because that would be to throw pearls before swine, or even because the age has advanced beyond the stage to which men of genius belonged to one more important. [...]

Let us now cast a glance at the belauded progress of the world. Wherein does it consist? how are we made happy? Progress in *art* one would not be warranted in rating highly; although our modern works of art are richer in ideas, yet the artistic *form* was more perfect in antiquity, and the resuscitated Greeks would with *perfect truth* declare our works of art in all departments to be thoroughly *barbarous*. (Think of our romances and stage-plays, of our statues and exhibitions of pictures, of our architecture, and the monotonous temperament in music!) The more the ideal content of our works of art threatens to burst the confining form, the further are these works removed from the *pure* notion of art, that is rooted in absolute harmony of form and matter. Space unfortunately prevents my working out these suggestions in detail.

Scientific progress contributes in a purely theoretical reference little or nothing to the happiness of the world, but in practical reference [science] stands in good stead political, social, moral and technical progress. The influence of science on moral progress I may regard as insignificant, as also in political and social respects it must not be rated too highly, since in these departments theory for the most part hobbles after instinctive practice. On the other hand, it is of incalculable importance in the progress of the *practical arts*. But what do these achieve for human happiness? Manifestly nothing but afford the possibility of social and political progress and increase the conveniences of life, and perhaps also superfluous luxury! Partly this takes place directly, partly by the facilitation and perfection of commercial communication. Factories, steamships, railways, and telegraphs have done nothing *positive* for the happiness of mankind; they have only diminished a part of the impediments and inconveniences by which man was previously confined and oppressed. If a more rational cultivation of the soil and a facilitated importation from less populated regions has placed a greater supply of food at the command of the civilised nations, this certainly has had the result that the member of the population of these civilised nations have in part very considerably increased; but is the *happiness* or the *misery* of the individual and the community thereby increased? Especially when we remember that with increasing population the number of the millions living on the verge of starvation likewise increases. The augmented food-supply of the earth, the augmented comfort and the augmented luxury taken together represent the augmented national wealth or terrestrial wealth. This latter, likewise, cannot be regarded as a growth of positive happiness. In the first place, it effects nothing but an increase of the population, and therefore of misery; secondly, its high appreciation depends on the illusion created by the instinctive acquisitive impulse; thirdly, its consequence is a diminution of pain, and an approximation to the zero-point of sensation that is never attainable. The only *positive* utility of the growth of opulence is that it *sets free for mental exertion energies* that before were absorbed in the struggle with want, and that it thereby *accelerates* the *progress of the world. This* result appertains, however, only to the process as such, by no means to the individuals or nations concerned in the process, who yet imagine that they are working *for themselves* in increasing their national wealth.

The last great advances of the world which remain to be considered are the *political* and *social*. Let us assume the most perfect state to be realised and the peoples of the earth to have solved their political problem in a complete manner. What then does one get by this political framework? A snail-shell without the snail, an empty form that waits its filling up. Mankind does not live in order to be governed, but it is governed in order to be able to *live* (in the highest sense of the term). All the well-known problems of the state are of a negative nature. They are *protection* against, *security* for, *defense* from, etc. Where the state fulfils positive objects (*e.g.*, instruction) it trespasses on the sphere of society, which, in the immaturity of the latter, may occasionally become necessity. The most perfect state does, therefore, nothing but place man in a situation where he can begin to live without fear of unwarranted attacks, *i.e.*, to unfold his forces and capabilities in all directions, which do not infringe the rights of others. Thus the ideal of the state also simply places man at the threshold of his felicity.

With the social ideals it is not different. They show how to lighten to a certain extent the struggle with want for the necessaries of life through the principle of the solidarity of the community and other expedients. They teach how to alleviate as far as possible the torments and cares which one draws upon oneself through the satisfaction of the instincts of founding a household by the best possible arrangement of the family relations; to fulfil the duties of the education of children at the least possible cost, etc. The question is always only the mitigation of evils, not attainment of positive happiness. The sole apparent exception is the increase of the collective wealth resulting from co-operation, but this has been already dealt with above.

These, then, would be the main lines of the world's progress. So far as they rest on *realities*, they agree in lifting man more and more from the depths of his misery towards the level of sensation. Were the ideal goals attained, the zero or indifference point of feeling as regards these phases of life would be attained; but as ideals always remain ideals, and the progress of humanity may indeed approach, but never reach them, even in these directions the world will never attain the height of the zero-point, but always remain below it, pain being still in excess.

One may become clear with regard to the *eudaemonological value* of the world's progress even without considering it in detail. One has only to reflect on the analogous case of the individual, he who comes into a better position in life will in passing from worse to better certainly feel pleasure. This pleasure, however, disappears with astonishing rapidity; the new and better circumstances are taken as matter of course, and the man does not feel himself a hair's-breadth the happier than in his former position. (The transition from better to worse produces a much more lasting pain.) It is just so with a nation, just so with humanity at large. Who feels himself better off now than thirty years ago because now there are railways and then there were none? And should the difference still be felt by older persons, assuredly not by those who have been born since the existence of railways. With the increased *means* nothing more has increased than *wishes* and *needs*, and in their train *discontent*. And even should mankind ever succeed in getting rid of the infectious diseases by preventive and eradicating measures, the hereditary by more rational sexual unions (contingent on a relaxation of the present unnaturally limited and almost blind struggle for existence), the rest by the progress of hygiene and medicine; should it ever succeed in preparing aliment from inorganic substances in chemical laboratories, and in limiting multiplication without restraining the instinct of propagation in accordance with the available means of subsistence, yet all this progress would offer nothing positive, but only remove or mitigate the worst, and in part most unnatural, evils of existing physical and social circumstances. But at the same time they would cause the question to become the more burning, What then to do with this life, with what substance of inner worth it is to *be filled*? what is to *compensate* for the bearing of the burden of life rendered placid by the simplest elementary considerations?

Whereas before the discomfort of existence, so far as it was felt, was referred to external evils and defects, and the attainment of a comfortable condition hoped for from the removal of the external evils most sensibly felt at the time, the error that lies in this projection of the cause of discomfort is the more perceived the more the palpable external ills of human life are removed by the world's progress; and in proportion as this escape from the pessimistic insight into the essential nature of the personal will is cut off, in the same degree grows the perception that pain is *immanent* to will; that the wretchedness of existence is founded in existence itself, and is dependent on external circumstances more in appearance than in reality. Consequently every approach to the ideal of the best life attainable on earth must make the question as to the absolute value of this life only an *ever more burning one*, since both the continually increasing perception of the illusory nature of most positive pleasures, as the ever clearer and clearer insight into the inevitableness of the misery lurking in one's own breast, like a goblin perpetually changing its shape, co-operates to this result. [...]

As the suffering of the world has increased with the development of organisation from the primitive cell to the origin of man, so will it farther increase with the progressive development of the human spirit until one day the goal is attained. It was a childish short-sightedness when Rousseau, from the perception of increasing suffering, drew the conclusion: the world must, if possible, turn back to the age of childhood. As if the childhood of humanity had not been misery! No; if once backwards, then farther, ever farther, to the creation of the world! But we have no choice. We must *forwards*, even if we desire it not. It is not, however, the golden age that lies before us, but the iron; and the dreams of the golden age of the future prove still more empty than those of the past. [...]

We began this chapter with the question whether the being or the not-being of the present world deserves the preference, and have been obliged to answer this question, after conscientious consideration, thus, that all secular existence brings with it more *pain* than *pleasure*. As cause of this disproportion we have seen those moments collected under (1.) in the first stage of the illusion, which bring it about that all volition must necessarily be attended by more pain than pleasure, that thus all volition is foolish and irrational. Even then the only possible result was clearly to be perceived; the whole subsequent inquiry was merely the empirical inductive proof of the correctness of that consequence, which we certainly could not omit if we were to proceed surely.

If this result *appears* to the reader who has had the patience to accompany me so far a cheerless one, I must assure him that he was in error if he sought to find consolation and hope in philosophy. For such ends there are books of religion and edification. Philosophy, however, has but a single eye for truth, unconcerned whether what it finds suits the *emotional judgment entangled in the illusion of instinct* or not. Philosophy is hard, cold, and insensitive as a stone; floating in the ether of pure thought, it endeavours after the icy cognition of what is, its causes, and its essences. If the strength of man is unequal to the task of enduring the results of thought, and the heart, convulsed with woe, stiffens with horror, breaks into despair, or softly dissolves into world-pain, and for any of these reasons the practical-psychological machinery gets out of gear through such knowledge—then philosophy registers these facts as valuable psychological material for its investigations. It likewise registers it when the result of these considerations in the sympathising soul of the more strongly-built natures is a righteous indignation, a manly wrath clenching the teeth, a fervid fury at the frenzied carnival of existence, or when this rage turns into a Mephistophelean gallows-humour, that with half-suppressed pity and half-unrestrained mockery looks down with a like sovereign irony both on those caught in the illusion of happiness and on those dissolved in tearful woe—or when the heart wrestling with fate spies after a last way of deliverance from this hell. [...]

Olga Plumacher, from "Pessimism"

In offering the following remarks on Pessimism, my object is not to advance any new arguments in its support, but only to review that critical survey of the doctrine which has recently been made by an English writer. Pessimism, as is well known, has of late been gaining ground both in Germany and elsewhere, and in view of this fact Mr. James Sully has presented us with an examination of the doctrine in a work entitled *Pessimism: A History and a Criticism.* Three points in particular have been dwelt upon by him: first, the systematic proof which the doctrine has found in the works of Schopenhauer and Hartmann; secondly, its chance of realisation in the present and future; and lastly, the conditions of its genesis in the individual mind, and the causes of its rapid propagation. Mr. Sully especially attacks the *Philosophy of the Unconscious* of E. von Hartmann. As this work has not yet been translated into English, it is hardly possible for English readers to estimate the justice of the charges that Mr. Sully has brought against it; and hence they may not be unwilling to listen to a voice out of the pessimistic camp raised in defense of its leader.

To the unreflective mind in the juvenile age of individuals as well as of the race, life in itself is no problem: it is a self-evident thing; that which must be, and cannot help being. But when pain, sickness, hunger, death appear, then, come doubts and questionings, stirring that feeling of wonder which is destined to become the mother of philosophy. Thus does meditation on the misery of life beget philosophy, while at the same time it prompts the desire to vanquish that misery, as a thing which ought not to be.

Mr. Sully in the first four chapters of his work gives an account of the struggles between pessimism and optimism, which will interest many readers. As we approach the present time, we find the voices of unreasoned pessimism swelling in number, while philosophic pessimism recedes more and more into the background. Schopenhauer first fully recognised the claim of pessimism to be regarded as an integral part of the system of philosophy; Mr. Sully, accordingly, next expounds his system. In relation to pessimism Dr. Hartmann may be considered the successor of Schopenhauer, but in respect of the principles of his system he can no more be called the successor of Schopenhauer than of Hegel. [...]

In Chapter VII, [Sully] begins the criticism of the metaphysical proof of pessimism. Like Hartmann—though from a very different motive—he designates the problem of pessimism a eudaemonistic or hedonistic one. As the ethical worth of the world is of account only as it influences the feelings, he shows that hedonism is the only principle whereby we can try the solution of the pessimistic question. Would the non-existence of the world be preferable to its existence? Pessimism, according to Schopenhauer and Hartmann, follows a priori from the nature of Will, as the principle of life. Every act of will refers to something which does not yet exist, else it would not be necessary to will it; and as long as the volition does not procure its satisfaction, there is a state of longing, restlessness. All these terms are of course but similes when the satisfaction of will is an unconscious representation. If a volition can become satisfied, it must be at the cost of another volition, which is proportionately repressed in its sphere of action. In the region of conscious life, whether the aim of will be the mere maintenance of life, or the realisation of an idea, it is at all times and at all points in collision with other volitions, tending in opposite directions, and those that give way in the struggle react as pain. Schopenhauer was content to deduce the misery of life a priori from the principle; but Hartmann, proceeding inductively, offers an a posteriori proof. [...]

We come now to Pleasure and Pain. According to Hartmann, Sensation is a special mode of consciousness. Pleasure and pain, on the physical side, are intensified forms of the specific affections of the different organs; on the mental side, they are intensified reactions of will upon representations. Unsatisfied will is pain, whether the accompanying representation is conscious or (as in the case of many uncertain and indefinite feelings) unconscious. But unconsciously satisfied will yields no pleasure; it is only when the consciousness is sufficiently established to allow of representations and sensations being compared with each other, that the satisfaction of will becomes known as pleasure, as a higher feeling than mere painlessness, which is the normal state. By this conception of pleasure and pain, Hartmann's doctrine that the difference between the two is merely quantitative, not qualitative, loses much of its apparently paradoxical character. [...]

If Mr. Sully thus far, in controverting the pessimistic theory, advances nothing in support of optimism, he is no more successful in his strictures upon Hartmann's arguments for the preponderance of pain. Hartmann maintains, (1) that through irritation and exhaustion of the nerves pain becomes more and more painful the longer it lasts, while positive pleasure in the like case is lessened and, prompting the will to seek relief, gives rise to a new pain if relief is not found; (2) that satisfaction of will is recognised as pleasure only where the individual mind is advanced enough to compare the different states of sensation, while the mere fact of unsatisfied will is consciously felt; (3) that the relief which follows a pain constitutes the highest degree of pleasure; (4) that the pleasure of satisfaction is only a fleeting one, while the pain of non-satisfaction lasts as long as the effort of volition. Mr. Sully strives to show that the pleasure that follows relief from pain is a real pleasure, and not mere painlessness. This Hartmann does not doubt, but he holds that, in any general estimate of the value of life according to the balance of pains or pleasures, the whole amount of such pleasure is not only not sufficient to outweigh pain, but is not even enough to redress the scale. Were there no pain in the world, there would not be any of this negative pleasure; but that it would be a good bargain to get rid of all positive pain at the cost of all such pleasure, will be doubted only by those who would assert that poverty is desirable in order that the rich may enjoy the pleasure of almsgiving. With regard to the first of Hartmann's arguments for the preponderance of pain, Mr. Sully admits the fact, but finds in it an argument against pessimism, since the insensibility produced by nervous exhaustion destroys the pain and diminishes the discontent at the absence of pleasure. Now it is true that there is a certain degree of pain at which insensibility sets in. But terrible suffering must be endured before the nerves are paralysed, while as the field of irritation spreads and new parts are affected, though the first may have become insensible, those last attacked are but just beginning to torment. After all, too, this painless exhaustion yields but a short respite: as soon as the nerve has recovered its energy, suffering begins again; or if the complete destruction of certain nerves, or of whole organs, does really bring permanent relief, then it is attended with peril to the existence of the individual. Physicians do not regard the cessation of pain as a favourable symptom as long as the source of the irritation remains or has become intensified. In Hartmann's view, although it is hardly possible to determine the equivalence of a certain quantity of pleasure to a certain quantity of pain, yet "the pleasure must be considerably greater in degree than the pain, if the two are so to counterbalance each other in consciousness as to amount in combination to the state of indifference, and be preferred to this if the pleasure is a little increased or the pain lessened." The true measure of the comparative value of pain and pleasure is the readiness with which a pain is accepted for the sake of an antecedent or succeeding pleasure, or a pleasure sacrificed to avoid such a pain; and even so there will be all manner of individual differences. Yet the mere possibility of such comparison implies an habitual endurance of pain, for to the naive mind every pain, if it is anticipated with any degree of accuracy, is absolutely great; or if often the opposite seems to be the case, this is due to the careless disregard of pain and determined exaggeration of the value of pleasure.

So much for pleasure and pain of the same kind: it is a still more difficult matter to furnish a standard of comparison of sensual pleasures or pains with mental pains or pleasures. For here the estimate will vary even more with differences of character and intelligence. We are not surprised to find Mr. Sully at variance with pessimists on this head also. He acknowledges its difficulty, but hopes to get over it thus: "The simplest method is to make the antagonistic feelings simultaneous. In this case it will be found that when they are of equal intensity, they tend to neutralise one another, that is, to produce a resultant state of feeling which has a zero-value." *Probatum est!*[5] It is a pity Mr. Sully does not deal in concrete examples, else we should have liked an illustration.

If, again, we turn from pain and pleasure to their causes, we shall find, as a general rule, that the natural and artificial circumstances that are productive of pain are present everywhere and at all times, while those productive of an over-balancing pleasure are limited and difficult of attainment; unless indeed we are content to regard the mere painless modifications of organic sensation as pleasures, as Mr. Sully does with the visual impressions of form and colour. As for *ennui*, on which Schopenhauer laid so much stress as the foe of human well-being, Mr. Sully regards it as only "the penalty inflicted on us for the non-fulfilment of some normal function, or the reminder which is given us by the natural impulse of an organ to discharge its recruited store of energy." Now certainly *ennui* is not in the common sense of the word an external evil, like poverty or sickness; but the circumstances that prevent us from actually removing this removable evil are very often either social or political ones, or are material organic conditions of our own body which are outside the mind of the individual. Many evils might be annihilated, if we so willed with all our power; unfortunately it only too often happens

5 [Thus it is proven! (Latin) (though Plumacher is here using it ironically).]

that we cannot will that which is reasonable and, if not positively pleasurable, at least painless. [...]

Mr. Sully finds that, in spite of all the efforts of philosophers from Aristotle to H. Spencer,[6] "a systematic science of hedonics has, as yet, no existence," and he aims at supplying the want by "a truly scientific attempt to define happiness and its conditions, and to determine whether the average external circumstances of human life realise these conditions." Now at first sight it does certainly seem easier to determine whether a person is happy than to say whether in the same person's life pleasure has predominated over pain; not because happiness is simply "a peculiar compound of pleasure," but because happiness may include a certain amount of pain, without ceasing to be counted as happiness. According to Mr. Sully, "a wise man" will not aim at single pleasures, but at those fixed and permanent relations of life which are ever sources of pleasure and safeguards against pain, and which, from being the originators of happiness, come to be identified with it. Surveying his mental and physical faculties, he will strive to gain wealth and riches; for the satisfaction of his inner life he will surround himself with friendship and love; and with works of charity—so far as they do not disturb his personal comfort—he will gratify his sense of pity. He will seek to counteract the bad influences of weather and climate by hardening and training his body, and enlarge his ability to enjoy mental pleasures by the acquisition of knowledge, which extends his mental horizon and improves his artistic skill. He will render his mental life, the sphere of sensations, thoughts and fancies, happy by the power of conscious volition, being careful to exclude all painful and sad representations, whether recollections or anticipations, and to cultivate sweet memories and hopes of a future more and more bright. Nor is it merely the attainment of these ends that is to be called happiness: the very act of striving after them is a source of felicity, since all (?) the varied activities of self-culture and bodily training are pleasurable. Thus, "when all the worst evils of life, such as sickness, bereavement, &c., are averted—when the conditions of large schemes of agreeable activity are present, when the person concerned manifests an habitual pleasurable interest in the events of the world which immediately surrounds him, and when the whole key of life is that of quiet, unfaltering devotion to large, inspiring and yet rational ends,

6 [Herbert Spencer (1820–1903) was an English psychologist and philosopher, and an early advocate of Darwinism, particularly as applied in societal and moral contexts.]

we may be said to have a fairly unambiguous presentation of human happiness." "Observing such a type of existence, we take upon ourselves to assure the person that he is and must (!) be happy, at moments when he is disposed to doubt the fact." "We have the fact that happiness has been and is now being realised. By this fact alone the fundamental idea of modern pessimism is amply refuted."

So far Mr. Sully, to whom we would say in reply: The fact that there are persons, and will be, at least as long as the development of our earth goes on undisturbed, whose life is to be declared a happy one, is not denied by pessimism. But the question with the pessimist is: (1) Has such a happy life really a higher value than pleasureless, but also painless, non-existence? and: (2) If [a] happy life really is preferable to non-existence, what is the proportion of this self-justified existence to that which we may call unjustified, as not including a greater amount of pleasure than of pain? To the philosopher, existence is not more reasonable, has no higher value, than non-existence; existence can become superior to non-existence only by its content. Mr. Sully everywhere conceives life as something that ought to be. This no doubt it is to the simple unreflective mind, from the fact of its being willed. But the point to be settled is, whether this willing is justifiable.

Mr. Sully makes the victory for optimism too easy when he claims the simple normal action of the senses as positive pleasure, and asserts that labour as such brings more pleasure than pain. Self-culture and mental improvement likewise are regarded by him as in themselves pleasurable. And, no doubt, in many cases the victory our reason gains over our instincts or over our bad impulses and habits, is accompanied by a pleasurable feeling of satisfaction; but in other cases the suppression of impulses condemned by reason is so painful that the succeeding pleasure would be no equivalent for it, if the future consequences were not taken into account. Besides, reason does not always get the victory, having often to be contented with such gains as only vanity can find satisfactory. Notwithstanding this, Mr. Sully conceives the way to happiness as a state of happiness itself, though he has to admit "that the quality of the happiness reached by most of those who are undoubtedly worthy to be called in a sense happy is anything but high if measured by an ideal standard." The question, then, as to what chance the majority have of securing this modest happiness becomes the more pressing. Mr. Sully allows further that "there are many persons who cannot, by any stretch of probability, be pronounced happy," the fact of suicide, of struggle with want and difficulty, and of sickness everywhere, sufficiently proving this. As one of the hindrances to happiness, he mentions the "gloomy temperament which seems to incapacitate one for accepting any of the cheering gifts of life," and adds, "oftener it is a weakness of active impulse and of will which shuts the person out from all those fields of interesting occupation which are the sole guarantee of an enduring happiness." Thus millions of men never have the opportunity of tracing a reasonable plan of happiness, though their heart craves intensely for it; and they struggle painfully to seize it by single unsystematic, and therefore useless, efforts. Now to us it seems quite as great a misfortune to miss the path to happiness, as to have no path at all. Not only are there many who refuse to see the way to happiness, there are also many who will their own misery and with full consciousness tread the path to unhappiness. And what more tragical fate than to be forced by one's inmost nature to struggle for that which to the struggler brings nothing but pain and destruction? Mr. Sully takes too superficial a view of the doctrine of determinism when he says it merely declares "that men will not aim at a thing till they feel the appropriate motives—in other words, till they begin to wish to possess it." For when the way which leads to happiness is clearly known, how many obstacles have to be overcome, how many enemies conquered, before the goal is reached! Even the mere protection against want is not so light a thing as Mr. Sully seems to think. Those who suffer from hunger and cold in our large towns, and the starving thousands of India, are they all people who did not will to work? Is it the case that the man, whose deepest feelings of love, friendship and trust in mankind are wounded, can seek and find satisfaction and happiness in other directions? Is sickness, whether of ourselves or those we love, less painful because, as "wise men," we are sure that under given circumstances a certain thing may or must happen? Are "the rough street Arab" and "the ragged urchin" really less to be pitied, because in moments, when the stomach does not rebel, the busy world around them makes them forget their miserable condition and the fact that within six hours they will be hungry without the means to satisfy their hunger? As regards death, Mr. Sully holds that, so far from being considered an evil, pessimism should laud it as the saviour from life's misery; while the consciousness of the shortness of life and of the certainty of death, instead of making life less valuable, should really enhance its pleasure, as long as it lasts. To the pessimist, who has learnt to look upon life from a philosophical point of view, his own death is indeed no evil (we say nothing here of the manner of death);

the summons to quit the ranks of the great army of sufferers is welcome, if only it does not bring too great sorrow to others. The death of those we love is, however, at all times an evil, even when we comfort ourselves with the thought that they are now safe from fate's cruel blows, nor can any pessimistic phrases make it otherwise; while to the optimist, death is an evil [absolutely], whose very thought is the destroyer of every joy. The frivolous and stupid may succeed in forgetting it, but never the "wise man," in face of the thousandfold reminders that surround him.

Turning next to the question of future progress, it is Mr. Sully's opinion that this "is a much more definite and tractable problem than that of the relative amount of happiness and misery co-existing now or at any past period in the world's history." And "if progress makes for an increase of happiness, it matters but little what are the exact proportions of joy or sorrow in the world at this fleeting point of time. Provided only happiness be shown to be possible under certain conditions, the demonstration that the onward movement of things tends, however slowly, to the fuller realisation of these conditions suffices to redeem the world as a whole from the damning charge of the pessimist." This, however, can only be admitted, if it be proved, first, that the peculiar conglomerate of feeling which Mr. Sully calls happiness, seems to an intellectual mind really preferable to the insensible state of non-existence; and, secondly, that what we call progress really acts in the supposed direction. But this Mr. Sully has not succeeded in proving. What makes his "wise man" an especially happy man is his bondage to illusions, his light-mindedness, which in spite of all present disappointments lulls him again and again in the flattering hopes of a better future, and his never-ceasing impulse to action, which prevents him from self-reflection. But if the man in question is really a wise man, sooner or later the moment of disillusion will come, and it will then be of no use to assure him, as Mr. Sully does, that he is and must be happy. To meet this contingency, Mr. Sully can only suggest a sustained faith in a happier world to come, or, failing that, at least in a happier future of posterity. It is this future that we will now for a little consider. [...]

No doubt, knowledge is expanding in all directions, and with the increase of knowledge of nature there is an increase of our power over it. But hitherto all positive increase of general wealth has had the character of a robbing of nature, and a time will come when the productiveness of the whole earth can no more be increased. Nevertheless, pessimists do not deny that increase of knowledge, directly as well as indirectly, tends to lessen and even remove many evils, and Hartmann, in particular, joins with his pessimism a political and social optimism that seems quite beyond the comprehension of Mr. Sully. It is generally admitted that epidemics may be prevented, or, where they already exist, may be confined within narrower limits by a more rational sanitary policy and improved medical art, while many diseases may be made wholly to disappear by proper physical training and the discovery of new remedies. Yet as long as the doom of death lasts, sickness and infirmity with its attendant sufferings will go before. Hartmann does not question the progress of the medical art, but only doubts whether it can keep up with the rapid increase of the more complex nervous diseases, and of that sensibility which causes slight disturbances of the normal functions to be more acutely felt than were greater disturbances in the earlier stages of man's existence, in consequence of the finer nervous organisation which is the condition of higher intelligence. The future will doubtless heal many wounds which now seem incurable. Even the social question will some day find a solution, though no one dare say whether it will be by gentle or by violent means. But the great sources of suffering will still abide in the future, for the reason that they spring from the very conditions of life. In fact, just in proportion as the different evils arising from passing social and political conditions are found to vanish, will the fact become more and more evident that life itself is the worst foe of happiness. Even if Mr. Sully had succeeded in proving that in the far-off future those existences that we call happy will become the majority, the fundamental idea of pessimism would still be far from being refuted. Should it be the doom of organic creation to perish by a general refrigeration, surely the sum total of pain arising from the pressure of more and more unfavourable climatic conditions on the animal and vegetable kingdoms would be infinitely greater than during the period of improving conditions; for with every backward movement a developed consciousness would have to be repressed. And, even if the cooling of our globe were to cease at the stage most favourable to human life and progress, the existence of a happy race during an indefinite future would tell against pessimism only on the supposition that the happy humanity of the future and the suffering humanity of the past and the present are one and the same. [...]

We will not follow Mr. Sully in his inquiry into the internal and external sources of pessimism and the causes of its rapid dissemination, but only note that he has too intelligent and keen an eye for natural, political and social shortcomings to throw himself unreservedly into the arms of optimism. He considers that, according to the side from which they are regarded, the facts may land us either in optimism or pessimism. In this we agree with him, but not when he goes on to say that the main source of pessimism is an abnormal sensitiveness to pain, and that pessimism itself is to be regarded in a large measure as a pathological phenomenon, which will cease to exist when the medical science of the future shall succeed in overcoming the peculiarities of temperament in which it is rooted. With certain limitations this may be true in cases of unreasoned pessimism—*Weltschmerz*,[7] but not of philosophical pessimism, which, uninfluenced by subjective feelings, rests exclusively on objective observation, and counts individual sensation as an object among other objects. Whatever can in this way be alleged against pessimism, can with equal force be alleged against optimism, and there is no reason why defects of temperament should be easier to eliminate in the one case than in the other. Nor is the attempt to hold the balance between optimism and pessimism that most worthy of "the man of philosophic mind"; it should rather be to find the synthesis of both. To the eye of cool reason the world seems as good as possible because it is a real logical process; in the eudaemonistic point of view, it is worse than no world, because the path whereon the logos strides from victory to victory is a path of suffering to the creature.

7 [Literally, "the pain of the world" (German), but here understood dismissively as an affected disposition of suffering.]

Chapter 9

SCHOPENHAUER AND NIETZSCHE ON REDEMPTION THROUGH ART

Introduction

PESSIMISTIC THINKERS CLAIM THAT HUMAN LIFE IS CHARAC-terized by insatiable and unceasing desire and the recurring pain of lack. We saw in Chapter 7 (in §58 of the first volume of *The World as Will and Representation*) that for Schopenhauer, the "unattainable nature of lasting satisfaction and the negativity of all happiness" follows from the fact that we are manifestations of the will and that it is itself "a striving without aim or end." Schopenhauer compares this situation to the fiery wheel that the Greek king Ixion was tied to and spun on for eternity. Our situation is, thus, fairly hopeless, but Schopenhauer does think that it is possible to find a measure of solace *in life*. What this solace consists in is a momentary release from the endless cycle—not the attainment of lasting happiness (since that is not possible) but a respite, even a brief one, from the pain and suffering that accompanies our ceaseless desire.

Schopenhauer thinks that this release comes through *aesthetic experience*. Aesthetic experience is our response when we behold a work of natural or artistic beauty, and Schopenhauer thinks (following Kant, as it happens) that this experience involves a stilling of our own desire, that our liking of the aesthetic object is not informed by any desire for the object or interest in it (as useful for some further end, for instance). As we will see, Schopenhauer has a rather complicated account of what, metaphysically speaking, is involved in aesthetic experience. Very briefly, he thinks that in our encounter with a beautiful object two things occur, one on the side of the *object* and the other on the side of the *subject*. On the one hand, the object itself is elevated to the form or *Idea* of which it is the expression (Schopenhauer deliberately invokes the Platonic theory of Ideas here). So, in this experience, we attain to a higher cognition of this object beyond what it is as an individual thing and instead grasp it in its essential, universal character. The object is thereby elevated beyond the complex of ordinary desires and uses to which we might put it and simply beheld as an object. On the other hand, the subject who experiences the object is elevated beyond their individuality into a "pure will-less subject of knowing." In Schopenhauer's terms, in this experience we simply become a "pure mirror" of the object. As a result, we are liberated from the striving of the will as the wheel of Ixion stands still and, even if only briefly, we experience a kind of peacefulness or tranquility.

Friedrich Nietzsche (1844–1900) was another philosopher who saw a redemptive potential in art. Early in his intellectual career, Nietzsche was a devoted admirer of Schopenhauer, and his first major philosophical work, *Die Geburt der Tragödie aus dem Geiste der Musik* (*The Birth of Tragedy from the Spirit of Music*), is very much a sympathetic engagement with Schopenhauer's pessimism. Nietzsche's book was first published in 1872 with a second revised edition in 1886 (from which the following selection is drawn), and in it Nietzsche does take issue with a number of Schopenhauer's claims, most importantly his contention that the Idea expressed in tragedy is merely that of the "resignation" of the tragic hero to the terrible truth of existence. Yet, this is against the backdrop of substantial agreement with Schopenhauer regarding, for instance, Schopenhauer's metaphysics of will and representation, and his account of aesthetic experience.

Nietzsche's aim in *The Birth of Tragedy* is to offer an account of why tragic plays, and particularly ancient Greek tragedies, produce the affect they do—in spite of representing terrible events, they nonetheless induce a sort of pleasure in the audience. By way of explaining this, Nietzsche introduces two different psychological drives or impulses, which he names after two Greek gods: the *Dionysian* and the *Apollonian*. The Dionysian impulse is that which seeks to push beyond the bounds of individuality, or the Schopenhauerian *principium individuationis*, to that which fundamentally unites every being into an undifferentiated whole. Nietzsche associates this impulse with the experience of intoxication and ecstasy. The Apollonian impulse is that which celebrates individuation and seeks expression in ever more precise forms, and Nietzsche associates this with aesthetic experience as Schopenhauer understands it, that is, as resulting in a kind of peaceful tranquility.

While each impulse has inspired distinct forms of art—the Apollonian infuses Homer's epics, and the Dionysian the "dithyramb" or an improvised choral hymn celebrating the life of Dionysus—it is in tragedy that both of these impulses come together. On Nietzsche's account, ancient Greek tragedies blend a Dionysian element, rooted in the musical chorus, with the Apollonian character of the dramatic action unfolding before the audience. The effect on the spectator is, accordingly, complex. Through the chorus, we feel the intoxication of the Dionysian impulse and a profound feeling of unity with all of nature—significantly, Nietzsche takes this experience to be positive, even exalting for us. However, this experience does not last and as we return to our individual existence we encounter a moment of danger as we long for the ecstatic state once again. This is where the dramatic action draws our attention, and through the dialogue and events played out on the stage, we are drawn out of our pessimistic reflections and seduced back to ordinary life. For Nietzsche, then, the classical examples of tragedy tell us much more than merely to resign ourselves to suffering, as they provide a model for how to continue to live in spite of the miseries of existence.

Arthur Schopenhauer, from *The World as Will and Representation*, Volume I

§38. In the aesthetical mode of contemplation we have found two inseparable constituent parts: the knowledge of the object, not as individual thing but as Platonic Idea, that is, as the enduring form of this whole species of things; and the self-consciousness of the knowing person, not as individual, but as pure will-less subject of knowledge. The condition under which both these constituent parts appear always united was found to be the abandonment of the method of knowing which is bound to the principle of sufficient reason, and which, on the other hand, is the only kind of knowledge that is of value for the service of the will and also for science. Moreover, we shall see that the pleasure which is produced by the contemplation of the beautiful arises from these two constituent parts, sometimes more from the one, sometimes more from the other, according to what the object of the aesthetical contemplation may be.

All willing arises from want, therefore from deficiency, and therefore from suffering. The satisfaction of a wish ends it; yet for one wish that is satisfied there remain at least ten which are denied. Further, the desire lasts long, the demands are infinite; the satisfaction is short and scantily measured out. But even the final satisfaction is itself only apparent; every satisfied wish at once makes room for a new one; both are illusions; the one is known to be so, the other not yet. No attained object of desire can give lasting satisfaction, but merely a fleeting gratification; it is like the alms thrown to the beggar, that keeps him alive today that his misery may be prolonged till the morrow. Therefore, so long as our consciousness is filled by our will, so long as we are given up to the throng of desires with their constant hopes and fears, so long as we are the subject of willing, we can never have lasting happiness nor peace. It is essentially all the same whether we pursue or flee, fear injury or seek enjoyment; the care for the constant demands of the will, in whatever form it may be, continually occupies and sways the consciousness; but without peace no true well-being is possible. The subject of willing is thus constantly stretched on the revolving wheel of Ixion, pours water into the sieve of the Danaids, is the ever-longing Tantalus.

But when some external cause or inward disposition lifts us suddenly out of the endless stream of willing, delivers knowledge from the slavery of the will, the attention is no longer directed to the motives of willing, but comprehends things free from their relation to the will, and thus observes them without personal interest, without subjectivity, purely objectively, gives itself entirely up to them so far as they are Ideas, but not in so far as they are motives. Then all at once the peace which we were always seeking, but which always fled from us on the former path of the desires, comes to us of its own accord, and it is well with us. It is the painless state which Epicurus prized as the highest good and as the state of the gods; for we are for the moment set free from the miserable striving of the will; we keep the Sabbath of the penal servitude of willing; the wheel of Ixion stands still.

But this is just the state which I described above as necessary for the knowledge of the Idea, as pure contemplation, as sinking oneself in perception, losing oneself in the object, forgetting all individuality, surrendering that kind of knowledge which follows the principle of sufficient reason, and comprehends only relations; the state by means of which at once and inseparably the perceived particular thing is raised to the Idea of its whole species, and the knowing individual to the pure subject of will-less knowledge, and as such they are both taken out of the stream of time and all other relations. It is then all one whether we see the sun set from the prison or from the palace.

Inward disposition, the predominance of knowing over willing, can produce this state under any circumstances. This is shown by those admirable Dutch artists who directed this purely objective perception to the most insignificant objects, and established a lasting monument of their objectivity and spiritual peace in their pictures of still life, which the aesthetic beholder does not look on without emotion; for they present to him the peaceful, still, frame of mind of the artist, free from will, which was needed to contemplate such insignificant things so objectively, to observe them so attentively, and to repeat this perception so intelligently; and as the picture enables the onlooker to participate in this state, his emotion is often increased by the contrast between it and the unquiet frame of mind, disturbed by vehement willing, in which he finds himself. In the same spirit, landscape painters, and particularly Ruisdael,[1] have

1 [Jacob van Ruisdael (1628–82), a pre-eminent Dutch landscape painter.]

often painted very insignificant country scenes, which produce the same effect even more agreeably.

All this is accomplished by the inner power of an artistic nature alone; but that purely objective disposition is facilitated and assisted from without by suitable objects, by the abundance of natural beauty which invites contemplation, and even presses itself upon us. Whenever it discloses itself suddenly to our view, it almost always succeeds in delivering us, though it may be only for a moment, from subjectivity, from the slavery of the will, and in raising us to the state of pure knowing. This is why the man who is tormented by passion, or want, or care, is so suddenly revived, cheered, and restored by a single free glance into nature: the storm of passion, the pressure of desire and fear, and all the miseries of willing are then at once, and in a marvellous manner, calmed and appeased. For at the moment at which, freed from the will, we give ourselves up to pure will-less knowing, we pass into a world from which everything is absent that influenced our will and moved us so violently through it. This freeing of knowledge lifts us as wholly and entirely away from all that, as do sleep and dreams; happiness and unhappiness have disappeared; we are no longer individual; the individual is forgotten; we are only pure subject of knowledge; we are only that one eye of the world which looks out from all knowing creatures, but which can become perfectly free from the service of will in man alone. Thus all difference of individuality so entirely disappears, that it is all the same whether the perceiving eye belongs to a mighty king or to a wretched beggar; for neither joy nor complaining can pass that boundary with us. So near us always lies a sphere in which we escape from all our misery; but who has the strength to continue long in it? As soon as any single relation to our will, to our person, even of these objects of our pure contemplation, comes again into consciousness, the magic is at an end; we fall back into the knowledge which is governed by the principle of sufficient reason; we know no longer the Idea, but the particular thing, the link of a chain to which we also belong, and we are again abandoned to all our woe. Most men remain almost always at this standpoint because they entirely lack objectivity, i.e., genius. Therefore they have no pleasure in being alone with nature; they need company, or at least a book. For their knowledge remains subject to their will; they seek, therefore, in objects, only some relation to their will, and whenever they see anything that has no such relation, there sounds within them, like a ground bass in music, the constant inconsolable cry, "It is of no use to me"; thus in solitude the most beautiful surroundings have for them a desolate, dark, strange, and hostile appearance.

Lastly, it is this blessedness of will-less perception which casts an enchanting glamour over the past and distant, and presents them to us in so fair a light by means of self-deception. For as we think of days long gone by, days in which we lived in a distant place, it is only the objects which our fancy recalls, not the subject of will, which bore about with it then its incurable sorrows just as it bears them now; but they are forgotten, because since then they have often given place to others. Now, objective perception acts with regard to what is remembered just as it would in what is present, if we let it have influence over us, if we surrendered ourselves to it free from will. Hence it arises that, especially when we are more than ordinarily disturbed by some want, the remembrance of past and distant scenes suddenly flits across our minds like a lost paradise. The fancy recalls only what was objective, not what was individually subjective, and we imagine that that objective stood before us then just as pure and undisturbed by any relation to the will as its image stands in our fancy now; while in reality the relation of the objects to our will gave us pain then just as it does now. We can deliver ourselves from all suffering just as well through present objects as through distant ones whenever we raise ourselves to a purely objective contemplation of them, and so are able to bring about the illusion that only the objects are present and not we ourselves. Then, as the pure subject of knowledge, freed from the miserable self, we become entirely one with these objects, and, for the moment, our wants are as foreign to us as they are to them. The world as representation alone remains, and the world as will has disappeared. [...]

§51. If now, with the exposition which has been given of art in general, we turn from plastic and pictorial art to poetry, we shall have no doubt that its aim also is the revelation of the Ideas, the grades of the objectification of will, and the communication of them to the hearer with the distinctness and vividness with which the poetical sense comprehends them. Ideas are essentially perceptible; if, therefore, in poetry only abstract conceptions are directly communicated through words, it is yet clearly the intention to make the hearer perceive the Ideas of life in the representatives of these conceptions, and this can only take place through the assistance of his own imagination. But in order to set the imagination to work for the accomplishment of this end, the abstract conceptions, which are the immediate material of poetry as of dry prose, must be so arranged that their spheres intersect each other in such a way that none of them can remain in its abstract universality; but, instead of it, a perceptible representative appears to the imagination; and this is always further modified by the words of the poet according to what his intention may be. As the chemist obtains solid precipitates by combining perfectly clear and transparent fluids; the poet understands how to precipitate, as it were, the concrete, the individual, the perceptible Idea, out of the abstract and transparent universality of the concepts by the manner in which he combines them. For the Idea can only be known by perception; and knowledge of the Idea is the end of art. The skill of a master, in poetry as in chemistry, enables us always to obtain the precise precipitate we intended. This end is assisted by the numerous epithets in poetry, by means of which the universality of every concept is narrowed more and more till we reach the perceptible. [...]

From the general nature of the material, that is, the concepts, which poetry uses to communicate the Ideas, the extent of its province is very great. The whole of nature, the Ideas of all grades, can be represented by means of it, for it proceeds according to the Idea it has to impart, so that its representations are sometimes descriptive, sometimes narrative, and sometimes directly dramatic. If, in the representation of the lower grades of the objectivity of will, plastic and pictorial art generally surpass it, because lifeless nature, and even brute nature, reveals almost its whole being in a single well-chosen moment; man, on the contrary, so far as he does not express himself by the mere form and expression of his person, but through a series of actions and the accompanying thoughts and emotions, is the principal object of poetry, in which no other art can compete with it, for here the progress or movement which cannot be represented in plastic or pictorial art just suits its purpose. [...]

Tragedy is to be regarded, and is recognised as the summit of poetical art, both on account of the greatness of its effect and the difficulty of its achievement. It is very significant for our whole system, and well worthy of observation, that the end of this highest poetical achievement is the representation of the terrible side of life. The unspeakable pain, the wail of humanity, the triumph of evil, the scornful mastery of chance, and the irretrievable fall of the just and innocent, is here presented to us; and in this lies a significant hint of the nature of the world and of existence. It is the strife of will with itself, which here, completely unfolded at the highest grade of its objectivity, comes into fearful prominence. It becomes visible in the suffering of men, which is now introduced, partly through chance and error, which appear as the rulers of the world, personified as fate, on account of their insidiousness, which even reaches the appearance of design; partly it proceeds from man himself, through the self-mortifying efforts of a few, through the wickedness and perversity of most. It is one and the same will that lives and appears in them all, but whose phenomena fight against each other and destroy each other. In one individual it appears powerfully, in another more weakly; in one more subject to reason, and softened by the light of knowledge, in another less so, till at last, in some single case, this knowledge, purified and heightened by suffering itself, reaches the point at which the phenomenon, the veil of Maya,[2] no longer deceives it. It sees through the form of the phenomenon, the *principum individuationis*. The egoism which rests on this perishes with it, so that now the motives that were so powerful before have lost their might, and instead of them the complete knowledge of the nature of the world, which has a tranquilizing effect on the will, produces resignation, the surrender not merely of life, but of the very will to live. Thus we see in tragedies the noblest men, after long conflict and suffering, at last renounce the ends they have so keenly followed, and all the pleasures of life for ever, or else freely and joyfully surrender life itself. So is it [...] with Hamlet, whom his friend Horatio would willingly follow, but is bade remain a while, and in this harsh world draw his breath in pain, to tell the story of Hamlet, and clear his memory [...]. The true sense of tragedy is the deeper insight, that it is not his own individual sins that the hero atones for, but original sin, i.e., the crime of existence itself [...].

§52. [T]here is still another fine art which has been excluded from our consideration, and had to be excluded, for in the systematic connection of our exposition there was no fitting place for it—I mean music. It stands alone, quite cut off from all the other arts. In it we do not recognise the copy or repetition of any Idea of existence in the world. Yet it is such a great and exceedingly noble art, its effect on the inmost nature of man is so powerful, and it is so entirely and deeply understood by him in his inmost consciousness as a perfectly universal language [...]. From our

2 [Schopenhauer borrows this concept from Indian philosophy, where *māyā* means illusion or appearance. For Schopenhauer, this pertains to the world considered as representation, that is, as a world of objects in space and time.]

standpoint, therefore, at which the aesthetic effect is the criterion, we must attribute to music a far more serious and deep significance, connected with the inmost nature of the world and our own self, and in reference to which the arithmetical proportions, to which it may be reduced, are related, not as the thing signified, but merely as the sign. That in some sense music must be related to the world as the representation to the thing represented, as the copy to the original, we may conclude from the analogy of the other arts, all of which possess this character, and affect us on the whole in the same way as it does, only that the effect of music is stronger, quicker, more necessary and infallible. Further, its representative relation to the world must be very deep, absolutely true, and strikingly accurate, because it is instantly understood by everyone, and has the appearance of a certain infallibility, because its form may be reduced to perfectly definite rules expressed in numbers, from which it cannot free itself without entirely ceasing to be music. Yet the point of comparison between music and the world, the respect in which it stands to the world in the relation of a copy or repetition, is very obscure. Men have practised music in all ages without being able to account for this; content to understand it directly, they renounce all claim to an abstract conception of this direct understanding itself. [...]

[We] may regard the phenomenal world, or nature, and music as two different expressions of the same thing, which is therefore itself the only medium of their analogy, so that a knowledge of it is demanded in order to understand that analogy. Music, therefore, if regarded as an expression of the world, is in the highest degree a universal language, which is related indeed to the universality of concepts, much as they are related to the particular things. Its universality, however, is by no means that empty universality of abstraction, but quite of a different kind, and is united with thorough and distinct definiteness. In this respect it resembles geometrical figures and numbers, which are the universal forms of all possible objects of experience and applicable to them all a priori, and yet are not abstract but perceptible and thoroughly determined. All possible efforts, excitements, and manifestations of will, all that goes on in the heart of man and that reason includes in the wide, negative concept of feeling, may be expressed by the infinite number of possible melodies, but always in the universal, in the mere form, without the material, always according to the thing-in-itself, not the phenomenon, the inmost soul, as it were, of the phenomenon, without the body. This deep relation which music has to the true nature of all things also explains the fact that suitable music played to any scene, action, event, or surrounding seems to disclose to us its most secret meaning, and appears as the most accurate and distinct commentary upon it. This is so truly the case, that whoever gives himself up entirely to the impression of a symphony, seems to see all the possible events of life and the world take place in himself, yet if he reflects, he can find no likeness between the music and the things that passed before his mind. For, as we have said, music is distinguished from all the other arts by the fact that it is not a copy of the phenomenon, or, more accurately, the adequate objectivity of will, but is the direct copy of the will itself, and therefore exhibits itself as the metaphysical to everything physical in the world, and as the thing-in-itself to every phenomenon. We might, therefore, just as well call the world embodied music as embodied will; and this is the reason why music makes every picture, and indeed every scene of real life and of the world, at once appear with higher significance, certainly all the more in proportion as its melody is analogous to the inner spirit of the given phenomenon. It rests upon this that we are able to set a poem to music as a song, or a perceptible representation as a pantomime, or both as an opera. Such particular pictures of human life, set to the universal language of music, are never bound to it or correspond to it with stringent necessity; but they stand to it only in the relation of an example chosen at will to a general concept. In the determinateness of the real, they represent that which music expresses in the universality of mere form. For melodies are to a certain extent, like general concepts, an abstraction from the actual. This actual world, then, the world of particular things, affords the object of perception, the special and individual, the particular case, both to the universality of the concepts and to the universality of the melodies. But these two universalities are in a certain respect opposed to each other; for the concepts contain particulars only as the first forms abstracted from perception, as it were, the separated shell of things; thus they are, strictly speaking, abstracta; music, on the other hand, gives the inmost kernel which precedes all forms, or the heart of things. [...]

Friedrich Nietzsche, from *The Birth of Tragedy*

I.

We shall have gained much for the science of aesthetics, when once we have perceived not only by logical inference, but by the immediate certainty of intuition, that the continuous development of art is bound up with the duality of the Apollonian and the Dionysian; in like manner as procreation is dependent on the duality of the sexes, involving perpetual conflicts with only periodically intervening reconciliations. These names we borrow from the Greeks, who disclose to the intelligent observer the profound mysteries of their view of art, not indeed in concepts, but in the impressively clear figures of their world of deities. It is in connection with Apollo and Dionysus, the two art-deities of the Greeks, that we learn that there existed in the Grecian world a wide antithesis, in origin and aims, between the art of the shaper, the Apollonian, and the non-plastic art of music, that of Dionysus. Both of these so heterogeneous tendencies run parallel to each other, for the most part openly at variance, and continually inciting each other to new and more powerful births, to perpetuate in them the strife of this antithesis—which is but seemingly bridged over by their mutual term 'art'—till at last, by a metaphysical miracle of the Hellenic will, they appear paired with each other, and through this pairing eventually generate the equally Dionysian and Apollonian artwork of Attic tragedy.

In order to bring these two tendencies within closer range, let us conceive them first of all as the separate artworlds of dreamland and drunkenness, between which physiological phenomena a contrast may be observed analogous to that existing between the Apollonian and the Dionysian. [...] The beauteous appearance of the dream-worlds, in the production of which every man is a perfect artist, is the presupposition of all plastic art, and in fact, as we shall see, of an important half of poetry also. We take delight in the immediate apprehension of form; all forms speak to us; there is nothing indifferent, nothing superfluous. But, together with the highest life of this dream-reality we also have, glimmering through it, the sensation of its appearance—such at least is my experience, as to the frequency, even normality of which I could adduce many proofs, as also the sayings of the poets. Indeed, the man of philosophic turn has a foreboding that underneath this reality in which we live and have our being, another and altogether different reality lies concealed, and that therefore it is also an appearance; and Schopenhauer actually designates the gift of occasionally regarding men and things as mere phantoms and dream-pictures as the criterion of philosophical ability. Accordingly, the man susceptible to art stands in the same relation to the reality of dreams as the philosopher to the reality of existence; he is a close and willing observer, for from these pictures he reads the meaning of life, and by these processes he trains himself for life. And it is perhaps not only the agreeable and friendly pictures that he realises in himself with such perfect understanding: the earnest, the troubled, the dreary, the gloomy, the sudden checks, the tricks of fortune, the uneasy presentiments, in short, the whole "divine comedy" of life, and the inferno, also pass before him, not merely like pictures on the wall—for he too lives and suffers in these scenes—and yet not without that fleeting sensation of appearance. And perhaps many a one will, like myself, recollect having sometimes called out cheeringly and not without success amid the dangers and terrors of dream-life: "It is a dream! I will dream on!" I have likewise been told of persons capable of continuing the causality of one and the same dream for three and even more successive nights; all of which facts clearly testify that our innermost being, the common substratum of all of us, experiences our dreams with deep joy and cheerful acquiescence.

This cheerful acquiescence in the dream-experience has likewise been embodied by the Greeks in their Apollo: for Apollo, as the god of all shaping energies, is also the soothsaying god. He, who (as the etymology of the name indicates) is the "shining one," the deity of light, also rules over the fair appearance of the inner world of fantasies. The higher truth, the perfection of these states in contrast to the only partially intelligible everyday world, even the deep consciousness of nature, healing and helping in sleep and dream, is at the same time the symbolical analogue of the faculty of soothsaying and, in general, of the arts, through which life is made possible and worth living. But also that delicate line, which the dream-picture must not overstep—lest it act pathologically (in which case appearance, being reality pure and simple, would impose upon us)—must not be wanting in the picture of Apollo: that measured limitation, that freedom from the wilder emotions, that philosophical calmness of the sculptor-god. His eye must be "sunlike," according to his origin; even when it is angry and looks displeased, the sacredness of his beauteous appearance is still there. And so we might apply to Apollo, in an eccentric sense, what Schopenhauer says of the man wrapped in the veil of Maya: "Just as in a stormy sea, unbounded in every direction, rising and falling with howling mountainous waves, a sailor sits in a boat and trusts in his frail barque: so in the midst of a world of sorrows the individual sits quietly supported by and trusting in his *principium individuationis*."[3] Indeed, we might say of Apollo, that in him the unshaken faith in this *principium* and the quiet sitting of the man wrapped therein have received their sublimest expression; and we might even designate Apollo as the glorious divine image of the *principium individuationis*, from out of the gestures and looks of which all the joy and wisdom of "appearance," together with its beauty, speak to us.

In the same work Schopenhauer has described to us the stupendous awe which seizes upon man, when of a sudden he is at a loss to account for the cognitive forms of a phenomenon, in that the principle of reason, in some one of its manifestations, seems to admit of an exception. Add to this awe the blissful ecstasy which rises from the innermost depths of man, indeed, of nature, at this same collapse of the *principium individuationis*, and we shall gain an insight into the being of the *Dionysian*, which is brought within closest ken perhaps by the analogy of *drunkenness*. It is either under the influence of the narcotic draught, of which the hymns of all primitive men and peoples tell us, or by the powerful approach of spring penetrating all nature with joy, that those Dionysian emotions awake, in the augmentation of which the subjective vanishes to complete self-forgetfulness. [...]

Under the charm of the Dionysian not only is the covenant between man and man again established, but also estranged, hostile or subjugated nature again celebrates her reconciliation with her lost son, man. Of her own accord earth proffers her gifts, and peacefully the beasts of prey approach from the desert and the rocks. The chariot of Dionysus is bedecked with flowers and garlands: panthers and tigers pass beneath his yoke. [...] Now, at the evangel of cosmic harmony, each one feels himself not only united, reconciled, blended with his neighbour, but as one with him, as if the veil of Maya had been torn and were now merely fluttering in tatters before the mysterious Primordial Unity. In song and in dance man exhibits himself as a member of a higher community: he has forgotten how to walk and speak, and is on the point of taking a dancing flight into the air. His gestures bespeak enchantment. Even as

3 [The quotation is from §63 of volume 1 of *The World as Will and Representation*.]

the animals now talk, and as the earth yields milk and honey, so also something supernatural sounds forth from him: he feels himself a god, he himself now walks about enchanted and elated like the gods whom he saw walking about in his dreams. Man is no longer an artist, he has become a work of art: the artistic power of all nature here reveals itself in the tremors of drunkenness to the highest gratification of the Primordial Unity. [...]

2.

Thus far we have considered the Apollonian and his antithesis, the Dionysian, as artistic powers which burst forth from nature herself *without the mediation of the human artist*, and in which her art-impulses are satisfied in the most immediate and direct way: first, as the pictorial world of dreams, the perfection of which has no connection whatever with the intellectual height or artistic culture of the individual man, and again, as drunken reality, which likewise does not heed the individual man, but even seeks to destroy and redeem him by a mystic feeling of oneness. Regarding these immediate art-states of nature, every artist is either an "imitator," that is, either an Apollonian, an artist in dreams, or a Dionysian, an artist in ecstasies, or finally—as for instance in Greek tragedy—an artist in both dreams and ecstasies; thus, we may perhaps picture him, as in his Dionysian drunkenness and mystical self-abnegation, lonesome and apart from the revelling choruses, he sinks down, and how now, through Apollonian dream-inspiration, his own state, i.e., his oneness with the primal source of the universe, reveals itself to him *in a symbolical dream-picture*.

After these general premisings and contrastings, let us now approach the Greeks in order to learn in what degree and to what height these *art-impulses of nature* were developed in them, whereby we shall be enabled to understand and appreciate more deeply the relation of the Greek artist to his archetypes, or, according to the Aristotelian expression, "the imitation of nature." In spite of all the dream-literature and the numerous dream-anecdotes of the Greeks, we can speak only conjecturally, though with a fair degree of certainty, of their *dreams*. Considering the incredibly precise and unerring plastic power of their eyes, as also their manifest and sincere delight in colours, we can hardly refrain (to the shame of everyone born later) from assuming for their very dreams a logical causality of lines and contours, colours and groups, a sequence of scenes resembling their best reliefs, the perfection of which would certainly justify us, if a comparison were possible, in designating the dreaming Greeks as Homers and Homer as a dreaming Greek: in a deeper sense than when modern man, in respect to his dreams, ventures to compare himself with Shakespeare.

On the other hand, we should not have to speak conjecturally, if asked to disclose the immense gap which separated the *Dionysian Greek* from the Dionysian barbarian. From all quarters of the ancient world—to say nothing of the modern—from Rome as far as Babylon, we can prove the existence of Dionysian festivals, the type of which bears, at best, the same relation to the Greek festivals as the bearded satyr, who borrowed his name and attributes from the goat, does to Dionysus himself. In nearly every instance the center of these festivals lay in extravagant sexual licentiousness, the waves of which overwhelmed all family life and its venerable traditions; the very wildest beasts of nature were let loose here, including that detestable mixture of lust and cruelty which has always seemed to me the genuine "witches' brew." For some time, however, it would seem that the Greeks were perfectly secure and guarded against the feverish agitations of these festivals (the knowledge of which entered Greece by all the channels of land and sea) by the figure of Apollo himself rising here in full pride, who could not have held out the Gorgon's head to a more dangerous power than this grotesquely uncouth Dionysian. It is in Doric art that this majestically-rejecting attitude of Apollo perpetuated itself. This opposition became more precarious and even impossible, when, from out of the deepest root of the Hellenic nature, similar impulses finally broke forth and made way for themselves: the Delphic god, by a seasonably effected reconciliation, was now contented with taking the destructive arms from the hands of his powerful antagonist. This reconciliation marks the most important moment in the history of the Greek cult: wherever we turn our eyes we may observe the revolutions resulting from this event. It was the reconciliation of two antagonists, with the sharp demarcation of the boundary-lines to be thenceforth observed by each, and with periodical transmission of testimonials—in reality, the chasm was not bridged over. But if we observe how, under the pressure of this conclusion of peace, the Dionysian power manifested itself, we shall now recognise in the Dionysian orgies of the Greeks, as compared with the Babylonian festivals with their retrogression of man to the tiger and the ape, the significance of festivals of world-redemption and days of transfiguration.

Not till then does nature attain her artistic jubilee; not till then does the rupture of the *principium individuationis* become an artistic phenomenon. That horrible "witches' brew" of sensuality and cruelty was here powerless: only the curious blending and duality in the emotions of the Dionysian revellers reminds one of it—just as medicines remind one of deadly poisons—the phenomenon, that is, that pains beget joy, that jubilation wrings painful sounds out of the breast. From the highest joy sounds the cry of horror or the yearning wail over an irretrievable loss. In these Greek festivals a sentimental trait, as it were, breaks forth from nature, as if she must sigh over her dismemberment into individuals. The song and pantomime of such dually-minded revellers was something new and unheard-of in the Homeric-Grecian world: and the Dionysian *music* in particular excited awe and horror. If music, as it would seem, was previously known as an Apollonian art, it was, strictly speaking, only as the wave-beat of rhythm, the formative power of which was developed to the representation of Apollonian conditions. The music of Apollo was Doric architectonics in tones, but in merely suggested tones, such as those of the cithara. *The* very element which forms the essence of Dionysian music (and hence of music in general) is carefully excluded as un-Apollonian; namely, the thrilling power of the tone, the uniform stream of the melody, and the thoroughly incomparable world of harmony. In the Dionysian dithyramb man is incited to the highest exaltation of all his symbolic faculties; something never before experienced struggles for utterance—the annihilation of the veil of Maya, oneness as genius of the race, indeed of nature. The essence of nature is now to be expressed symbolically; a new world of symbols is required, for once the entire symbolism of the body, not only the symbolism of the lips, face, and speech, but the whole pantomime of dancing which sets all the members into rhythmical motion. Thereupon the other symbolic powers, those of music, in rhythmics, dynamics, and harmony, suddenly become impetuous. To comprehend this collective discharge of all the symbolic powers, a man must have already attained that height of self-abnegation, which wills to express itself symbolically through these powers: the Dithyrambic votary of Dionysus is therefore understood only by those like himself! With what astonishment must the Apollonian Greek have beheld him! With an astonishment, which was all the greater the more it was mingled with the shuddering suspicion that all this was in reality not so very foreign to him, yes, that, like unto a veil, his Apollonian consciousness only hid this Dionysian world from his view.

3.

In order to comprehend this we must take down the artistic structure of the *Apollonian culture*, as it were, stone by stone, till we behold the foundations on which it rests. Here we observe first of all the glorious *Olympian* figures of the gods, standing on the gables of this structure, whose deeds, represented in far-shining reliefs, adorn its friezes. Though Apollo stands among them as an individual deity, side by side with others, and without claim to priority of rank, we must not allow this fact to mislead us. The same impulse which embodied itself in Apollo has, in general, given birth to this whole Olympian world, and in this sense we may regard Apollo as the father thereof. What was the enormous need from which proceeded such an illustrious group of Olympian beings?

Whosoever, with another religion in his heart, approaches these Olympians and seeks among them for moral elevation, even for sanctity, for incorporeal spiritualisation, for sympathetic looks of love, will soon be obliged to turn his back on them, discouraged and disappointed. Here nothing suggests asceticism, spirituality, or duty: here only an exuberant, even triumphant life speaks to us, in which everything existing is deified, whether good or bad. And so the spectator will perhaps stand quite bewildered before this fantastic exuberance of life, and ask himself what magic potion these madly merry men could have used for enjoying life, so that, wherever they turned their eyes, Helena, the ideal image of their own existence "floating in sweet sensuality," smiled upon them. But to this spectator, already turning backwards, we must call out: "depart not hence, but hear rather what Greek folk-wisdom says of this same life, which with such inexplicable cheerfulness spreads out before thee." There is an ancient story that king Midas hunted in the forest a long time for the wise Silenus, the companion of Dionysus, without capturing him. When at last he fell into his hands, the king asked what was best of all and most desirable for man. Fixed and immovable, the demon remained silent until at last, forced by the king, he broke out with shrill laughter into these words: "Oh, wretched ephemeral race, children of chance and misery, why do you compel me to tell you that which would be most expedient for you not to hear? What is best of all is for ever beyond your reach: not to be born, not to be, to be nothing. The second best for you, however, is soon to die."

How is the Olympian world of deities related to this folk-wisdom? Even as the rapturous vision of the tortured martyr to his sufferings.

Now the Olympian magic mountain opens, as it were, to our view and shows to us its roots. The Greek knew and felt the terrors and horrors of existence: to be able to live at all, he had to interpose the shining dream-birth of the Olympian world between himself and them. The excessive distrust of the titanic powers of nature, the fates enthroned inexorably over all knowledge, the vulture of the great philanthropist Prometheus, the terrible fate of the wise Oedipus, the family curse of the Atride which drove Orestes to matricide; in short, that entire philosophy of the sylvan god, with its mythical exemplars, which wrought the ruin of the melancholy Etruscans, was again and again surmounted anew by the Greeks through the artistic *middle world* of the Olympians, or at least veiled and withdrawn from sight. To be able to live, the Greeks had, from direst necessity, to create these gods: which process we may perhaps picture to ourselves in this manner that, out of the original Titan thearchy of terror the Olympian thearchy of joy was evolved, by slow transitions, through the Apollonian impulse to beauty, even as roses break forth from thorny bushes. How else could this so sensitive people, so vehement in its desires, so singularly qualified for *suffering*, have endured existence, if it had not been exhibited to them in their gods, surrounded with a higher glory? The same impulse which calls art into being, as the complement and consummation of existence, seducing to a continuation of life, caused also the Olympian world to arise, in which the Hellenic "will" held up before itself a transfiguring mirror. Thus do the gods justify the life of man, in that they themselves live it—the only satisfactory theodicy! Existence under the bright sunshine of such gods is regarded as that which is desirable in itself, and the real *grief* of Homeric men has reference to parting from it, especially to early parting: so that we might now say of them, with a reversion of the Silenian wisdom, that "to die early is worst of all for them, the second worst is—some day to die at all." If once the lamentation is heard, it will ring out again, of the short-lived Achilles, of the leaf-like change and vicissitude of the human race, of the decay of the heroic age. It is not unworthy of the greatest hero to long for a continuation of life, even as a day-labourer. So vehemently does the "will," at the Apollonian stage of development, long for this existence, so completely at one does the Homeric man feel himself with it, that the very lamentation becomes its song of praise.

[...] Wherever we meet with the "naïve" in art,[4] it behooves us to recognise the highest effect of the Apollonian culture, which in the first place has always to overthrow some titanic empire and slay monsters, and which, through powerful dazzling representations and pleasurable illusions, must have triumphed over a terrible depth of world-contemplation and a most keen susceptibility to suffering. But how seldom is the naïve—that complete absorption in the beauty of appearance—attained! And hence how inexpressibly sublime is Homer, who, as an individual being, bears the same relation to this Apollonian folk-culture as the dream-artist does to the dream-faculty of the people and of nature in general. The Homeric "naïveté" can be comprehended only as the complete triumph of the Apollonian illusion: it is the same kind of illusion as nature so frequently employs to compass her ends. The true goal is veiled by a phantasm: we stretch out our hands for the latter, while nature attains the former through our illusion. In the Greeks the "will" desired to contemplate itself in the transfiguration of the genius and the world of art; in order to glorify themselves, its creatures had to feel themselves worthy of glory; they had to behold themselves again in a higher sphere, without this consummate world of contemplation acting as an imperative or reproach. Such is the sphere of beauty, in which, as in a mirror, they saw their images, the Olympians. With this mirroring of beauty the Hellenic will combated its talent—correlative to the artistic—for suffering and for the wisdom of suffering: and, as a monument of its victory, Homer, the naïve artist, stands before us.

7.

We shall now have to avail ourselves of all the principles of art hitherto considered, in order to find our way through the labyrinth, as we must designate *the origin of Greek tragedy*. I shall not be charged with absurdity in saying that the problem of this origin has as yet not even been seriously stated, not to say solved, however often the fluttering tatters of ancient tradition have been sewed together in sundry combinations and torn asunder again. This tradition tells us in the most unequivocal terms, *that tragedy sprang from the tragic chorus*, and was originally only chorus and nothing but chorus: and hence we feel it our duty to

4 [That is, the innocent, natural, or instinctive. The notion was introduced by the famous philosopher, poet, and playwright, Friedrich Schiller (1759–1805).]

look into the heart of this tragic chorus as being the real proto-drama, without in the least contenting ourselves with current art-phraseology, according to which the chorus is the ideal spectator, or represents the people in contrast to the regal side of the scene. [...]

Much more celebrated than this political explanation of the chorus is the notion of A.W. Schlegel,[5] who advises us to regard the chorus, in a manner, as the essence and extract of the crowd of spectators—as the "ideal spectator." This view when compared with the historical tradition that tragedy was originally only chorus, reveals itself in its true character, as a crude, unscientific, yet brilliant assertion, which, however, has acquired its brilliancy only through its concentrated form of expression, through the truly Germanic bias in favour of whatever is called "ideal," and through our momentary astonishment. [...] For hitherto we always believed that the true spectator, be he who he may, had always to remain conscious of having before him a work of art, and not an empirical reality: whereas the tragic chorus of the Greeks is compelled to recognise real beings in the figures of the stage. The chorus of the Oceanides really believes that it sees before it the Titan Prometheus, and considers itself as real as the god of the scene. And are we to own that he is the highest and purest type of spectator, who, like the Oceanides, regards Prometheus as real and present in body? And is it characteristic of the ideal spectator that he should run on the stage and free the god from his torments? We had believed in an aesthetic public, and considered the individual spectator the better qualified the more he was capable of viewing a work of art as art, that is, aesthetically; but now the Schlegelian expression has intimated to us that the perfect ideal spectator does not at all suffer the world of the scenes to act aesthetically on him, but corporeo-empirically. Oh, these Greeks! we have sighed; they will upset our aesthetics! But once accustomed to it, we have reiterated the saying of Schlegel, as often as the subject of the chorus has been broached.

But the tradition which is so explicit here speaks against Schlegel: the chorus as such, without the stage—the primitive form of tragedy—and the chorus of ideal spectators do not harmonise. What kind of art would that be which was extracted from the concept of the spectator, and whereof we are to regard the "spectator as such" as the true form? The spectator without the play is something absurd. We fear that the birth

5 [A.W. von Schlegel (1767–1845) was a German philosopher, poet, and critic, well-known for his translation of Shakespeare into German.]

of tragedy can be explained neither by the high esteem for the moral intelligence of the multitude nor by the concept of the spectator without the play; and we regard the problem as too deep to be even so much as touched by such superficial modes of contemplation.

An infinitely more valuable insight into the signification of the chorus had already been displayed by Schiller in the celebrated Preface to his "Bride of Messina," where he regarded the chorus as a living wall which tragedy draws round herself to guard her from contact with the world of reality, and to preserve her ideal domain and poetical freedom.

It is with this, his chief weapon, that Schiller combats the ordinary conception of the natural, the illusion ordinarily required in dramatic poetry. He contends that while indeed the day on the stage is merely artificial, the architecture only symbolical, and the metrical dialogue purely ideal in character, nevertheless an erroneous view still prevails in the main: that it is not enough to tolerate merely as a poetical license *that* which is in reality the essence of all poetry. The introduction of the chorus is, he says, the decisive step by which war is declared openly and honestly against all naturalism in art. [...]

It is indeed an "ideal" domain, as Schiller rightly perceived, upon which the Greek satyric chorus, the chorus of primitive tragedy, was wont to walk, a domain raised far above the actual path of mortals. The Greek framed for this chorus the suspended scaffolding of a fictitious *natural state* and placed thereon fictitious *natural beings*. It is on this foundation that tragedy grew up, and so it could of course dispense from the very first with a painful portrayal of reality. Yet it is not an arbitrary world placed by fancy between heaven and earth; rather is it a world possessing the same reality and trustworthiness that Olympus with its dwellers possessed for the believing Hellene. The satyr, as being the Dionysian chorist, lives in a religiously acknowledged reality under the sanction of the myth and cult. That tragedy begins with him, that the Dionysian wisdom of tragedy speaks through him, is just as surprising a phenomenon to us as, in general, the derivation of tragedy from the chorus. Perhaps we shall get a starting-point for our inquiry, if I put forward the proposition that the satyr, the fictitious natural being, is to the man of culture what Dionysian music is to civilisation. [...] In like manner, I believe the Greek man of culture felt himself neutralised in the presence of the satyric chorus: and this is the most immediate effect of the Dionysian tragedy, that the state and society, and, in general, the gaps between man and man give way to an overwhelming feeling of oneness, which leads back to the heart of nature. The metaphysical comfort—with which, as I have here intimated, every true tragedy dismisses us—that, in spite of the perpetual change of phenomena, life at bottom is indestructibly powerful and pleasurable, this comfort appears with corporeal lucidity as the satyric chorus, as the chorus of natural beings who live ineradicable as it were behind all civilisation, and who, in spite of the ceaseless change of generations and the history of nations, remain for ever the same.

With this chorus the deep-minded Hellene, who is so singularly qualified for the most delicate and severe suffering, consoles himself: he who has glanced with piercing eye into the very heart of the terrible destructive processes of so-called universal history, as also into the cruelty of nature, and is in danger of longing for a Buddhistic negation of the will. Art saves him, and through art life saves him—for herself.

For we must know that in the rapture of the Dionysian state, with its annihilation of the ordinary bounds and limits of existence, there is a *lethargic* element, wherein all personal experiences of the past are submerged. It is by this gulf of oblivion that the everyday world and the world of Dionysian reality are separated from each other. But as soon as this everyday reality rises again in consciousness, it is felt as such, and nauseates us; an ascetic, will-paralysing mood is the fruit of these states. In this sense the Dionysian man may be said to resemble Hamlet: both have for once seen into the true nature of things—they have *perceived*, but they are loathe to act, for their action cannot change the eternal nature of things; they regard it as shameful or ridiculous that one should require of them to set aright the time which is out of joint. Knowledge kills action, action requires the veil of illusion—it is this lesson which Hamlet teaches, and not the cheap wisdom of John-a-Dreams who from too much reflection, as it were from a surplus of possibilities, does not arrive at action at all. Not reflection, no! true knowledge, insight into appalling truth, preponderates over all motives inciting to action, in Hamlet as well as in the Dionysian man. No comfort avails any longer; his longing goes beyond a world after death, beyond the gods themselves; existence with its glittering reflection in the gods, or in an immortal other world is abjured. In the consciousness of the truth he has perceived, man now sees everywhere only the awfulness or the absurdity of existence, he now understands the symbolism in the fate of Ophelia, he now discerns the wisdom of the sylvan god Silenus: and loathing seizes him.

Here, in this extremest danger of the will, *art* approaches, as a saving and healing enchantress; she alone is able to transform these nauseating reflections on the awfulness or absurdity of existence into representations with which it is possible to live: these are the representations of the *sublime* as the artistic subjugation of the awful, and the *comic* as the artistic delivery from the nausea of the absurd. The satyric chorus of dithyramb is the saving deed of Greek art; the paroxysms described above spent their force in the intermediary world of these Dionysian followers.

8.

The satyr, like the idyllic shepherd of our more recent time, is the offspring of a longing after the primitive and the natural; but mark with what firmness and fearlessness the Greek embraced the man of the woods, and again, how coyly and mawkishly the modern man dallied with the flattering picture of a tender, flute-playing, soft-natured shepherd! Nature, on which as yet no knowledge has been at work, which maintains unbroken barriers to culture—this is what the Greek saw in his satyr, which still was not on this account supposed to coincide with the ape. On the contrary: it was the archetype of man, the embodiment of his highest and strongest emotions, as the enthusiastic reveller enraptured by the proximity of his god, as the fellow-suffering companion in whom the suffering of the god repeats itself, as the herald of wisdom speaking from the very depths of nature, as the emblem of the sexual omnipotence of nature, which the Greek was wont to contemplate with reverential awe. The satyr was something sublime and godlike: he could not but appear so, especially to the sad and wearied eye of the Dionysian man. He would have been offended by our spurious tricked-up shepherd, while his eye dwelt with sublime satisfaction on the naked and unstuntedly magnificent characters of nature: here the illusion of culture was brushed away from the archetype of man; here the true man, the bearded satyr, revealed himself, who shouts joyfully to his god. Before him the cultured man shrank to a lying caricature. Schiller is right also with reference to these beginnings of tragic art: the chorus is a living bulwark against the onsets of reality, because it—the satyric chorus—portrays existence more truthfully, more realistically, more perfectly than the cultured man who ordinarily considers himself as the only reality. The sphere of poetry does not lie outside the world, like some fantastic impossibility of a poet's imagination: it seeks to be the very opposite, the unvarnished expression of truth, and must for this very reason cast aside the false finery of that supposed reality of the cultured man. The contrast between this intrinsic truth of nature and the falsehood of culture, which poses as the only reality, is similar to that existing between the eternal kernel of things, the thing in itself, and the collective world of phenomena. And even as tragedy, with its metaphysical comfort, points to the eternal life of this kernel of existence, notwithstanding the perpetual dissolution of phenomena, so the symbolism of the satyric chorus already expresses figuratively this primordial relation between the thing in itself and phenomenon. The idyllic shepherd of the modern man is but a copy of the sum of the illusions of culture which he calls nature; the Dionysian Greek desires truth and nature in their most potent form; he sees himself metamorphosed into the satyr.

The revelling crowd of the votaries of Dionysus rejoices, swayed by such moods and perceptions, the power of which transforms them before their own eyes, so that they imagine they behold themselves as reconstituted genii of nature, as satyrs, The later constitution of the tragic chorus is the artistic imitation of this natural phenomenon, which of course required a separation of the Dionysian spectators from the enchanted Dionysians. However, we must never lose sight of the fact that the public of the Attic tragedy rediscovered itself in the chorus of the orchestra, that there was in reality no antithesis of public and chorus: for all was but one great sublime chorus of dancing and singing satyrs, or of such as allowed themselves to be represented by the satyrs. The Schlegelian observation must here reveal itself to us in a deeper sense. The chorus is the "ideal spectator" in so far as it is the only *beholder*, the beholder of the visionary world of the scene. A public of spectators, as known to us, was unknown to the Greeks. In their theatres the terraced structure of the spectators' space rising in concentric arcs enabled everyone, in the strictest sense, to overlook the entire world of culture around him, and in surfeited contemplation to imagine himself a chorist. According to this view, then, we may call the chorus in its primitive stage in proto-tragedy, a self-mirroring of the Dionysian man: a phenomenon which may be best exemplified by the process of the actor, who, if he be truly gifted, sees hovering before his eyes with almost tangible perceptibility the character he is to represent. The satyric chorus is first of all a vision of the Dionysian throng, just as the world of the stage is, in turn, a vision of the satyric chorus, the power of this vision is great enough to render the eye dull and insensible to the impression of "reality," to the presence of the cultured men occupying the tiers of seats on every side. The form of the Greek theatre reminds one of a lonesome mountain-valley: the architecture of the scene appears like a luminous cloud-picture which the Bacchants swarming on the mountains behold from the heights, as the splendid encirclement in the midst of which the image of Dionysus is revealed to them. [...]

The Dionysian excitement is able to impart to a whole mass of men this artistic faculty of seeing themselves surrounded by such a host of spirits, with whom they know themselves to be inwardly one. This function of the tragic chorus is the *dramatic* proto-phenomenon: to see one's self transformed before one's self, and then to act as if one had really entered into another body, into another character. This function stands at the beginning of the development of the drama. Here we have something different from the rhapsodist, who does not blend with his pictures, but only sees them, like the painter, with contemplative eye outside of him; here we actually have a surrender of the individual by his entering into another nature. Moreover this phenomenon appears in the form of an epidemic: a whole throng feels itself metamorphosed in this way. [...]

This enchantment is the prerequisite of all dramatic art. In this enchantment the Dionysian reveller sees himself as a satyr, *and as satyr he in turn beholds the god*, that is, in his transformation he sees a new vision outside him as the Apollonian consummation of his state. With this new vision the drama is complete.

According to this view, we must understand Greek tragedy as the Dionysian chorus, which always disburdens itself anew in an Apollonian world of pictures. The choric parts, therefore, with which tragedy is interlaced, are in a manner the mother-womb of the entire so-called dialogue, that is, of the whole stage-world, of the drama proper. In several successive outbursts does this primordial basis of tragedy beam forth the vision of the drama, which is a dream-phenomenon throughout, and, as such, epic in character: on the other hand, however, as objectivation of a Dionysian state, it does not represent the Apollonian redemption in appearance, but, conversely, the dissolution of the individual and his unification with primordial existence. Accordingly, the drama is the Apollonian embodiment of Dionysian perceptions and influences, and is thereby separated from the epic as by an immense gap.

The *chorus* of Greek tragedy, the symbol of the mass of the people moved by Dionysian excitement, is thus fully explained by our conception of it as here set forth. Whereas, being accustomed to the position of a chorus on the modern stage, especially an operatic chorus, we could never comprehend why the tragic chorus of the Greeks should be older, more primitive, indeed, more important than the "action" proper, as has been so plainly declared by the voice of tradition; whereas, furthermore, we could not reconcile with this traditional paramount importance and primitiveness the fact of the chorus' being composed only of humble, ministering beings; indeed, at first only of goatlike satyrs; whereas, finally, the orchestra before the scene was always a riddle to us; we have learned to comprehend at length that the scene, together with the action, was fundamentally and originally conceived only as a vision, that the only reality is just the chorus, which of itself generates the vision and speaks thereof with the entire symbolism of dancing, tone, and word. This chorus beholds in the vision its lord and master Dionysus, and is thus for ever the *serving* chorus: it sees how he, the god, suffers and glorifies himself, and therefore does not itself *act*. But though its attitude towards the god is throughout the attitude of ministration, this is nevertheless the highest expression, the Dionysian expression of *nature*, and therefore, like nature herself, the chorus utters oracles and wise sayings when transported with enthusiasm: as *fellow-sufferer* it is also the *sage* proclaiming truth from out of the heart of nature. Thus, then, originates the fantastic figure, which seems so shocking, of the wise and enthusiastic satyr, who is at the same time "the dumb man" in contrast to the god: the image of nature and her strongest impulses, indeed, the symbol of nature, and at the same time the herald of her art and wisdom: musician, poet, dancer, and visionary in one person. [...]

9.

Whatever rises to the surface in the dialogue of the Apollonian part of Greek tragedy, appears simple, transparent, beautiful. In this sense the dialogue is a copy of the Hellene, whose nature reveals itself in the dance, because in the dance the greatest energy is merely potential, but betrays itself nevertheless in flexible and vivacious movements. The language of the Sophoclean heroes, for instance, surprises us by its Apollonian precision and clearness, so that we at once imagine we see into the innermost recesses of their being, and marvel not a little that the way to these recesses is so short. But if for the moment we disregard the character of the hero which rises to the surface and grows visible—and which at bottom is nothing but the light-picture cast on a dark wall, that is, appearance through and through—if rather we enter into the myth which projects itself in these bright mirrorings, we shall of a sudden experience a phenomenon which bears a reverse relation to one familiar in optics.

When, after a vigorous effort to gaze into the sun, we turn away blinded, we have dark-coloured spots before our eyes as restoratives, so to speak; while, on the contrary, those light-picture phenomena of the Sophoclean hero—in short, the Apollonian of the mask—are the necessary productions of a glance into the secret and terrible things of nature, as it were shining spots to heal the eye which dire night has seared. Only in this sense can we hope to be able to grasp the true meaning of the serious and significant notion of "Greek cheerfulness"; while of course we encounter the misunderstood notion of this cheerfulness, as resulting from a state of unendangered comfort, on all the ways and paths of the present time.

Chapter 10

THE NEGATION AND AFFIRMATION OF LIFE: SCHOPENHAUER AND NIETZSCHE

Introduction

SCHOPENHAUER AND (THE EARLY) NIETZSCHE FIND IN AESthetic experience a brief respite from the miseries of existence. This is not, however, sufficient to redeem life itself and to make existence preferable to non-existence. Ultimately, for Schopenhauer the only appropriate attitude to take towards life is one of *negation*. At one point in his *The World as Will and Representation*, Schopenhauer identifies the will as the *will to life*—what the will *wills* is the continuation of existence and the cycle of birth and death in endless succession. In our case, the will to life is expressed most concretely in our bodies: our hunger, thirst, and sexual desire are all in the service of our preservation and procreation, and the bodily organs that fulfill these functions are direct manifestations of the will to life working in us. And while we naturally and instinctively act in accordance with the will to life, once we have come to be aware of its operation in us (as only human beings can), we have the freedom to consciously choose whether we deliberately *affirm* the will to life, and so actively promote our own individual existence, or *negate* it, and so actively oppose the will's activity in us.

Schopenhauer distinguishes two routes to the negation of the will to life: the first is through our *knowledge* of the nature of the world of representation and its basis in the will; the second is through the experience of profound suffering. Either way, the most extreme form this negation takes for Schopenhauer is *asceticism*, or adopting an exceedingly strict form of life in which we deprive the body of nourishment and even mortify the flesh to root out desire altogether. The result of this, for the ascetic, is a peace and tranquility comparable to aesthetic experience, but more lasting, culminating in a death that is not feared but welcomed.

Shortly after he published *The Birth of Tragedy*, Nietzsche became much more critical of Schopenhauer, and among his targets was Schopenhauer's promotion of what Nietzsche calls the *ascetic ideal*. For Nietzsche, an ascetic ideal is any ideal through commitment to which we are led to prioritize some value or state as more important than this sensible life and our own physical well-being. Where Schopenhauer thinks the ascetic ideal is attainable only rarely and under extraordinary circumstances (as in monastic life), Nietzsche thinks that the ascetic ideal is widespread throughout modern culture. In the third essay of *Zur Genealogie der Moral* (*On the Genealogy of Morals*) published in 1887, Nietzsche shows how ascetic ideals have pervaded all areas of modern culture, including art, philosophy, and religion, and even in the uncompromising scientific commitment to truth. Nietzsche finds the widespread endorsement of the ascetic ideal baffling, since what is involved in willing these ideals is a kind of *nihilism*, or a complete devaluation of this life in favor of the chosen ideal. This reveals a peculiar feature of the human will, namely, that it must will *something*, some ideal, provided that it gives significance to its own strivings and sufferings. To not will at all would be to have to confront the meaninglessness of existence—that ultimately all ideals, all values, with reference to which human actions find meaning, are human inventions and not grounded in some transcendental beyond. This realization of the death of the old system of values, and the resulting disorientation of the deeper meaninglessness of life, are dramatically presented in the famous aphorism 125 of *Die fröhliche Wissenschaft* (*The Joyful Wisdom*) of 1882.

Nietzsche does not leave the issue here, however, as in a number of texts through the 1880s he attempts to think through the challenge of Schopenhauer's pessimism. Where Schopenhauer promotes the ascetic ideal and its negation of life, Nietzsche champions a perspective where we "say yes" to life, and affirm it. Of course, this is not merely in the Schopenhauerian sense of affirming our own preservation but in the sense that we affirm life by continuing to engage in creative activity (especially aesthetic) in spite of a clear-eyed recognition of its ultimate meaninglessness. Doing so, Nietzsche claims, requires an exuberant vitality that is strong enough to bear up to this darkest of truths, and here again he finds inspiration in the Greeks. Returning to his *Birth of Tragedy* in the second edition of that text, published in 1886 (and with a new subtitle: "On Hellenism and Pessimism"), Nietzsche reconsiders the significance of Greek tragedy in light of this challenge. Now, instead of offering a kind of distraction from the terrors of existence through its Apollonian elements, tragedy instead documents a gifted people with the daring and vitality of youth showing that creative activity can be a response to the Dionysian character of reality. The Greeks now provide an example of a "pessimism of strength" which, in contrast to the "weak" pessimism of Schopenhauer, is able to acknowledge the truth of things but still find reason to affirm, even celebrate life. The Greeks thus offer a life-affirming inspiration to us moderns, though the bar is set very high indeed. Returning to von Hartmann's thought experiment (not to mention Leibniz's and Kant's thoughts on the subject), Nietzsche crafts his own test to determine whether we have truly succeeded in affirming life when he asks us, in aphorism 341 of *The Joyful Wisdom*, whether we could imagine ourselves living not once more but *eternally* over again and still say yes to life.

Arthur Schopenhauer, from *The World as Will and Representation*, Volume I

§ 68. [...] We saw before that hatred and wickedness are conditioned by egoism, and egoism rests on the entanglement of knowledge in the *principium individuationis*. Thus we found that the penetration of that *principium individuationis* is the source and the nature of justice, and when it is carried further, even to its fullest extent, it is the source and nature of love and nobility of character. For this penetration alone, by abolishing the distinction between our own individuality and that of others, renders possible and explains perfect goodness of disposition, extending to disinterested love and the most generous self-sacrifice for others.

If, however, this penetration of the *principium individuationis*, this direct knowledge of the identity of will in all its manifestations, is present in a high degree of distinctness, it will at once show an influence upon the will which extends still further. If that veil of Maya, the *principium individuationis*, is lifted from the eyes of a man to such an extent that he no longer makes the egotistical distinction between his person and that of others, but takes as much interest in the sufferings of other individuals as in his own, and therefore is not only benevolent in the highest degree, but even ready to sacrifice his own individuality whenever such a sacrifice will save a number of other persons, then it clearly follows that such a man, who recognises in all beings his own inmost and true self, must also regard the infinite suffering of all suffering beings as his own, and take on himself the pain of the whole world. No suffering is any longer strange to him. All the miseries of others which he sees and is so seldom able to alleviate, all the miseries he knows directly, and even those which he only knows as possible, work upon his mind like his own. It is no longer the changing joy and sorrow of his own person that he has in view, as is the case with him who is still involved in egoism; but, since he sees through the *principium individuationis*, all lies equally near him. He knows the whole, comprehends its nature, and finds that it consists in a constant passing away, vain striving, inward conflict, and continual suffering. He sees wherever he looks suffering humanity, the suffering brute creation, and a world that passes away. But all this now lies as near him as his own person lies to the egoist. Why should he now, with such knowledge of the world, affirm this very life through constant acts of will, and thereby bind himself ever more closely to it, press it ever more firmly to himself? Thus he who is still involved in the *principium individuationis*, in egoism, only knows particular things and their relation to his own person, and these constantly become new *motives* of his volition. But, on the other hand, that knowledge of the whole, of the nature of the thing-in-itself which has been described, becomes a *tranquilizer* of all and every volition. The will now turns away from life; it now shudders at the pleasures in which it recognises the affirmation of life. Man now attains to the state of voluntary renunciation, resignation, true indifference, and perfect will-lessness. If at times, in the hard experience of our own suffering, or in the vivid recognition of that of others, the knowledge of the vanity and bitterness of life draws nigh to us also who are still wrapped in the veil of Maya, and we would like to destroy the sting of the desires, close the entrance against all suffering, and purify and sanctify ourselves by complete and final renunciation; yet the illusion of the phenomenon soon entangles us again, and its motives influence the will anew; we cannot tear ourselves free. The allurement of hope, the flattery of the present, the sweetness of pleasure, the well-being which falls to our lot, amid the lamentations of a suffering world governed by chance and error, draws us back to it and rivets our bonds anew. Therefore Jesus says: "It is easier for a camel to go through the eye of a needle, than for a rich man to enter into the kingdom of God."

If we compare life to a course or path through which we must unceasingly run—a path of red-hot coals, with a few cool places here and there; then he who is entangled in delusion is consoled by the cool places, on which he now stands, or which he sees near him, and sets out to run through the course. But he who sees through the *principium individuationis*, and recognises the real nature of the thing-in-itself, and thus the whole, is no longer susceptible of such consolation; he sees himself in all places at once, and withdraws. His will turns round, no longer affirms its own nature, which is reflected in the phenomenon, but negates it. The phenomenon by which this change is marked, is the transition from virtue to asceticism. That is to say, it no longer suffices for such a man to love others as himself, and to do as much for them as for himself; but there arises within him a horror of the nature of which his own phenomenal existence is an expression, the will to life, the kernel and inner nature of that world which is recognised as full of misery. He therefore disowns this nature which appears in him, and is already expressed through his body, and his action gives the lie to his phenomenal existence, and appears in open contradiction to it. Essentially nothing else but a manifestation of will, he ceases to will anything, guards against attaching his will to anything, and seeks to confirm in himself the greatest indifference to everything. His body, healthy and strong, expresses through the genitals, the sexual impulse; but he negates the will and gives the lie to the body; he desires no sensual gratification under any condition. Voluntary and complete chastity is the first step in asceticism or the negation of the will to life. It thereby negates the affirmation of the will which extends beyond the individual life, and gives the assurance that with the life of this body, the will, whose manifestation it is, ceases. [...]

Asceticism then shows itself further in voluntary and intentional poverty, which not only arises *per accidens*,[6] because the possessions are given away to mitigate the sufferings of others, but is here an end in itself, is meant to serve as a constant mortification of will, so that the satisfaction of the wishes, the sweet of life, shall not again arouse the will, against which self-knowledge has conceived a horror. He who has attained to this point, still always feels, as a living body, as concrete manifestation of will, the natural disposition for every kind of volition; but he intentionally suppresses it, for he compels himself to refrain from doing all that he would like to do, and to do all that he would like not to do, even if this has no further end than that of serving as a mortification of will. Since he himself negates the will which appears in his own person, he will not resist if another does the same, i.e., inflicts wrongs upon him. Therefore every suffering coming to him from without, through chance or the wickedness of others, is welcome to him, every injury, ignominy, and insult; he receives them gladly as the opportunity of learning with certainty that he no longer affirms the will, but gladly sides with every enemy of the manifestation of will which is his own person. Therefore he bears such ignominy and suffering with inexhaustible patience and meekness, returns good for evil without ostentation, and allows the fire of anger to rise within him just as little as that of the desires. And he mortifies not only the will itself, but also its visible form, its objectivity, the body. He nourishes it sparingly, lest its excessive vigour and prosperity should animate and excite more strongly the will, of which it is merely the expression and the mirror. So he practices fasting, and even resorts to chastisement and self-inflicted torture, in order that, by

6 [Accidentally (Latin).]

constant privation and suffering, he may more and more break down and destroy the will, which he recognises and abhors as the source of his own suffering existence and that of the world. If at last death comes, which puts an end to this manifestation of that will, whose existence here has long since perished through free negation of itself, with the exception of the weak residue of it which appears as the life of this body, it is most welcome, and is gladly received as a longed-for deliverance. Here it is not, as in the case of others, merely the manifestation which ends with death, but the inner nature itself is abolished, which here existed only in the manifestation, and that in a very weak degree; this last slight bond is now broken. For him who thus ends, the world has ended also.

And what I have here described with feeble tongue and only in general terms, is no philosophical fable, invented by myself, and only of today; no, it was the enviable life of so many saints and beautiful souls among Christians, and still more among Hindus and Buddhists, and also among the believers of other religions. However different were the dogmas impressed on their reason, the same inward, direct, intuitive knowledge, from which alone all virtue and holiness proceed, expressed itself in precisely the same way in the conduct of life. For here also the great distinction between intuitive and abstract knowledge shows itself; a distinction which is of such importance and universal application in our whole investigation, and which has hitherto been too little attended to. There is a wide gulf between the two, which can only be crossed by the aid of philosophy, as regards the knowledge of the nature of the world. Intuitively or *in concreto*, every man is really conscious of all philosophical truths, but to bring them to abstract knowledge, to reflection, is the work of philosophy, which neither ought nor is able to do more than this.

Thus it may be that the inner nature of holiness, self-renunciation, mortification of our own will, asceticism, is here for the first time expressed abstractly, and free from all mythical elements, as negation of the will to life, appearing after the complete knowledge of its own nature has become a tranquilizer of all volition. On the other hand, it has been known directly and realised in practice by saints and ascetics, who had all the same inward knowledge, though they used very different language with regard to it, according to the dogmas which their reason had accepted, and in consequence of which an Indian, a Christian, or a Lama saint must each give a very different account of his conduct, which is, however, of no importance as regards the fact. A saint may be full of the absurdest superstition, or, on the contrary, he may be a philosopher, it is all the same. His conduct alone certifies that he is a saint, for, in a moral regard, it proceeds from knowledge of the world and its nature, which is not abstractly but intuitively and directly apprehended, and is only expressed by him in any dogma for the satisfaction of his reason. It is therefore just as little needful that a saint should be a philosopher as that a philosopher should be a saint; just as it is not necessary that a perfectly beautiful man should be a great sculptor, or that a great sculptor should himself be a beautiful man. In general, it is a strange demand upon a moralist that he should teach no other virtue than that which he himself possesses. To repeat the whole nature of the world abstractly, universally, and distinctly in concepts, and thus to store up, as it were, a reflected image of it in permanent concepts always at the command of the reason; this and nothing else is philosophy. [...]

I only wish to add a little to the general indication of the nature of this state. We saw above that the wicked man, by the vehemence of his volition, suffers constant, consuming, inward pain, and finally, if all objects of volition are exhausted, quenches the fiery thirst of his self-will by the sight of the suffering of others. He, on the contrary, who has attained to the negation of the will to life, however poor, joyless, and full of privation his condition may appear when looked at externally, is yet filled with inward joy and the true peace of heaven. It is not the restless strain of life, the jubilant delight which has keen suffering as its preceding or succeeding condition, in the experience of the man who loves life; but it is a peace that cannot be shaken, a deep rest and inward serenity, a state which we cannot behold without the greatest longing when it is brought before our eyes or our imagination, because we at once recognise it as that which alone is right, infinitely surpassing everything else, upon which our better self cries within us the great *sapere aude*.[7] Then we feel that every gratification of our wishes won from the world is merely like the alms which the beggar receives from life today that he may hunger again on the morrow; resignation, on the contrary, is like an inherited estate, it frees the owner forever from all care.

It will be remembered[8] [...] that the aesthetic pleasure in the beautiful consists in great measure in the fact that in entering the state of pure contemplation we are lifted for the moment above all willing, i.e., all wishes and cares; we become, as it were, freed from ourselves. We are

7 [Dare to know (Latin).]

8 [See the selections from Schopenhauer in Chapter 9.]

no longer the individual whose knowledge is subordinated to the service of its constant willing, the correlative of the particular thing to which objects are motives, but the eternal subject of knowing purified from will, the correlative of the Platonic Idea. And we know that these moments in which, delivered from the ardent strain of will, we seem to rise out of the heavy atmosphere of earth, are the happiest which we experience. From this we can understand how blessed the life of a man must be whose will is silenced, not merely for a moment, as in the enjoyment of the beautiful, but forever, indeed altogether extinguished, except as regards the last glimmering spark that retains the body in life, and will be extinguished with its death. Such a man, who, after many bitter struggles with his own nature, has finally conquered entirely, continues to exist only as a pure, knowing being, the undimmed mirror of the world. Nothing can trouble him more, nothing can move him, for he has cut all the thousand cords of will which hold us bound to the world, and, as desire, fear, envy, anger, drag us hither and thither in constant pain. He now looks back smiling and at rest on the delusions of this world, which once were able to move and agonise his spirit also, but which now stand before him as utterly indifferent to him, as the chess-men when the game is ended, or as, in the morning, the cast-off masquerading dress which worried and disquieted us in a night in Carnival. Life and its forms now pass before him as a fleeting illusion, as a light morning dream before half-waking eyes, the real world already shining through it so that it can no longer deceive; and like this morning dream, they finally vanish altogether without any violent transition. [...]

We must not, however, suppose that when, by means of the knowledge which acts as a tranquilizer of will, the negation of the will to life has once appeared, it never wavers or vacillates, and that we can rest upon it as on an assured possession. Rather, it must ever anew be attained by a constant battle. For since the body is the will itself only in the form of objectivity or as manifestation in the world as representation, so long as the body lives, the whole will to life exists potentially, and constantly strives to become actual, and to burn again with all its ardour. Therefore that peace and blessedness in the life of holy men which we have described is only found as the flower which proceeds from the constant victory over the will, and the ground in which it grows is the constant battle with the will to life, for no one can have lasting peace upon earth. We therefore see the histories of the inner life of saints full of spiritual conflicts, temptations, and absence of grace, i.e., the kind of knowledge which makes all motives ineffectual, and as a universal tranquilizer silences all volition, gives the deepest peace and opens the door of freedom. Therefore also we see those who have once attained to the negation of the will to life strive with all their might to keep upon this path, by enforced renunciation of every kind, by penance and severity of life, and by selecting whatever is disagreeable to them, all in order to suppress the will, which is constantly springing up anew. Hence, finally, because they already know the value of salvation, their anxious carefulness to retain the hard-won blessing, their scruples of conscience about every innocent pleasure, or about every little excitement of their vanity, which here also dies last, the most immovable, the most active, and the most foolish of all the inclinations of man. By the term asceticism, which I have used so often, I mean in its narrower sense this intentional breaking of the will by the refusal of what is agreeable and the selection of what is disagreeable, the voluntarily chosen life of penance and self-chastisement for the continual mortification of the will.

We see this practised by him who has attained to the negation of the will in order to enable him to persist in it; but suffering in general, as it is inflicted by fate, is a second way of attaining to that negation. Indeed, we may assume that most men only attain to it in this way, and that it is the suffering which is personally experienced, not that which is merely known, which most frequently produces complete resignation, often only at the approach of death. For only in the case of a few is the mere knowledge which, seeing through the *principium individuationis*, first produces perfect goodness of disposition and universal love of humanity, and finally enables them to regard all the suffering of the world as their own; only in the case of a few, I say, is this knowledge sufficient to bring about the negation of the will. Even with him who approaches this point, it is almost invariably the case that the tolerable condition of his own body, the flattery of the moment, the delusion of hope, and the satisfaction of the will, which is ever presenting itself anew, i.e., lust, is a constant hindrance to the negation of the will, and a constant temptation to the renewed affirmation of it. Therefore in this respect all these illusions have been personified as the devil. Thus in most cases the will must be broken by great personal suffering before its self-conquest appears. Then we see the man who has passed through all the increasing degrees of affliction with the most vehement resistance, and is finally brought to the verge of despair, suddenly retire into himself, know himself and the world, change his whole nature, rise above himself and all suffering, as if purified and sanctified by it, in inviolable peace, blessedness, and sublimity, willingly renounce everything he previously desired with all his might, and joyfully embrace death. It is the refined silver of the negation of the will to life that suddenly comes forth from the purifying flame of suffering. It is salvation. Sometimes we see even those who were very wicked purified to this degree by great grief; they have become new beings and are completely changed. Therefore their former misdeeds trouble their consciences no more, yet they willingly atone for them by death, and gladly see the end of the manifestation of that will which is now foreign to them and abhorred by them. [...]

In actual life we see that those unfortunate persons who have to drink to the dregs the greatest cup of suffering, since when all hope is taken from them they have to face with full consciousness a shameful, violent, and often painful death on the scaffold, are very frequently changed in this way. We must not indeed assume that there is so great a difference between their character and that of most men as their fate would seem to indicate, but must attribute the latter for the most part to circumstances; yet they are guilty and to a considerable degree bad. We see, however, many of them, when they have entirely lost hope, changed in the way referred to. They now show actual goodness and purity of disposition, true abhorrence of doing any act in the least degree bad or unkind. They forgive their enemies, even if it is through them that they innocently suffer; and not with words merely and a sort of hypocritical fear of the judges of the lower world, but in reality and with inward earnestness and no desire for revenge. Indeed, their sufferings and death at last becomes dear to them, for the negation of the will to life has appeared; they often decline the deliverance when it is offered, and die gladly, peacefully, and happily. To them the last secret of life has revealed itself in their excessive pain; the secret that misery and wickedness, sorrow and hate, the sufferer and the inflicter of suffering, however different they may appear to the knowledge which follows the principle of sufficient reason, are in themselves one, the manifestation of that one will to life which objectifies its conflict with itself by means of the *principium individuationis*. They have learned to know both sides in full measure, the badness and the misery; and since at last they see the identity of the two, they reject them both at once; they negate the will to life. In what myths and dogmas they account to their reason for this intuitive and direct knowledge and for their own change is, as has been said, a matter of no importance. [...]

All suffering, since it is a mortification and a call to resignation, has potentially a sanctifying power. This is the explanation of the fact that every great misfortune or deep pain inspires a certain awe. But the sufferer only really becomes an object of reverence when, surveying the course of his life as a chain of sorrows, or mourning some great and incurable misfortune, he does not really look at the special combination of circumstances which has plunged his own life into suffering, nor stops at the single great misfortune that has befallen him; for in so doing his knowledge still follows the principle of sufficient reason, and clings to the particular phenomenon; he still wills life only not under the conditions which have happened to him; but only then, I say, is he truly worthy of reverence when he raises his glance from the particular to the universal, when he regards his suffering as merely an example of the whole, and for him, since in a moral regard he partakes of genius, one case stands for a thousand, so that the whole of life conceived as essentially suffering brings him to resignation. [...]

According to what has been said, the negation of the will to life, which is just what is called absolute, entire resignation, or holiness, always proceeds from that tranquilizer of the will which the knowledge of its inner conflict and essential vanity, expressing themselves in the suffering of all living things, becomes. The difference, which we have represented as two paths, consists in whether that knowledge is called up by suffering which is merely and purely known, and is freely appropriated by means of the penetration of the *principium individuationis*, or by suffering which is directly felt by a man himself. True salvation, deliverance from life and suffering, cannot even be imagined without complete negation of the will. Till then, everyone is simply this will itself, whose manifestation is an ephemeral existence, a constantly vain and empty striving, and the world full of suffering we have represented, to which all irrevocably and in like manner belong. For we found above that life is always assured to the will to life, and its one real form is the present, from which they can never escape, since birth and death reign in the phenomenal world. The Indian myth expresses this by saying "they are born again." The great ethical difference of character means this, that the bad man is infinitely far from the attainment of the knowledge from which the negation of the will proceeds, and therefore he is in truth actually exposed to all the miseries which appear in life as possible, for even the present fortunate condition of his personality is merely a phenomenon produced by the *principium individuationis*, and a delusion of Maya, the happy dream of a beggar. The sufferings which in the vehemence and ardour of his will he inflicts upon others are the measure of the suffering, the experience of which in his own person cannot break his will, and plainly lead it to the negation of itself. All true and pure love, on the other hand, and even all free justice, proceed from the penetration of the *principium individuationis*, which, if it appears with its full power, results in perfect sanctification and salvation, the phenomenon of which is the state of resignation described above, the unbroken peace which accompanies it, and the greatest delight in death.

Friedrich Nietzsche, from *The Genealogy of Morals*, Essay III

1.

What is the meaning of ascetic ideals? In artists, nothing, or too much; in philosophers and scholars, a kind of "flair" and instinct for the conditions most favourable to advanced intellectualism; in women, at best an *additional* seductive fascination, a little *morbidezza* on a fine piece of flesh, the angelhood of a fat, pretty animal; in physiological failures and whiners (in the majority of mortals), an attempt to pose as "too good" for this world, a holy form of debauchery, their chief weapon in the battle with lingering pain and *ennui*; in priests, the actual priestly faith, their best engine of power, and also the supreme authority for power; in saints, finally a pretext for hibernation, their *novissima glories cupido*,[9] their peace in nothingness ("God"), their form of madness.

But in the very fact that the ascetic ideal has meant so much to man, lies expressed the fundamental feature of man's will, his *horror vacui*:[10] *he needs a goal*—and he will sooner will nothingness than not will at all.—Am I understood?—Have I not been understood?—"Certainly not, sir?" Well, let us begin at the beginning.

6.

Schopenhauer has made use of the Kantian treatment of the aesthetic problem—though he certainly did not regard it with the Kantian eyes. Kant thought that he showed honour to art when he favoured and placed in the foreground those of the predicates of the beautiful which constitute the honour of knowledge: impersonality and universality. This is not the place to discuss whether this was not a complete mistake; all that I wish to emphasize is that Kant, just like other philosophers, instead of envisaging the aesthetic problem from the standpoint of the experiences of the artist (the creator), has only considered art and beauty from the

9 [Most recent desire for glory (Latin).]

10 [Abhorrence of a vacuum (Latin).]

standpoint of the spectator, and has thereby imperceptibly imported the spectator himself into the idea of the "beautiful"! But if only the philosophers of the beautiful had sufficient knowledge of this "spectator"!—Knowledge of him as a great fact of personality, as a great experience, as a wealth of strong and most individual events, desires, surprises, and raptures in the sphere of beauty! But, as I feared, the contrary was always the case. And so we get from our philosophers, from the very beginning, definitions on which the lack of a subtler personal experience squats like a fat worm of crass error, as it does on Kant's famous definition of the beautiful. "That is beautiful," says Kant, "which pleases without interesting." Without interesting! Compare this definition with this other one, made by a real "spectator" and "artist"—by Stendhal,[11] who once called the beautiful *une promesse de bonheur*. Here, at any rate, the one point which Kant makes prominent in the aesthetic position is repudiated and eliminated—*le désintéressement*. Who is right, Kant or Stendhal? When, forsooth, our aesthetes never get tired of throwing into the scales in Kant's favour the fact that, under the magic of beauty, men can look at even naked female statues "without interest," we can certainly laugh a little at their expense:—in regard to this ticklish point the experiences of artists are more "interesting," and at any rate Pygmalion was not necessarily an "unaesthetic man."[12] Let us think all the better of the innocence of our aesthetes, reflected as it is in such arguments; let us, for instance, count to Kant's honour the country-parson naïveté of his doctrine concerning the peculiar character of the sense of touch! And here we come back to Schopenhauer, who stood in much closer neighbourhood to the arts than did Kant, and yet never escaped outside the pale of the Kantian definition: how was that? The circumstance is marvellous enough: he interprets the expression, "without interest," in the most personal fashion, out of an experience which must in his case have been part and parcel of his regular routine. On few subjects does Schopenhauer speak with such certainty as on the working of aesthetic contemplation: he says of it that it simply counteracts sexual interest, like lupulin and camphor; he never gets tired of glorifying this escape from the "will to life" as the

11 [Stendahl (1783–1842), a French novelist known for his precise psychological portraits of his characters. The French phrase to follow translates as "A promise of happiness."]

12 [Pygmalion was the Greek mythological sculptor who fell in love with one of his own statues.]

great advantage and utility of the aesthetic state. In fact, one is tempted to ask if his fundamental conception of will and Idea, the thought that there can only exist freedom from the "will" by means of "Idea," did not originate in a generalisation from this sexual experience. (In all questions concerning the Schopenhauerian philosophy, one should, by the bye, never lose sight of the consideration that it is the conception of a youth of twenty-six, so that it participates not only in what is peculiar to Schopenhauer's life, but in what is peculiar to that special period of his life.) [...] But granted that Schopenhauer was a hundred times right for himself personally, how does that help our insight into the nature of the beautiful? Schopenhauer has described one effect of the beautiful—the calming of the will—but is this effect really normal? As has been mentioned, Stendhal, an equally sensual but more happily constituted nature than Schopenhauer, gives prominence to another effect of the "beautiful." "The beautiful *promises* happiness." To him it is just the *excitement* of the will (the "interest") by the beauty that seems the essential fact. And does not Schopenhauer ultimately lay himself open to the objection, that he is quite wrong in regarding himself as a Kantian on this point, that he has absolutely failed to understand in a Kantian sense the Kantian definition of the beautiful—that the beautiful pleased him as well by means of an interest, by means, in fact, of the strongest and most personal interest of all, that of the victim of torture who escapes from his torture?—And to come back again to our first question, "What is the meaning of a philosopher paying homage to ascetic ideals?" We get now, at any rate, a first hint: he wishes to *escape from a torture*.

8.

These philosophers, you see, are by no means uncorrupted witnesses and judges of the *value* of the ascetic ideal. They think *of themselves*—what is the "saint" to them? They think of that which to them personally is most indispensable; of freedom from compulsion, disturbance, noise; freedom from business, duties, cares; of a clear head; of the dance, spring, and flight of thoughts; of good air—rare, clear, free, dry, as is the air on the heights, in which every animal creature becomes more intellectual and gains wings; they think of peace in every cellar; all the hounds neatly chained; no baying of enmity and uncouth rancour; no remorse of wounded ambition; quiet and submissive internal organs, busy as mills, but unnoticed; the heart alien, transcendent, future, posthumous—to summarise, they mean by the ascetic ideal the joyous asceticism of a deified and newly fledged animal, sweeping over life rather than resting. We know what the three great catch-words of the ascetic ideal are: poverty, humility, chastity; and now just look closely at the life of all the great fruitful inventive spirits—you will always find again and again these three qualities up to a certain extent. Not for a minute, as is self-evident, as though, perchance, they were part of their virtues—what has this type of man to do with virtues?—but as the most essential and natural conditions of their best existence, their finest fruitfulness. In this connection it is quite possible that their predominant intellectualism had first to curb an unruly and irritable pride, or an insolent sensualism, or that it had all its work cut out to maintain its wish for the "desert" against perhaps an inclination to luxury and dilettantism, or similarly against an extravagant liberality of heart and hand. But their intellect did effect all this, simply because it was the dominant instinct, which carried through its orders in the case of all the other instincts. It effects it still; if it ceased to do so, it would simply not be dominant. But there is not one iota of "virtue" in all this. [...]

10.

[...] The oldest philosophers were well versed in giving to their very existence and appearance, meaning, firmness, background, by reason whereof men learned to fear them; considered more precisely, they did this from an even more fundamental need, the need of inspiring in themselves fear and self-reverence. For they found even in their own souls all the valuations turned against themselves; they had to fight down every kind of suspicion and antagonism against "the philosophic element in themselves." Being men of a terrible age, they did this with terrible means: cruelty to themselves, ingenious self-mortification—this was the chief method of these ambitious hermits and intellectual revolutionaries, who were obliged to force down the gods and the traditions of their own soul, so as to enable themselves to believe in their own revolution. [...] Let us compress the facts into a short formula. The philosophic spirit had, in order to be *possible* to any extent at all, to masquerade and disguise itself as one of the *previously fixed* types of the contemplative man, to disguise itself as priest, wizard, soothsayer, as a religious man generally: the *ascetic ideal* has for a long time served the philosopher as a superficial form, as a condition which enabled him to exist. ... To be able to be a philosopher he had to exemplify the ideal; to exemplify it, he was bound to *believe* in it. The peculiarly etherealised abstraction of philosophers, with their negation of the world, their enmity to life, their disbelief in the senses, which has been maintained up to the most recent time, and has almost thereby come to be accepted as the ideal *philosophic attitude*—this abstraction is the result of those enforced conditions under which philosophy came into existence, and continued to exist; inasmuch as for quite a very long time philosophy would have been *absolutely impossible* in the world without an ascetic cloak and dress, without an ascetic self-misunderstanding. Expressed plainly and palpably, the *ascetic priest* has taken the repulsive and sinister form of the caterpillar, beneath which and behind which alone philosophy could live and slink about....

Has all that really changed? Has that flamboyant and dangerous winged creature, that "spirit" which that caterpillar concealed within itself, has it, I say, thanks to a sunnier, warmer, lighter world, really and finally flung off its hood and escaped into the light? Can we today point to enough pride, enough daring, enough courage, enough self-confidence, enough mental will, enough will for responsibility, enough freedom of the will, to enable the philosopher to be now in the world really—*possible*?

11.

And now, after we have caught sight of the *ascetic priest*, let us tackle our problem. What is the meaning of the ascetic ideal? It now first becomes serious—vitally serious. We are now confronted with the *real representatives of the serious*. "What is the meaning of all seriousness?" This even more radical question is perchance already on the tip of our tongue: a question, fairly, for physiologists, but which we for the time being skip. In that ideal the ascetic priest finds not only his faith but also his will, his power, his interest. His *right* to existence stands and falls with that ideal. What wonder that we here run up against a terrible opponent (on the supposition, of course, that we are the opponents of that ideal), an opponent fighting for his life against those who repudiate that ideal! [...] The idea, which is the subject of this dispute, is the *value* of our life from the standpoint of the ascetic priests: this life, then (together with the whole of which it is a part, "Nature," "the world," the whole sphere of becoming and passing away), is placed by them in relation to an existence of quite another character, which it excludes and to which it is opposed, unless it *negate* its own self: in this case, the case of an ascetic life, life is taken as a bridge to another existence. The ascetic treats life as a maze, in which one must walk backwards till one comes to the place where it starts; or he treats it as an error which one may, nay *must*, refute by action: for he *demands* that he should be followed; he enforces, where he can, *his* valuation of existence. What does this mean? Such a monstrous valuation is not an exceptional case, or a curiosity recorded in human history: it is one of the most general and persistent facts that there are. The reading from the vantage of a distant star of the capital letters of our earthly life, would perchance lead to the conclusion that the earth was the especially *ascetic planet*, a den of discontented, arrogant, and repulsive creatures, who never got rid of a deep disgust of themselves, of the world, of all life, and did themselves as much hurt as possible out of pleasure in hurting—presumably their one and only pleasure! Let us consider how regularly, how universally; how practically at every single period the ascetic priest puts in his appearance: he belongs to no particular race; he thrives everywhere; he grows out of all classes. Not that he perhaps bred this valuation by heredity and propagated it—the contrary is the case. It must be a necessity of the first order which makes this species, *hostile*, as it is, to *life*, always grow again and always thrive again. *Life* itself must certainly *have an interest* in the continuance of such a type of self-contradiction. For an ascetic life is a self-contradiction: here rules resentment without parallel, the resentment of an insatiate instinct and ambition, that would be master, not over some element in life, but over life itself, over life's deepest, strongest, innermost conditions; here is an attempt made to utilise power to dam the sources of power; here does the green eye of jealousy turn even against physiological well-being, especially against the expression of such well-being, beauty, joy; while a sense of pleasure is experienced and *sought* in abortion, in decay, in pain, in misfortune, in ugliness, in voluntary punishment, in the exercising, flagellation, and sacrifice of the self. All this is in the highest degree paradoxical: we are here confronted with a rift that *wills* itself to be a rift, which *enjoys* itself in this very suffering, and even becomes more and more certain of itself, more and more triumphant, in proportion as its own presupposition, physiological vitality, *decreases*. "Triumph at the moment of supreme agony": under this extravagant emblem did the ascetic ideal fight from of old; in this mystery of seduction, in this picture of rapture and torture, it recognised its brightest light, its salvation, its final victory. *Crux, nux, lux*[13]—it has all these three in one.

13 [Cross, nut, light (Latin).]

25.

No! You can't get round me with science, when I search for the natural antagonists of the ascetic ideal, when I put the question: "Where is the opposed will in which the opponent ideal expresses itself?" Science is not, by a long way, independent enough to fulfil this function; in every department science needs an ideal value, a power which creates values, and in whose *service* it *can believe* in itself—science itself never creates values. Its relation to the ascetic ideal is not in itself antagonistic; speaking roughly, it rather represents the progressive force in the inner evolution of that ideal. Tested more exactly, its opposition and antagonism are concerned not with the ideal itself, but only with that ideal's outworks, its outer garb, its masquerade, with its temporary hardening, stiffening, and dogmatising—it makes the life in the ideal free once more, while it repudiates its superficial elements. These two phenomena, science and the ascetic ideal, both rest on the same basis—I have already made this clear—the basis, I say, of the same over-appreciation of truth (more accurately the same belief in the *impossibility* of valuing and of criticising truth), and consequently they are *necessarily* allies, so that, in the event of their being attacked, they must always be attacked and called into question together. A valuation of the ascetic ideal inevitably entails a valuation of science as well; lose no time in seeing this clearly, and be sharp to catch it! [...] Considered physiologically, moreover, science rests on the same basis as does the ascetic ideal: a certain *impoverishment of life* is the presupposition of latter as of the former—add, frigidity of the emotions, slackening of the *tempo*, the substitution of dialectic for instinct, *seriousness* impressed on mien and gesture (seriousness, that most unmistakable sign of strenuous metabolism, of struggling, toiling life). Consider the periods in a nation in which the learned man comes into prominence; they are the periods of exhaustion, often of sunset, of decay—the effervescing strength, the confidence in life, the confidence in the future are no more. [...] No! this "modern science"—mark you this well—is at times the best ally for the ascetic ideal, and for the very reason that it is the ally which is most unconscious, most automatic, most secret, and most subterranean! They have been playing into each other's hands up to the present, have these "poor in spirit" and the scientific opponents of that ideal (take care, by the bye, not to think that these opponents are the antithesis of this ideal, that they are the *rich* in spirit—that they are not; I have called them the *hectic* in spirit). As for these celebrated *victories* of science; there is no doubt that they are victories—but victories over what? There was not for a single minute any victory among their list over the ascetic ideal, rather was it made stronger, that is to say, more elusive, more abstract, more insidious, from the fact that a wall, an outwork, that had got built on to the main fortress and disfigured its appearance, should from time to time be ruthlessly destroyed and broken down by science. Does anyone seriously suggest that the downfall of the theological astronomy signified the downfall of that ideal?—Has, perchance, man grown *less in need* of a transcendental solution of his riddle of existence, because since that time this existence has become more random, casual, and superfluous in the visible order of the universe? Has there not been since the time of Copernicus an unbroken progress in the self-belittling of man and his will for belittling himself? Alas, his belief in his dignity, his uniqueness, his irreplaceableness in the scheme of existence, is gone—he has become animal, literal, unqualified, and unmitigated animal, he who in his earlier belief was almost God ("child of God," "demi-God"). Since Copernicus, man seems to have fallen on to a steep plane—he rolls faster and faster away from the center—whither? into nothingness? *into the "thrilling sensation of his own nothingness"*?—Well! This would be the straight way—to the old ideal? All science (and by no means only astronomy, with regard to the humiliating and deteriorating effect of which Kant has made a remarkable confession, "it annihilates my own importance"), all science, natural as much as unnatural—by *unnatural* I mean the self-critique of reason—nowadays sets out to talk man out of his present opinion of himself, as though that opinion had been nothing but a bizarre piece of conceit; you might go so far as to say that science finds its peculiar pride, its peculiar bitter form of stoical ataraxia,[14] in preserving man's *contempt of himself*, that state which it took so much trouble to bring about, as man's final and most serious claim to self-appreciation [...].

28.

If you except the ascetic ideal, man, the *animal* man had no meaning. His existence on earth contained no end; "What is the purpose of man at all?" was a question without an answer; the *will* for man and the world

14 [*Ataraxia* (Greek) was a state of profound equanimity thought by the Stoics to be possessed by the Sage.]

was lacking; behind every great human destiny rang as a refrain a still greater "Vanity!" The ascetic ideal simply means this: that something *was lacking*, that a tremendous *void* encircled man—he did not know how to justify himself, to explain himself, to affirm himself, he *suffered* from the problem of his own meaning. He suffered also in other ways, he was in the main a *diseased* animal; but his problem was not suffering itself, but the lack of an answer to that crying question: "*For what purpose do we suffer?*" Man, the bravest animal and the one most inured to suffering, does *not* repudiate suffering in itself: he *wills* it, he even seeks it out, provided that he is shown a meaning for it, a *purpose* of suffering. *Not* suffering, but the senselessness of suffering was the curse which till then lay spread over humanity—*and the ascetic ideal gave it a meaning*! It was up till then the only meaning; but any meaning is better than no meaning; the ascetic ideal was in that connection the "*faute de mieux*"[15] *par excellence* that existed at that time. In that ideal suffering *found an explanation*; the tremendous gap seemed filled; the door to all suicidal nihilism was closed. The explanation—there is no doubt about it—brought in its train new suffering, deeper, more penetrating, more venomous, gnawing more brutally into life; it brought all suffering under the perspective of *guilt*, but in spite of all that—man was *saved* thereby, he had a *meaning*, and from henceforth was no more like a leaf in the wind, a shuttlecock of chance, of nonsense, he could now "will" something—absolutely immaterial to what end, to what purpose, with what means he wished: *the will itself was saved*. It is absolutely impossible to disguise *what* in point of fact is made clear by every complete will that has taken its direction from the ascetic ideal: this hatred of the human, and even more of the animal, and more still of the material, this horror of the senses, of reason itself, this fear of happiness and beauty, this desire to get right away from all illusion, change, growth, death, wishing and even desiring—all this means—let us have the courage to grasp it—a will for nothingness, a will opposed to life, a repudiation of the most fundamental conditions of life, but it is and remains *a will*!—and to say at the end that which I said at the beginning—man will will *nothingness* rather than *not will at all*.

15 [For want of a better alternative (French).]

Friedrich Nietzsche, *The Birth of Tragedy*, from "An Attempt at Self-Criticism"

1.

Whatever may lie at the bottom of this doubtful book[16] must be a question of the first rank and attractiveness, moreover a deeply personal question—in proof thereof observe the time in which it originated, *in spite* of which it originated, the exciting period of the Franco-German war of 1870–71. While the thunder of the battle of Wörth rolled over Europe, the ruminator and riddle-lover, who had to be the parent of this book, sat somewhere in a nook of the Alps, lost in riddles and ruminations, consequently very much concerned and unconcerned at the same time, and wrote down his meditations on the Greeks,—the kernel of the curious and almost inaccessible book, to which this belated prologue (or epilogue) is to be devoted. A few weeks later: and he found himself under the walls of Metz, still wrestling with the notes of interrogation he had set down concerning the alleged "cheerfulness" of the Greeks and of Greek art; till at last, in that month of deep suspense, when peace was debated at Versailles, he too attained to peace with himself, and, slowly recovering from a disease brought home from the field, made up his mind definitely regarding the "Birth of Tragedy from the Spirit of Music."—From music? Music and tragedy? Greeks and tragic music? Greeks and the artwork of pessimism? A race of men, well-fashioned, beautiful, envied, life-inspiring, like no other race hitherto, the Greeks—indeed? The Greeks were *in need* of tragedy? Yea—of art? Wherefore—Greek art? ...

We can thus guess where the great note of interrogation concerning the value of existence had been set. Is pessimism *necessarily* the sign of decline, of decay, of failure, of exhausted and weakened instincts?—as was the case with the Indians, as is, to all appearance, the case with us "modern" men and Europeans? Is there a pessimism of strength? An intellectual predilection for what is hard, awful, evil, problematical in existence, owing to well-being, to exuberant health, to fullness of existence?

16 [A reference to *The Birth of Tragedy* itself.]

Is there perhaps suffering in overfullness itself? A seductive fortitude with the keenest of glances, which yearns for the terrible, as for the enemy, the worthy enemy, with whom it may try its strength? from whom it is willing to learn what "fear" is? What means tragic myth to the Greeks of the best, strongest, bravest era? And the prodigious phenomenon of the Dionysian? And that which was born thereof, tragedy?—And again: that of which tragedy died, the Socratism of morality, the dialectics, contentedness and cheerfulness of the theoretical man—indeed? might not this very Socratism be a sign of decline, of weariness, of disease, of anarchically disintegrating instincts? And the "Hellenic cheerfulness" of the later Hellenism merely a glowing sunset? The Epicurean will *counter* to pessimism merely a precaution of the sufferer? And science itself, our science—ay, viewed as a symptom of life, what really signifies all science? Whither, worse still, *whence*—all science? Well? Is scientism perhaps only fear and evasion of pessimism? A subtle defense against—*truth*? Morally speaking, something like falsehood and cowardice? And, unmorally speaking, an artifice? O Socrates, Socrates, was this perhaps *thy* secret? Oh mysterious ironist, was this perhaps thine—irony? ...

4.

Ay, what is Dionysian?—In this book may be found an answer,—a "knowing one" speaks here, the votary and disciple of his god. Perhaps I should now speak more guardedly and less eloquently of a psychological question so difficult as the origin of tragedy among the Greeks. A fundamental question is the relation of the Greek to pain, his degree of sensibility—did this relation remain constant? or did it veer about?—the question, whether his ever-increasing *longing for beauty*, for festivals, gaieties, new cults, did really grow out of want, privation, melancholy, pain? For suppose even this to be true, [...] whence then the opposite longing which appeared first in the order of time, the *longing for the ugly*, the good, resolute desire of the Old Hellene for pessimism, for tragic myth, for the picture of all that is terrible, evil, enigmatical, destructive, fatal at the basis of existence—whence then must tragedy have sprung? Perhaps from *joy*, from strength, from exuberant health, from over-fullness. And what then, physiologically speaking, is the meaning of that madness, out of which comic as well as tragic art has grown, the Dionysian madness? What? perhaps madness is not necessarily the symptom of degeneration, of decline, of belated culture? Perhaps there are—a question for psychiatrists—neuroses of health? of folk-youth and -youthfulness? What does that synthesis of god and goat in the Satyr point to? What self-experience what "stress," made the Greek think of the Dionysian reveller and primitive man as a satyr? And as regards the origin of the tragic chorus: perhaps there were endemic ecstasies in the eras when the Greek body bloomed and the Greek soul brimmed over with life? Visions and hallucinations, which took hold of entire communities, entire cult-assemblies? What if the Greeks in the very wealth of their youth had the will *to be* tragic and were pessimists? What if it was madness itself, to use a word of Plato's, which brought the *greatest* blessings upon Hellas? And what if, on the other hand and conversely, at the very time of their dissolution and weakness, the Greeks became always more optimistic, more superficial, more histrionic, also more ardent for logic and the logicising of the world—consequently at the same time more "cheerful" and more "scientific"? Ay, despite all "modern ideas" and prejudices of the democratic taste, may not the triumph of *optimism*, the *common sense* that has gained the upper hand, the practical and theoretical *utilitarianism*, like democracy itself, with which it is synchronous—be symptomatic of declining vigour, of approaching age, of physiological weariness? And *not* at all—pessimism? Was Epicurus an optimist—because a *sufferer*? ... We see it is a whole bundle of weighty questions which this book has taken upon itself—let us not fail to add its weightiest question! Viewed through the optics of *life*, what is the meaning of—morality? ...

Friedrich Nietzsche, from *The Joyful Wisdom*

125. *The Madman*—Have you ever heard of the madman who on a bright morning lighted a lantern and ran to the market-place calling out unceasingly: "I seek God! I seek God!"—As there were many people standing about who did not believe in God, he caused a great deal of amusement. Why! is he lost? said one. Has he strayed away like a child? said another. Or does he keep himself hidden? Is he afraid of us? Has he taken a sea-voyage? Has he emigrated?—the people cried out laughingly, all in a hubbub. The insane man jumped into their midst and transfixed them with his glances. "Where is God gone?" he called out. "I mean to tell you! We have killed him, you and I! We are all his murderers! But how have we done it? How were we able to drink up the sea? Who gave us the sponge to wipe away the whole horizon? What did we do when we loosened this earth from its sun? Whither does it now move? Whither do we move? Away from all suns? Do we not dash on unceasingly? Backwards, sideways, forwards, in all directions? Is there still an above and below? Do we not stray, as through infinite nothingness? Does not empty space breathe upon us? Has it not become colder? Does not night come on continually, darker and darker? Shall we not have to light lanterns in the morning? Do we not hear the noise of the grave-diggers who are burying God? Do we not smell the divine putrefaction?—for even Gods putrefy! God is dead! God remains dead! And we have killed him! How shall we console ourselves, the most murderous of all murderers? The holiest and the mightiest that the world has hitherto possessed, has bled to death under our knife,—who will wipe the blood from us? With what water could we cleanse ourselves? What festivals of atonement, what sacred games shall we have to devise? Is not the magnitude of this deed too great for us? Shall we not ourselves have to become Gods, merely to seem worthy of it? There never was a greater event—and on account of it, all who are born after us belong to a higher history than any history hitherto!"—Here the madman was silent and looked again at his hearers; they also were silent and looked at him in surprise. At last he threw his lantern on the ground, so that it broke in pieces and was extinguished. "I come too early," he then said, "I am not yet at the right time. This prodigious event is still on its way, and is travelling—it has not yet reached men's ears. Lightning and thunder need time, the light of the stars needs

time, deeds need time, even after they are done, to be seen and heard. This deed is as yet further from them than the furthest star—and yet they have done it!"—It is further stated that the madman made his way into different churches on the same day, and there intoned his *Requiem aeternam deo.*[17] When led out and called to account, he always gave the reply: "What are these churches now, if they are not the tombs and monuments of God?"

341. *The Heaviest Burden*—What if a demon crept after thee into thy loneliest loneliness some day or night, and said to thee: "This life, as thou livest it at present, and hast lived it, thou must live it once more, and also innumerable times; and there will be nothing new in it, but every pain and every joy and every thought and every sigh, and all the unspeakably small and great in thy life must come to thee again, and all in the same series and sequence—and similarly this spider and this moonlight among the trees, and similarly this moment, and I myself. The eternal sand-glass of existence will ever be turned once more, and thou with it, thou speck of dust!"—Wouldst thou not throw thyself down and gnash thy teeth, and curse the demon that so spake? Or hast thou once experienced a tremendous moment in which thou wouldst answer him: "Thou art a God, and never did I hear aught more divine!" If that thought acquired power over thee, as thou art, it would transform thee, and perhaps crush thee; the question with regard to all and everything: "Dost thou want this once more, and also for innumerable times?" would lie as the heaviest burden upon thy activity! Or, how wouldst thou have to become favourably inclined to thyself and to life, so as to long for nothing more ardently than for this last eternal sanctioning and sealing?

17 [Eternal rest in God (Latin).]

SOURCES

Chapter 1

Bayle, Pierre. *The Dictionary Historical and Critical of Mr. Peter Bayle.* 2nd ed. Translated by Pierre Desmaizeaux. London: J.J. and P. Knapton, 1737.

Chapter 2

Pope, Alexander. "An Essay on Man." *Moral Essays and Satires.* London: Cassell & Company, 1891.
Leibniz, Gottfried Wilhelm. *Theodicy: Essays on the Goodness of God, the Freedom of Man, and the Origin of Evil.* Translated by E.M. Huggard. La Salle: Open Court, 1985.

Chapter 3

Voltaire. *Toleration and Other Essays.* Translated by Joseph McCabe. New York: G.P. Putnam's Sons, 1912.
Rousseau, Jean-Jacques. *The Miscellaneous Works of Mr. J.J. Rousseau.* 5 vols. T. Becket and P.A. De Hondt, 1767.
Cugoano, Ottobah. *Thoughts and Sentiments on the Evil and Wicked Traffic of the Slavery and Commerce of the Human Species.* London, 1787.

Chapter 4

Hume, David. *Dialogues Concerning Natural Religion.* London, 1779.
Kant, Immanuel. *Essays and Treatises on Moral, Political, Religious and various Philosophical Subjects.* 2 vols. London, 1799.

Chapter 5

Bayle, Pierre. *The Dictionary Historical and Critical of Mr. Peter Bayle.* 2nd ed. Translated by Pierre Desmaizeaux. London: J.J. and P. Knapton, 1737.
Hume, David. *Dialogues concerning Natural Religion.* London, 1779.

Chapter 6

Rousseau, Jean-Jacques. *A Discourse upon the Origin and Foundation of the Inequality of Mankind*. London, 1761.

Astell, Mary. *Some Reflections upon Marriage. The Third Edition. To Which Is Added a Preface, in Answer to Some Objections*. London, 1706.

Chapter 7

Schopenhauer, Arthur. *The World as Will and Idea*. 2 vols. Translated by R.B. Haldane and J. Kemp. London: Trübner & Co., 1883/86.

Chapter 8

von Hartmann, Eduard. *Philosophy of the Unconscious*. 3 vols. Translated by W.C. Coupland. London: Kegan Paul, Trench, Trübner & Co., 1893.

Plumacher, Olga, "Pessimism," *Mind* 4 (13), 1879: 68–89.

Chapter 9

Schopenhauer, Arthur. *The World as Will and Idea*. 2 vols. Translated by R.B. Haldane and J. Kemp. London: Trübner & Co., 1883/86.

Nietzsche, Friedrich. *The Birth of Tragedy or Hellenism and Pessimism*. Translated by W.A. Haussmann. London: George Allen and Unwin, 1909.

Chapter 10

Schopenhauer, Arthur. *The World as Will and Idea*. 2 vols. Translated by R.B. Haldane and J. Kemp. London: Trübner & Co., 1883/86.

Nietzsche, Friedrich. *The Genealogy of Morals. A Polemic*. Translated by H.B. Samuel. Edinburgh: Foulis, 1913.

Nietzsche, Friedrich. *The Birth of Tragedy or Hellenism and Pessimism*. Translated by W.A. Haussmann. London: George Allen and Unwin, 1909.

Nietzsche, Friedrich. *The Joyful Wisdom*. Translated by T. Common. Edinburgh: Foulis, 1910.

ABOUT THE PUBLISHER

The word "broadview" expresses a good deal of the philosophy behind our company. Our focus is very much on the humanities and social sciences—especially literature, writing, and philosophy—but within these fields we are open to a broad range of academic approaches and political viewpoints. We strive in particular to produce high-quality, pedagogically useful books for higher education classrooms—anthologies, editions, sourcebooks, surveys of particular academic fields and subfields, and also course texts for subjects such as composition, business communication, and critical thinking. We welcome the perspectives of authors from marginalized and underrepresented groups, and we have a strong commitment to the environment. We publish English-language works and translations from many parts of the world, and our books are available world-wide; we also publish a select list of titles with a specifically Canadian emphasis.

broadview press

This book is made of paper from well-managed FSC® - certified forests, recycled materials, and other controlled sources.